THE PANZA MONOLOGUES

The Panza Monologues

script also features

stories contributed by

Bárbara Renaud González,

Petra A. Mata, and

María R. Salazar

the

PANZA
MONOLOGUES

SECOND EDITION

WRITTEN, COMPILED, AND COLLECTED BY

VIRGINIA GRISE AND IRMA MAYORGA

FOREWORD BY TIFFANY ANA LÓPEZ

UNIVERSITY OF TEXAS PRESS / AUSTIN

NOTICE: Professionals and amateurs are hereby warned
that the script of *The Panza Monologues* contained in
this book, being fully protected under the Copyright Laws
of the United States of America and all other countries
of the Berne and Universal Copyright Conventions, is
subject to a royalty. All rights including, but not limited
to, professional, amateur, recording, motion picture,
recitation, lecturing, public reading, radio and television
broadcasting, and the rights of translation into foreign
languages are expressly reserved. Particular emphasis is
placed on readings and all uses of the script of *The Panza
Monologues* by educational institutions. Requests for
permission should be sent to Permissions, University of
Texas Press, at the address above.

♾ The paper used in this book meets the minimum
requirements of ANSI/NISO Z39.48-1992 (R1997)
(Permanence of Paper).

Library of Congress Cataloging-in-Publication Data

Grise, Virginia.
The panza monologues / written, compiled, and collected by
Virginia Grise & Irma Mayorga. — Second edition.
    pages   cm
"The Panza Monologues script also features stories contributed by
Barbara Renaud González, Petra A. Mata, and María R. Salazar."
Includes bibliographical references and index.
ISBN 978-0-292-74909-2 (cloth : alk. paper) —
ISBN 978-0-292-75405-8 (pbk. : alk. paper)
1. Mexican American women—Drama. 2. Body image—Drama.
3. Monologues. I. Mayorga, Irma. II. Title.
PS3607.R569P36 2013
812'.6—dc23

                        2013008529

doi: 10.7560/749092

The script of the play *The Panza Monologues* was first
published by ALLGO & Evelyn Street Press, 2004.

\ ꜚ | ꜙ /

to all the *PANZAS* in the world

for which there is hunger, pain, or sorrow . . .

you inspire us to work harder

/ ꜚ | \ ꜙ

CONTENTS

FOREWORD

The Panza Monologues is a collaborative project by Virginia Grise and Irma Mayorga crafted from conversations among fellow activists, artists, friends, and neighbors with whom they worked, played, and broke bread in San Antonio, Texas. The play enacts a series of composite stories performed in the first person, with the lead actor taking on multiple personas; in this way, the "I" voice of the actor speaks to the "we" of community. Through well-crafted storytelling driven by humor, frankness, and realness to the nth degree, *The Panza Monologues* reframes our thinking and stages a conversation about the body, the politics of food, matters of violence and trauma, and the necessity of self-love. As theater, it documents a complex range of women's experiences by exploring how they come to perceive the body as a site of struggle and empowerment, particularly in direct relationship to the stomach as a gateway to emotional and physical health. This type of bold invitation calls women and their allies to investigate not only their bodies but also the context of the body in the broader spectrum of communal health. *The Panza Monologues* thereby joins the ranks of such plays as Ntozake Shange's *For colored girls who have considered suicide, when the rainbow is enuf,* Cherríe Moraga's *Giving up the Ghost,* Josefina López's *Real Women Have Curves,* and Eve Ensler's *The Vagina Monologues,* works recognized as pivotal for the ways they have shifted consciousness about the female body as a personal storehouse of knowledge and a source of cultural memory.

From Carmen Miranda to Selena, JLo, and Shakira, the *panza* has been showcased as a symbol of creative power and sexual energy. Latina cultural icons such as these deliver potent *panza* imagery that reminds us of our ancestors' celebration of fertility. The *panza* also serves as a barometer of womanhood (youth and the onset of menses), the original home space of the child (pregnancy), and a signifier of wisdom born from life experience (menopause). If the *panza* has phases, these are its big three. The *panza* clearly plays an important role in the construction of identity. However, as one journeys through life, shifting one's thinking about the *panza* is not always a simple matter. How *do* we think about the *panza* and come into consciousness about what it represents to others but especially to ourselves? *The Panza Monologues* takes this question, which encourages articulations and connections, as its launching point for staging larger conversations about women, their sense of the *panza*, and, by extension, the world.

My own *panza* story begins with experiencing menopause in my early 40s. By age 43, my periods had completely ceased. Since my late 30s, I had been diagnosed as showing early signs of menopause and told this was not all that unusual for someone with thyroid disease. When it finally happened, I did not perceive the cessation of my menstrual cycle as a compromise to my sense of womanhood. When it came to the issue of motherhood, I had chosen not to have children, seeing myself more as a public mother than a biological one. When they started to manifest themselves, I worked hard not to dwell too much on the symptoms of menopause (mood swings, hot flashes, insomnia, diminished libido) that are normalized as a result of the ways they are so widely made light of in popular culture and often outright dismissed in the medical community. When my symptoms became exacerbated, I shared concerns about the ways they were starting to become intrusive, to which my doctor replied, "Some women go through menopause without much discomfort, and others have a much harder time of it." I felt forced to just accept what was happening to my body and move forward into the next stage of my life. I did my best to do so as gracefully as possible, patiently waiting out the transition my body was making—that is, until my *panza* started to shape shift in most disturbing ways.

Overnight it seemed my once pleasantly curvy *panza* morphed into the proverbial lumpy spare tire. While driving in the car, I could feel my *panza* becoming more of a presence. I recalled a woman's testimony I once heard about why she had joined Weight Watchers: "Well, I was on the edge of the bed, getting ready for work, struggling to pull on my pants, when I glanced into the mirror and was so startled, I cried out, 'My Lord! Who's that sitting in my lap!'" I was starting to get what she meant. Indeed, my *panza* had inflated in an unprecedented manner, such that I could cradle a big heap of it in my hand, as if I were cupping the fleshy shoulder of a young child.

Admittedly, these concerns about my *panza* initially arose in large part from vanity. The mound of flab that appeared around my midsection and obliterated my hourglass figure had made a dramatically rapid and unwarranted entrance. I am a passionate devotee to my wardrobe and the collection of clothes I've amassed since my 30s when I decided life was too short not to dress well. If my 20s were about using fashion to hide or flaunt the *panza*, the 30s were about refusing to worry about the *panza* by styling it to look nothing less than fabulous. In the past, a bit more attention to diet and exercise would yield a fairly quick and visible firming up. After 40, however, the *panza* slowed down and stopped responding to anything predictably or cooperatively. It was becoming a source of discomfort as well as unhappiness that needed to be acknowledged as something aside from concerns about aesthetics.

Practitioners who specialize in metabolic function and adrenal health assert that the belly holds our most vital organs apart from the heart, and they postulate that the optimal functioning of these organs depends on high-quality food and sufficient sleep to sustain biological processes, many of which greatly affect neurological functions and thereby control a sense of emotional well-being. The way Western culture recognizes the *panza* as inhabiting only two extremes—sexy or repulsive—thwarts the ability to think about *panza* wellness in more intricate ways and toward more pressing matters. Apart from the condition of pregnancy, a woman's concerns about her *panza* are for the most part viewed as the ravings of an emotionally dissatisfied or hormonally imbalanced woman. How do we get the culture to refocus thinking about the stomach, away from aesthetics (how it looks) to health (how it functions)?

The Panza Monologues engages this question by introducing a vocabulary that enables thinking about the force of the *panza* in defining the many phases of one's life. It dares to speak about aspects of our life experiences for which there is a dearth of meaningful shared public vocabulary. The play's themes and stories encouraged my growing rebellion against all the dismissive rhetoric about menopausal women and their disintegrating bodies, inspiring me to listen attentively to my body and become a fierce advocate for my own *panza* health and well-being.

As a result of my tenacious insistence that my discomfiting symptoms were not the side effects of menopause, doctors ran tests that enabled them to discover a rare tumor on my urethra. We know that the vagina and the *panza* are connected through reproduction. We also know that eating certain foods (such as oysters, caffeine, and sugar) can have an impact on the vagina's ecosystem and cause a range of responses, from increased libido to yeast infection. Throughout life, from puberty to menopause, the *panza* and the vagina journey through vast changes in tandem. It is paramount that we not lose sight of the intimate connection between the two. After surgical removal of my tumor, as one would expect, I started to feel infinitely better. Gone was the feeling that my *panza* is a disconcerting place. Now I'm consciously taking care of her, getting exercise, eating right, and practicing stress management. In other words, I am actively listening to her needs and acknowledging the *panza*'s existence as a powerful gauge of wellness. As a result, my health is being restored; I feel aglow again. And I'm marveling at the changes and improvements in both my *panza* and *su comadre* (aka the vagina), the moon to her sun. The *panza* is about infinitely much more than just hunger. Reading *The Panza Monologues* as I recovered from surgery provided good medicine. This work lyrically affirms the *panza* as the epicenter of a woman's physical, emotional, and spiritual lives. Laughter is healing, but so is coming into critical consciousness.

Before the publication of this new edition—which makes the play available to a much wider readership—and with the permission of Grise and Mayorga, I taught *The Panza Monologues* as part of my courses on Chicana/o literature, feminist drama, Latina/o theater and film, and theater for social change at the University of California, Riverside, one of the nation's three most ethnically and economically diverse campuses and a Hispanic-Serving Institution. The classroom fills with the laughter of recognition, and the play sparks conversation about cultural taboos and embodied knowledge, and inspires creative projects in which my students use their own *panza* narratives as a springboard for critical engagement. With the availability of a DVD of the play as a reference (see www.panzamonologues.com), this volume becomes a valuable teaching resource for students to study the transition of theatrical work from page to stage and the conceptual moments between art, feminism, and activism.

Theater is always about the body, which makes it critically rich terrain for both articulating and grappling with feminist concerns. A very short representative list of pivotal theater practitioners whose work directs, illustrates, and informs the making of feminist theory includes María Irene Fornés, Adrienne Kennedy, Cherríe Moraga, Emily Mann, Paula Vogel, Caryl Churchill, Suzan-Lori Parks, Holly Hughes, Karen Finley, Carmelita Tropicana (Alina Troyano), Anna Deavere Smith, Lynne Nottage, Velina Hasu Houston, Jessica Hagedorn, Dael Orlandersmith, Diana Son, and Denise Uyehara, as well as Spiderwoman Theater, to name just a few leading figures. What distinguishes theater as a genre is its singular ability to spotlight the body as a principal vehicle of expression, with the language of performance conveying what remains partially or wholly unspeakable in verbal communication alone. (For example, Annie Rogers has written two astounding books about her process of learning to read performative gestures during her work with children and adolescents who are survivors of trauma.) When we lack the words to say it, the body often takes over as our speaker. Theater artists tap into the dynamics of embodiment that define live performance in order to reconstruct the public space of the theater as an arena of witnessing where affect and feeling palpably inform the experience of listening to a story and watching it unfold. Theater intensifies communication and heightens one's ability to come into awareness. As Bertolt Brecht maintained in his work and contemporary practitioners such as Anne Bogart illustrate in theirs, theater has a direct connection to social change because it has the power not only to show a character's response but also to reflect the conditions that led to that response. And in the hegemony of a patriarchal culture it's a very significant thing for women to take the stage. This is illustrated in the titles of several key works in Latina feminist theater studies: *Holy Terrors: Latin American Women Perform*, Diana Taylor and Roselyn Constantino's edited anthology of Latin American contemporary women's theater and performance artists; *Latina Performance: Traversing the Stage*, Alicia Arrizón's critical volume on Latina theater; and *Stages of Life: Transcultural Performance and Identity in U.S. Latina Theater* and *Puro Teatro, a Latina Anthology*, Alberto Sandoval-Sánchez and Nancy Saporta Sternback's anthologies of Latina plays and performance texts. Just the act of entering the theater affirms that women's experiences are worthy of sharing as the subject of art and merit documentation within the archive of public discourse.

The Panza Monologues evolved from the Chicana practice of everyday life and the conversations Grise and Mayorga observed, cultivated, imagined, recorded, re-created, and enacted in and for their Mexican-majority hometown, San Antonio, Texas. Grise and Mayorga's goal in beginning to draft the play by observing and collecting *panza* stories and writing their own was to create a piece of theater that conveyed the kind of epiphanic moments when one connects with a story being told and feels genuinely moved to higher ground personally, politically, critically, and spiritually. In their introductory comments, Grise and Mayorga write, "Separating *The Panza Monologues* from its origins in San Antonio would be to eviscerate the work's heart, for it was in the afflictions of our city that we found the play's focus and its voice." As the theorist Mary Pat Brady emphasizes in her work, place and space inform affect. A connection to place (home, community, nation) structures feelings; how we think and act result from the range of emotional responses created and caused by place. This is seen in the titles of landmark critical volumes, such as *Telling to Live: Latina Feminist Testimonios* and *Living Chicana Theory*, as well as in the signal phrasings of key theoretical works, such as Gloria Anzaldúa's "mestiza consciousness," Chela Sandoval's "a hermeneutics of love," and Emma Perez's "*sitios y lenguas.*"

Yet Grise and Mayorga do not intend *The Panza Monologues* for their telling or their Tejana/o city alone. It can be interpreted as a declaration of its authors' commitment to forging Chicana discourse about embodiment and epistemology. Indeed, it participates in bearing witness to the complexities of Chicana and Latina experience and inscribes *panza* narratives into the historical record across disciplines.

This new edition of the play has been specifically designed to illicit continued action. An unprecedented range of source materials and creative documents are included in this second edition. This makes the work readily teachable and an extraordinary tool for classrooms of all sorts and students and scholars of many disciplines. This is also an important pedagogical development, as so many plays are often left out of curriculum or theater seasons simply because of a lack of source materials. No other collection of Chicana theater has included such a rich and diverse range of materials in connection with a single play. Together with UT Press's 2008 anthology, *Teatro Chicana: A Collective Memoir and Selected Plays*, by the Chicana collective Teatro de las Chicanas (who have worked together since their college days in the late 1970s), this volume offers a strong sense of the trajectory of Chicana theater history. This edition of *The Panza Monologues* contains additional documents: the book's fourth chapter is a veritable do-it-yourself primer for cultural production and pedagogical possibilities. One also finds "guidelines, advice, and good wishes for staging a production" of *The Panza Monologues* and creative activities that spur readers into consciousness raising and creativity that compels new narratives and intimate connections about subjectivity, identity, place, and gender. Grise and Mayorga's frank and generous sharing about the spectrum of the production process also includes helpful details for intricate matters such as permissions, royalties, and promotion to stage community productions of the play or hold screenings of the DVD, which gives readers a comprehensive sense of the work involved in being a professional theater artist, a burgeoning community organizer, or an agent of social change.

I've been most fortunate to attend and participate in a "Love Your Body *Panza* Party" that was organized in Riverside, California, by Christina Albidrez and the committee for Ladyfest Inland Empire 2012. I found the event tremendously inspiring for the ways it embraced the play on DVD in order to bring together a diverse spectrum of community members: women, men, queer, straight, allies, baby dykes, uber-femmes, teenagers, old heads, model-thin waifs, curvy gals, riots grrrls, shy girls. They screened sections from the DVD, had a copy of the script available, invited members of the community to enact selected stories (I read "Political *Panza*"), and set up a makeshift public mural space for guests to trace their body and post their own *panza* stories. They had been in contact with Grise and Mayorga and honored the "DIY Production Manual" protocol with a great sense of pride about shepherding the work and making it accessible to their community. Here, in the energy and work of the *"Panza* Party," one could see how the play—apart from Grise and Mayorga—has its own life.

The Panza Monologues is a landmark work for many reasons, including how it uses storytelling to bring awareness to the cultural specificity of food and body image in Mexican American and Chicana/o culture. Complete with its dramaturgical materials and pedagogical blueprints, this new edition illustrates the artistic and critical richness of collaborative work. It is also significant because it teaches us about a new generation of Latina practitioners and theorists and the skills they bring to their work as well as the stories they tell. Notably, both Grise and Mayorga are the daughters of working-class families, came into adulthood after the crucible of the Chicana/o Civil Rights movement of the 1960s and early 1970s, and are first-generation college-educated women who turned to the arts as a form of expression and documentation. Both are also the children of military families and had the opportunity to travel and move across multiple types of borders, achieve advanced degrees as theater artists, and freely pursue careers in the arts. Such experiences among Chicanas have yet to be fully documented, and their narratives here begin this essential work that describes changes within the U.S. Latina/o population. In this, *The Panza Monologues* illuminates the generational shifts among our artists and serves as a benchmark that describes how Chicanas/Latinas engage in theater as a form of social change.

Despite the appearance of solo authorship, there are many collaborative forces that inform the making of a work and coming into voice. Here, the result is a more detailed picture about the complexity of social issues and women's lives. *The Panza Monologues'* final gesture is to invite further voicing of the work by empowering readers to stage their own *panza* storytelling event or craft their own performances through the avenue of creative writing. In this way, *The Panza Monologues* not only serves as a mirror, helping women to see themselves, but goes much further by extending a formal invitation to others to add to the archive of *panza* narratives and create new actions.

DR. TIFFANY ANA LÓPEZ

Tomás Rivera Endowed Chair of Theatre, Creative Writing, and English, University of California, Riverside

MUCHAS MANY THANK-YOUS
TO ALL OUR PANZA ALLIES

This second edition of *The Panza Monologues* provides us with an opportunity to acknowledge our many astounding, supportive, and dedicated *panza* allies who over the years have helped us move ever forward as theater artists in countless, benevolent ways. We could never have made theater without the openhearted support of these vital collaborators and companions; their help has been paramount to materializing our work as *teatristas*.

We would especially like to thank María Berriozabal, Petra A. Mata, Bárbara Renaud-González, Cindy Rodríguez, and María R. Salazar, who took time out of their busy lives to answer our plea for stories about their *panzas*. Each of these women has generously allowed us to perform a moment from her life experiences. We always strive to honor their stories. The gifts of their words and insights make *The Panza Monologues* sing with a deeper truth.

We give our unending thanks to the Austin Latina/Latino Lesbian and Gay Organization (ALLGO) in Austin, Texas, for believing in *panza* power and for fighting for *panza* positive policies in the state of Tejas. ALLGO, then under the leadership of Lorenzo Herrera y Lozano and the artistic direction of Sharon Bridgforth, nurtured the world premiere of *The Panza Monologues* in November 2004. Lorenzo, Sharon, and ALLGO proved to be magnificent hosts and bestowed us with their magnanimous spirits along with the support of invaluable resources. ALLGO joined forces with Evelyn Street Press, owned by the sagacious Jackie Cuevas and Jennifer Margulies, to jointly publish the first edition of *The Panza Monologues*. *Estamos pero bien* grateful to these beautiful people for their collaboration and shared vision for our work.

Muchas many thank-yous to all the student groups, academic institutional centers and programs, and stalwart cultural and political organizations who scraped and saved their pennies, petitioned their institutions for aid, wrote grants to foundations, and had the temerity to bring Chicana *teatro* such as ours into their communities. These cultural warriors have been inspirations, and we are honored by their efforts. Formal and informal groups such as these have always fought (literally and figuratively) to make productions of *The Panza Monologues* for audiences of all types. We also have awe and admiration for the student-led groups that have organized and produced their own readings of *The Panza Monologues* at their universities and cultural centers, the professors who have invited us into their classrooms to speak about the work, the scholars who have written about the performance, and teachers of all sorts who use our play in their classrooms.

In many ways, the journey to reach this second edition began with the creation of *The Panza Monologues* DVD. Therefore, we take this opportunity to offer gratitude to our DVD collaborators. We thank with all our love Los Flacasos, our masterly and mind-blowing musicians, who include Eduardo Arenas, Laura Cambrón, and Jacqueline Mungía. Alexandro Hernández Gutiérrez served as lead composer, performer, and organizer of this exceptionally talented group. His generosity of time, creativity, and intense musicality helped move our work to the next level of its *destino*. Thank you, Tejarocho, for the unbounded force that is your heart. Mirasol Riojas, another multitalented Tejana from San Antonio, lent her careful eye and passionate commitment to the task of making our raw video footage a cohesive work through patient and sharp video editing skills. From the earliest origins of *The Panza Monologues*, Marissa Ramirez has served as our source of unending support and has been our leading *flaca* ally. Filming in L.A. would have been impossible without her presence and boundless moral and physical assistance. Unlike either of us, this woman can climb a ladder like nobody's business.

We are grateful for the resources and funding provided by Florida State University and Dartmouth College that aided the completion of this book. Most particularly, *muchas* many thank-yous for support provided by the FSU Theatre Department and the Dartmouth Department of Theater.

We are also grateful to the following groups, organizations, and individuals who, in no small way, have made the things that needed to happen, happen—somewhere in the course of the play's journey—by breaking down doors or showing up with the keys whenever we faced a barrier. These allies lent us their homes, hands, or hearts, allowed us to borrow endlessly from their caches of goodwill, or served as much-needed protectors, imprimaturs, or conspirators: Adelina Anthony, Glenna Avila, Natalya Baldyga, Marlene Beltran, Vini Bhansali, Ricardo A. Bracha, Jen Cardenas, Rosemary Cano, Cara Mía Theatre, Jessica Cerda and Café Latino, Lydia de los Rios, East Side Café, Dr. Mary Karen Dahl, Esperanza Garza, Emma and Ronald Grise, Cordelia Guevara, María Jimenez-Torres, Karla Legaspy, Hildegaard Mayorga, Juanita G. Mayorga, Matthew McKibben, Elizabeth Osborne, the Playwrights' Center, Jamila Reyes-Gutiérrez, Dr. Laura Harris, Mujeres Activas en Letras y Cambio Social, Muerta Paz Corazón, Plaza de la Raza, Sheree Ross, Raquel Ruiz, raúl r. salinas, Resistencia Bookstore, Dawn Surrat, Teatro Q, Rosie Torres, Jan Townsend, the Austin Project, and David Zamora-Casas.

Sincere thank-yous to the Gender and Sexuality Center at the University of Texas at Austin and the willing hands of its director, Ana Ixchel Rosal. Our performance presentation at UT, Austin, instigated by Ixchel in March 2010, was also a foundational step to realizing this new edition of *The Panza Monologues*.

Nuestro más profundo agradecimiento to the University of Texas Press and especially for the prescient, attentive, and generous abetment of our editor Theresa May, who welcomed our book project with vigor, excitement, and *cariño*. *Mil gracias* to Celeste Guzman Mendoza, San Antonio *escritora*, whose generous encouragement guided us to the auspices of UT Press.

To help complete our book, we were again aided by the talents of a community of caring supporters and allies. Thank you *estimada* Dr. Tiffany Ana López for your thoughtfulness and camaraderie. We are indebted to Dr. López's scrupulous scholarly insights, her dedication to Latina/o *teatro*, and the labor put toward creating her illuminating foreword. With generous and timely attention, Dr. Patricia Herrera contributed many valuable comments to our working manuscript. We also owe a debt of gratitude to the guidance and grace bestowed on us by Dr. Alberto Sandoval-Sánchez. We have drawn on the depth of his scholarship on Latina/o theater, which helped to sharpen and shape the contents of our book. We would also like to acknowledge

Dr. Sandoval-Sánchez's decades-long, unwavering commitment to the development of Latina theater artists in the United States and his interminable efforts through his scholarship to document and foreground the import of women of color. Lorenzo Herrera y Lozano stepped in a second time to help, and his fluency in *español* proved invaluable to tightening our *lenguas pochas*. *Tlazocamatli* to Xicana artist Debora Kuetzpal Vasquez, another San Anto *mujer* and a true *compañera* and *hermana* in the struggle, for her support of our work over the years and the generous contribution of her bold and sentient artwork adorning this book's pages.

Finally, all of this playmaking, filming, touring, and publishing would not have been possible throughout the years without the sincere, devoted participation of our impassioned, encouraging, affirming, and *loud* live audiences in places such as Arizona, Califas, Colorado, *y* Tejas. From the depths of our *panzas, muchísimas gracias.*

V.G. & I.M.
a/f

INTRODUCCIÓN TO THE SECOND EDITION

We are seated in a broadcast booth for Dallas's local NPR station, KERA. Our white male radio host, roughly in his early sixties, is interviewing us for his weekly arts and culture program with an extremely even keeled "public radio voice," politely inquiring about our work. We are his guests—seizing all means possible to drum up an audience for our two-week run of *The Panza Monologues* in Dallas and Fort Worth produced under the Cara Mía Theatre Co. The brief on-air interview gives us a chance to explain to his metroplex North Texas audience that *panza* is the Spanish word for "belly." Usually it suggests a big belly, a round, protruding belly, but skinny people use the word too. It can be used with affection, a way to indicate that there's more of you around to love—especially around your midsection—or, cruelly, that you have a pot-bellied paunch for a stomach. The term does not discriminate: both sexes and all genders can have a *panza*. That's part of its cultural brilliance. We explain that our play spins out the word, widens its possibility to think about bellies and bodies, the rise of obesity among Latina/os, the conditions in people's lives. In our eyes, *panza* is a catalyst for looking at the social, political, geographic, and historical significance of women, of Latina/os, of ourselves. This is what we call thinking about *panza* politics.

The host nods and smiles. He begins to take phone calls from the public—a standard feature of his program. An excited woman's voice suddenly spills into our headsets:

Panza to Panza by I. Mayorga © 2005. Courtesy of I. Mayorga. Virginia Grise in *The Panza Monologues*, presented by the Austin Latino/Latina Lesbian, Gay, Bisexual, and Transgender Organization (ALLGO) at the Tillery Street Theater, Austin, Texas, 2004.

I just had to call! I was driving in my car, and I heard the word PANZA on the radio!? And I pulled over to listen because I'm driving, you know . . . and I can't believe you said PANZA on the radio! I haven't heard that word since I was a little girl! I haaaaadd to call in . . .

She goes on to exclaim that she couldn't believe we had made a whole play about *panzas*, and where could she buy tickets? As she kept talking, even in her excitement, she was able to filter her present concerns about her body through her childhood memories of *panzas*. She was in effect creating theory, right there on the air, generating ideas about connections between her body, her culture, her history, our play—completely unprompted, simply by examining the word *panza*. We immediately discerned the slight remnant of Spanish-inflected vowels in her otherwise unaccented English. The accentuation of her words and the cadences of her phrasing were all in the distinct dialect of English spoken by Texas Mexican people. She was a Tejana. We laughed along with her enthusiasm and exchanged *panza* stories between the three of us as our host's eyebrows arched higher and higher, displaying his surprise at the woman's loud, gushing, and boisterous call. And as her excitement intensified, he began to appear uncomfortable with her bubbly excess, her effusive recognition, her happiness just to talk about *panzas*. Measured by his reaction, it seemed this was clearly not the typical caller who phoned in to NPR to discuss "arts and culture."

We, however, were used to this response—after two years of producing *The Panza Monologues ya sabíamos*. We knew the word's simple, provocative power because we had seen this type of rhapsodic response in every place we had toured our show. We had known almost since those first days in an office, years before, where we had worked together down south in San Antonio, when we had laughed and sighed mightily about the plight of *panzas*.

It was this type of instantaneous resonance, hilarity, and culturally inspired excitement among Mexican American women that motivated us to write a play about what we heard, which then became a book, followed by a DVD, and finally the script republished as a second, expanded edition—the book we are elated beyond measure to present here.

The ideas that became *The Panza Monologues* began in San Antonio, Texas, our hometown. Separating *The Panza Monologues* from its origins in San Antonio would be to eviscerate the work's heart, for it was in the afflictions of our city that we found the play's focus and its voice. In the collective memory of the United States, San Antonio is best *remembered* (pun intended) as that place in Texas where the Alamo, "The Cradle of Texas Liberty," can be found. The Alamo and its historical significance have cast a long, dense shadow over San Antonio, a pall that in numerous ways continues to dim our city's present. While the Alamo pulls historical focus to San Anto, what gets left behind, most often hidden or ejected, is the story of Mexican Americans in our city—a tale pockmarked by a legacy of institutionalized racism, systematic segregation, disenfranchisement, and act after act of underhanded, crooked politics wielded against Texas Mexican residents and other peoples of color, most of them poor (which then comes to include poor white people).

Less well known is the fact that San Antonio also reigns as the "Tejano Capital" of Texas and anchors the northernmost edge of a distinct subregion of Mexican American culture, "South Texas."[1] Stretching from San Antonio to Corpus Christi on the Gulf Coast, South Texas also runs south to the Rio Grande, which divides Mexico from the United States, and after pressing toward Del Rio to the west gradually fades away. In this southern "horn of Texas," as the region is also commonly called (look at a map of Texas upside down . . . see the horn?), resides the state's majority of Mexican American people. Across the state, Texans of all sorts understand that the euphemism "South Texas" points to both a place and the predominance of Mexican American peoples and cultural ways that saturate its southern reaches.

The Panza Monologues is a solo performance piece that articulates our concerns about the plight of San Antonio's Mexican American population. We often characterize the play as our "love letter" to the city (often a brutal love letter) whose heartbreaking Texas Mexican past has deeply influenced the content and themes of our theater making and also our philosophies as Tejana-Chicana artists. The *panza*, our *panzas* and your *panza*, became very important to us mostly because we were too politically and socially aware to ignore the fact that our bodies were dangerously overweight. And we weren't alone. When we looked around our South Texas city, we couldn't help but notice that a great majority of San Antonio's Mexican American population were *panzones y panzonas* and that the majority of the city's Mexican Americans were also poor, often scraping by on the lower end of a "living wage" scale. As a line in our play asks, ". . . why is it that San Antonio is one of the largest cities in the nation and at the same time one of the poorest?" Here, we use "large" to indicate both the size of its people and the size of its population. Back in 2002–2003 we couldn't help but think that a predominance of obesity and poverty were somehow linked to the disenfranchisement of generations of Tejana/os that has had an impact on our *cultura* economically, legally, spatially, physically, and also psychically. Our *panzas* were not only a matter of individual responsibility in regard to health and diet but also deeply connected to the material, spatial, historical, and embodied legacy we have lived as Tejanas.

Ten years ago, these types of connections were first articulated through flip one-liners, brief scintillating thoughts, casual conversations, jokes, reflections, headlines, and the many *cuentos* we exchanged between ourselves and with other women as we started to animate the term *panza*. With our activist scrutiny and artists' imaginations, we began to interrogate the fleshiness of our Texas Mexican bodies by positioning our pronounced *panzas* front and center as deeply resonant cultural symbols that we could use metaphorically and figuratively to reveal a wide range of information about the conditions connected to women's bodies in San Antonio and Texas. These conditions were inevitably then linked to women's loves, abuses, health, and socioeconomic circumstances.

We used the content and spirit of these conversations and ideas to help generate *The Panza Monologues*. We are the play's lead writers and dramaturgs: the two women who collaborated to conceive of, gather, and eventually make manifest a collection of materials for theatrical production.[2] In thinking about how to stage the materials we had written and collected, we chose to feature Virginia in a solo performance format. Irma then shifted to the role of the show's director and also served as its producer. Visibility can be misleading; people often leave performances of *The Panza Monologues* with the impression that Virginia wrote the entire show. This is a credit to our collaboration as writers and our working relationship as performer and director—and also to the *duende* of Virginia's performance. The wider truth is that both of us created the live performance by working together in constant conversation and close-knit collaboration—each contributing individually authored performance pieces and theatrical ideas about how to stage *panza* politics.

But as the names in our book's front pages indicate, we also worked with contributed materials. This was a form of our feminist theater practice. In conceiving the show, we petitioned a group of San Antonio Tejanas for materials in order to add other women's voices to the play. We created our show from a feminist ethos that believes a collection of voices does in fact paint a more detailed picture about the complexity of social issues, historical circumstances, and the individual plights of women. As lead writers, in order to render a script, we pulled forward similarities, patterns, *and* contradictions from this rich bounty of original writings; we crafted the journey of the story we wanted to tell. As playwrights working with a wealth of voices and life experiences, we tried not to shy away from the contradictions between the women's voices. Therefore our work has been conceived by, written in part by, and compiled by the two of us with important contributions culled from writing and life stories offered by Bárbara Renaud González, Petra Mata, and María Salazar.[3]

Working together as playwrights who also function as performer and director requires an unyielding commitment to collaboration. As "A Chronological Production History of *The Panza Monologues*" shows, the play we formulated had a variety of developmental milestones as we staged it at many different types of venues each of which helped us to arrive at the final form, style, and sequential order of the show. In its early stages, we sought to refine the play in terms of the writing, acting, dramaturgy, presentation, and design, as well as the overall feel of the theater event for our audiences—from arrival to departure. In its early stages, we sought to refine the play in terms of the writing, acting, dramaturgy, presentation, and design, as well as the overall feel of the theater event for our audiences—from arrival to departure. Each new performance provided us with an opportunity to shape the arc of the play's emotional journey. We listened closely to our audiences' responses in order to sharpen the staging and aesthetics of the piece, often rearranging the sequence of the monologues after learning something new from our observations. We also drew heavily from the lessons of immediately responsive forms such as street and guerrilla theater to capture our audiences' attention as we continuously sought to create a work that was tightly hewn—something that had "lightness *and* exactitude."[4] This particular aesthetic goal could not take place overnight or within just a few hours, days, or weeks of rehearsal. It had to be gained from presenting the show publicly one, two, three, four . . . *many* times in order to look at the work, critically examine it, and then reconfigure. The script included in this book is the result of all that thinking, talking, trying, rewriting, heated exchanges, personal proclivities, and resolutions between us—these are the phases of a long and sustained conversation about creativity.

Yet the script of a play is not the play. Technically, a play exists only when it is played out in performance, when it is *playing*—on bodies, in space, in a visual, visceral conversation with an audience. However, this marked difference between print and live performance has not slowed the tidal wave of requests we've received for the physical pages: "Where can I buy the play?" Today people in the United States do not commonly go out and buy plays or sit down to read them in the same numbers as other forms of literature. Why then do our people of color–majority, mostly woman-populated audiences, almost always want something to hold on to, to have in their possession, that seems to assure them that they *did* see it. This hunger for both memento and knowledge plays out in our own ravenous consumption of literature, especially books that lend insight into our lives as Chicanas. We suspect our audiences' hunger highlights the ephemerality of a play in performance, which lasts only for an evening or afternoon. On the other hand, a printed script is solid, *forevers*—you know, like Selena.[5]

We have never taken the publication of our work, *a play*, lightly; very few plays make it into print. Even fewer printed plays are made by Latino playwrights. And even less of published drama in the U.S. features work made by Latinas. Yet it is now through printed texts that plays are largely disseminated; printed plays form an essential part of the archive of theatrical effort and thought. So what conclusions are made if you can't find any plays in print written by Latinas? Would you think that *perhaps* Latinas don't write plays? Would you think that *perhaps* Latinas don't make theater? We/they do/have. Our desire to have our play in print not only acknowledges requests from our audiences and allies but also seeks to interject a Chicana feminist worldview into the conversation held through U.S. American theater. Self-representations, such as this book, forsake our silence not only in theater's discussions but also in those held in our city, in our Latina/o communities, in our nation.

We didn't start off our playmaking journey by imagining an end point that consisted of our play as a published text. We simply wanted to create, to speak through theater. Yet over time it became clear to us that creating a testimony through print (and in the same regard through recorded performance) was part of a necessary material politics that could not only address the transitory quality of live theater's appearance and disappearance but could also amplify the cultural role theater has to play in publicly articulating and circulating facets of Latinas' agency, their/our *self-described* subjectivity. As the contextual materials that you'll find in this book hope to suggest, publication of our script offers an occasion for redress, provocation, and an invitation to create further actions that ameliorate generations of silence.

We both consider ourselves Chicana feminists. This simple proclamation, which expresses our desire to receive equal rights and treatment for ourselves as women of color and for all women, has proven to be a contentious position—even in our present day and age. Bringing forward a feminist and racial and class critique that also interrogates heteronormativity magnifies that aggression. The term *Chicana feminist* can often draw suspicion, disbelief, or disdain from our communities, whether Latina/o or Anglo. However, we have found that publicly identifying ourselves as Chicana feminists is a powerful declamation that we must offer to help nurture agency and self-determination in other women—of many different racial identities and ethnic origins. We persevere in identifying ourselves as Chicana feminists in deed, action, *arte*, and word because of the work public declamation accomplishes: it encourages women to articulate the forces of misogyny, racism, classism, and homophobia in their own lives (as well as the lives of their loved ones). While both of us not only had the propensity to want to be artists in theater and performance, we also desired to manifest a Chicana feminist ethos and practice *through* and *in* our creative activity as artists.

Through embodied practices of representation, theater has the ability to tell stories about the social contexts, crises, dilemmas, challenges, and questions that characterize the circumstances of people's lives and/or the communities to which they form attachments. This "theatrical mirror" can also offer affirmation. It's a politics of visibility. In this, the theater affords a constitutive space that summons identifications—however tangential or direct—and, hopefully in turn, a spectator/witness's critical thought about her lived conditions. Over the years many interactions with our audience members have borne witness to how powerfully affected a woman can be after considering some semblance of the racialized, gendered story that is her life in *The Panza Monologues*. The monologue "Praying," written and contributed to our performance by María Salazar, relates the physical and psychic violence an abusive father exerts on his children and pregnant wife. This monologue has always drawn women forward after our show. In the rush of postshow greetings, these women seek us out to share their personal testimonies of surviving child abuse—specifically citing "Praying"'s scene of subjection, which is told from the perspective of a girl still a child. The majority of these women have been Latinas. We believe that because "Praying" not only depicts the unspoken terror of domestic abuse but also specifically articulates its force within the structure of a Latina/o family—a representation rarely if ever portrayed in the dominant media or Latina/o *teatro*—it often serves as a catalyst for these women to speak, to find the fortitude to name, or mark their life experiences in spite of the cultural values that ask only for their shame or silence. This action is important—for them, to us, for our culture. Their voices testify to the efficacy of staging our stories, our very Latina/o stories. Our best hope is that witnessing *The Panza Monologues'* stories enables women to realize that they are not alone in their struggles, questions, or ideas. We hope that they make connections to the nature of their own feminism inherent in self-initiated actions that hope to eradicate oppression in their lives. Any measure of consciousness our work can materialize forms a crucial step toward resistance, enablement, and change.

The first edition of *The Panza Monologues* has been out of print for roughly four years. It sold quicker than *barbacoa* on a Sunday morning. On the one hand, we are glad; it means that our work is circulating in the world. On the other hand, it means that we have run out of copies of the play to circulate. Yet we continue to receive requests for the script. In this regard, the occasion of a second, expanded edition of *The Panza Monologues* has been a gift for us, a rare opportunity that arrived from new events surrounding our play and an improbable opportunity from the University of Texas Press. Sometimes, good people, new ideas, and new possibilities arrive exactly when and how they should. This kind of serendipity characterizes not only our path to publication but also much of our play's journey through the years.

In February 2010 we received an invitation to present a performance of *The Panza Monologues* for Women's History Month at the University of Texas in Austin. Like many of our invitations to perform at academic institutions, this request did not come from a theater department or organizers of campus arts offerings. Rather it arrived from the Gender and Sexuality Center (GSC) at UT and, more specifically, from the Center's director, Ana Ixchel Rosal. Although the GSC wanted to bring the full show, on the Center's dime no less, it could not secure a theater space (lights, sound, stage) on campus.

This circumstance inspired us to rethink the totality of the show's live presentation and imagine a new incarnation that we eventually called a "Performance *Plática* [Conversation]." Our UT presentation gave us the opportunity to think between our performance DVD of *The Panza Monologues* and a full-out live performance. We decided to make use of the DVD by screening segments from it and then expanding on the themes or backstory of the monologues we showed, something along the lines of VH-1's *Storyteller* series. The multisensory experience of four large flat-screen

Panza to Panza, The Panza Monologues DVD still © 2012. Courtesy of the authors. Virginia Grise in *The Panza Monologues* at Plaza de la Raza in Los Angeles for a special one-night performance on August 2, 2008, to record the play for DVD. Live music by Los Flacasos, pictured left to right: Jacqueline Mungía, Laura Cambrón, Alexandro Hernández Gutiérrez, and Eduardo Arenas.

TVs, positioned around the circumference of the audience, was also a welcome surprise and added a striking visual dimension to the "Performance *Plática*." To prepare for this new shift in presentation, we had to dig into remembering the backstory of the play's development—to revisit the challenges we had faced as well as our discoveries. Careful excavation brought forth a more complete account of creating the work, elaborations of our guiding principles, and articulations of the path to creating a performance DVD. To that end, our reflective backtracking served as a seedbed of ideas that would eventually be included in the materials found in this second edition of our book. Yet it was the fact that Celeste Guzman, who at the time worked at UT Press, happened to attend our "Performance *Plática*" that led to the reality of publication. After the *plática*, she asked us an unexpected question: "Would you consider a publisher like UT Press for the second edition of the play?"

Celeste's thought—followed quickly by her stewardship—reached out to us at exactly the right moment. You hold the results of her question in your hands.

The story of our play and its multiyear development documented in these pages describes an artistic trek by two Chicana *teatristas* in our efforts to create theater. The play, information, and accounts that follow have as much to say about theater in the United States as they do about trying to work through a methodology that embraces social and political consciousness. Our book also has as much to say about our struggle to work as feminist cultural workers as it does about the possibilities for making theater. And our story also speaks about our aesthetic sensibilities and artistic visions even as it describes the local history and contexts of our Texas Mexican hometown, San Antonio. With all these factors in the mix, our artistic work has often been defined by unpredictable twists and turns just as much as it has been a source of plenitude and affirmation from our audiences and for us. We are most likely stronger and better working artists for having traveled the contours of this journey.

In many ways, this second edition brings our play as well as a sense of ourselves home to Texas. Home not only to a press that bears our state's name but also home to Austin, the city where *The Panza Monologues* premiered and where the first edition was published. We couldn't imagine a more felicitous homecoming. We come full circle to a psychic, cultural, and geographic space that resides "deep in the heart," mind, and body of each of us, however far away we travel from it physically. Texas, with all the *historia* and mythology that it possesses, was the place that yielded these Tejana stories, important Chicana testimonies that became part of the work to keep silence at bay and creativity at the leading edge of explication. We hope that in its localized specificity our work can reach out to embrace places and peoples that find, see, and in some cases directly share the same tones and textures of strife, joy, humor, and inductions of hope. We don't come home empty-handed; we bring with us a book. And we hope that our work will encourage readers to think about and perhaps create new actions.

I.M. & V.G.
Hanover, NH, & Brooklyn, NY
27 julio 2012

ORGANIZATION OF THE BOOK

For the second edition of *The Panza Monologues*, we always envisioned including support materials beyond our script. As we monitored various manifestations and implementations of our work, we wanted to help the play live the life it is finding in the world by creating materials that enable its use as an imprimatur for action. We believe the release of our performance DVD has begun to motivate these possibilities. With this goal in mind, we have used several models of organization for the materials you will find here such as the guiding tenets of creative writing and activist workbooks or manuals; we want our materials to offer ideas for praxis-based activities, for actions.

Models from theater practice such as the dramaturgical casebook also inspired us. The dramaturgical casebook, a long-standing tradition in theater making, is a collection of materials that serve to inspire, inform, and shape a theater project's conception or execution by providing contextual information about a play. Among its inclusions, a casebook typically offers essential social, political, material, and historical contexts about a play, and in this, it serves as an invaluable source of knowledge that can illuminate a project's themes, its form, and the context of its creators and their creative process. The casebook also can function as an archive of participants' activity—a record of the process. For theater making, it's an invaluable tool. Here, each chapter of *The Panza Monologues*, Second Edition, serves a purpose for all these ends. We believe each chapter stands on its own as independent sections of information, and yet in total, the chapters are deeply interconnected.

To provide some of the background about creating and producing the play, our book opens with the origin story of *The Panza Monologues*. In Chapter One/*Uno*, "*The Panza Monologues:* From *Cuentos* to DVD," we offer a narrative that describes the play's earliest moments of conception and our incentives, our collaborative process as cowriters and as performer and director, the play's development over years, and finally its transformation into a performance taped for DVD. Tracing this history is important to us, for we believe laying bare details of our artistic life and travels with *The Panza Monologues* in the past decade illustrates the challenges Chicanas often face in their efforts to make theater—a difficult task that deserves description to appreciate its many facets.

In Chapter *Dos*/Two, "Script of *The Panza Monologues*," you will find the complete script for the play. Although it has changed over the course of its development, Chapter *Dos*/Two is our most definitive version, honed over many years and now set down in publication. This version of the script is faithful to the play as recorded on our performance DVD and also includes staging notes that describe the exciting addition of our band, Los Flacasos (roughly translated as "Skinny Minnies"). Yes, we know the word *flacasos* is all twisted up and doesn't make sense in terms of formal Spanish-language gender agreement. Its misconstruction is the band's playful effort to reflect the composition of their genders: two women and two men, all talented, all *eskinny*.

In addition to the script, Chapter *Dos*/Two includes a glossary for the play, mined from the extensive storehouse of Virginia's cultural and historical knowledge of Texas Mexican San Antonio. The glossary not only defines various words but also annotates many of the cultural references in *The Panza Monologues*. For ease of use, we have first divided the glossary according to the order of individual monologues. Next, in these sections words are listed in the order of their appearance in the monologue. We think this organization makes it easier for readers (and performers) to locate definitions without tracking through a longer, continuous alphabetical list. We hope our glossary is helpful to those uninitiated in the linguistic vernacular of South Texas and also provides thicker (often humorous) cultural descriptions of the many Spanish, Spanglish, Tejana/o citations, and other historical references used in our play's languages and theatrical antics.

At the end of the chapter we also include the more traditional chronological production history that accompanies a published script. The chronology documents the play's production history to render a picture of its development through time, including performance dates, participating artists, and geographic locations. However, we urge readers to refer to "*The Panza Monologues: From Cuentos to* DVD," which describes the richer story behind the deceptively simple list of dates, people, and places.

Chapter Three/*Tres*, "Tejana Topographies," opens by offering a sense of place: a cultural-historical map of San Antonio, which we commissioned from Debora Kuetzpal Vasquez, a nationally recognized San Antonio Xicana artist whose work often honors women, Xicana history, and San Anto. This map offers one form of "counter-topography" of San Antonio that records not only well-known landmarks and roads but also lesser-known Tejana/o cultural treasures and hot spots in the city. Chapter Three/*Tres* also seeks to set our work within the broader Texas landscape from which it arises. The essay "San Antonio Paint(ed) by Numbers" presents the numbers and sociopolitical circumstances shaping our city's geographic and psychic landscape. The numbers concerning economics, education, and health are hard. We hope they help to reposition the horizon line and create a newly considered view of our city's topographic relations. These two counter topographies set the scene for our personal autogeographies. By including these creatively driven autogeographies, we hope to sketch out and connect aspects of our familial origins, our development as artists, and the context of our individual art making as well as speak to a few of the life experiences that have influenced our thoughts as Chicana *teatristas*.

Do you want to produce your own staging of *The Panza Monologues*? Host a "*Panza* Party" with friends and family? Or create some type of community-based event to screen the DVD? Chapter *Cuatro*/Four, "A DIY Production Manual," contains helpful advice, guidance, and suggestions on how to accomplish all these activities. Hopefully you'll be inspired. We often receive requests from individuals and groups who want to stage the play in their communities, teach the play with groups of women or youth, or create a community event around the DVD. Over time, we have drawn up guidelines to help future producers and planners with the details for all these initiatives, which we hope provides some important guidance for theater making in general—especially if this is your first go at it (*ándale*, look at you!).

Chapter Five/*Cinco*, "Pedagogy of the *Panza*: A Reading, Creative Writing, and Discussion Guide for *The Panza Monologues*," sets down some starting points and activities for book clubs, teachers, discussion groups, and community groups. We also offer creative writing exercises that might help you add your *panza* stories to the ones we have found. "Further Reading" at the end of this chapter names some of our influences. These pathbreakers' and hell raisers' works have fortified us, inspired us, or put it to us straight. Their books have helped form a material *and* psychic testimony to the fact that we exist as a people, that the events that wrought our families, our communities, and ourselves have cast important auras on our lives. This list is in no way exhaustive; rather we recommend it as a starting point for all types of readers, especially those who have found *The Panza Monologues* outside the context of the academy; our desire is to use this opportunity to proliferate resources of all kinds.

"*Panza Pilón*: A Manifesto for *Panza* Positive Cultural Production" forms a cultural coda of sorts. Through our journey to create *The Panza Monologues*, we have generated many thoughts, observations, and philosophies that grew from our production efforts as well as our endeavors as artists who are attempting to negotiate making theater in the United States on our own terms and toward our own ends. This journey has inspired us to create a manifesto that highlights our concerns, especially in terms of our experiences as Tejana cultural producers and activists. The manifesto addresses knotty issues connected to art making, and we have articulated these concerns in order to draw urgent attention to art and life practices that we believe must be addressed for healthier—mind, body, and spirit—approaches to cultural production. Our manifesto gives us an opportunity to not only think on our work in theater but also link our efforts to the shifting national attitudes and conditions about, and within, Latina/o communities.

We have written this book to engage with many potential readers: those curious about the play; those seeking to produce the play; those desiring to use the play for the classroom or in another pedagogical setting; and all types of women, activists, young people, people of color, scholars, and theater makers. Given this expansive audience that we have imagined, throughout our book we have taken care not to write toward one particular type of reader, audience, or discipline. Therefore, we often take the time to explain fully terms ubiquitous in theater and theater making, and we take some space to explain more well known Latina/o terms, concepts, and ideas. As ever, we are working between cultures, between worlds, between ideas, and between realities—all with the intention to provide clarity for everyone.

In the end, this second, expanded edition of *The Panza Monologues* attempts to create a critical pedagogy within, about, and around our work—something beyond publication of the script alone—as a way for us to pass forward to future theater makers, *panza* allies, teachers, organizers, and creative people of all kinds the important insights and information we have gathered and gained as Chicana cultural producers.

ONE/UNO

THE PANZA MONOLOGUES
FROM *CUENTOS* TO DVD

In the ten years since we began this creative work, we have imagined *The Panza Monologues'* many possibilities as theater and Chicana feminist cultural production. Every play has an origin story, when an idea somehow found its way into words on a page and then action on a stage. Our play is no different. However, it's so rare that Chicanas have the opportunity to make theater in collaboration that we would like to take time to discuss more fully the context and way in which the play developed: from its inception as shared stories between us as friends to its existence as a performance DVD. Many people have asked, how did we think of talking about the *panza*—in a play, of all things? This is that story.

The development of *The Panza Monologues* mirrors our history as collaborators, the play's lead creators, writers, and organizers. Yet in our collaboration I have always functioned as the play's director and, perhaps more important, its producer overall: the woman who not only shaped the work onstage but also coordinated, calculated, and facilitated all production aspects of the show in addition to attending to management tasks connected to touring the piece such as coordination with our performance venues, lodging, travel, and finances. In the throes of our project, I've always had a great concern for taking care of Virginia as the solo performer, to allow her the space and distance to focus on her performance, which requires an enormous amount of physical and psychic energy. Considering this division of our roles, I offer this essay about the many phases and dimensions of our production history as a first-person account, written from the point of view of a producer and creator, someone who took care of all the *detallitos*.

An Extraordinary Group of Strong Smart Women

Before we were the lead co-creators of *The Panza Monologues*, we were coworkers at a social justice organization/cultural center in San Antonio. The story of our collaboration on the play starts with our relationship as activists and coworkers. In the summer of 2002, I chose to return to San Antonio after spending two years in New England. There I had been trying to finish a doctoral dissertation (with varied success), taught playwriting at a college, and worked full-time as both an artistic associate and the education and access director for New World Theater in Massachusetts, a theater company that at the time strove to develop contemporary theater and performance work primarily by people of color. My return to San Antonio formed a homecoming of sorts after also spending a number of years in California. By returning to San Antonio, I had made the decision to forgo embedding myself in an academic institution and instead to immerse myself directly in community-based work, in my hometown. Moreover, after my time away I wanted to come home to live in this fascinating and compelling city in a meaningful manner. I had a fortunate landing spot in the city, the Esperanza Peace and Justice Center (EPJC), which afforded me a community of progressive people, a place to consider a conversation in motion between art and social change, a job (thus a living wage) while I kept writing. I also wanted a sense of meaning in my work as an artist/scholar beyond the academy. While the East Coast had been an eye-opening adventure and California a political revelation, living in both of these places had only demonstrated to me how very Tejana I really was. Living in these distinct locations had also shown me the important ethnic differences between, for example, a California Mexican sense of being or a Nuyorican sense of being, as I had the opportunity to observe both in motion. I discovered that one only feels more Tejana, more Texas Mexican, when you are in the midst of negotiating these intracultural nuances—in other words, when you *aren't* living in Texas.

At the EPJC, I had the unanticipated good fortune to meet and work with an extraordinary group of strong, smart, savvy, and politically sophisticated Chicanas and *mexicanas* who formed the majority of its staff.[1] And here, among this group of women, I met Virginia Grise, who began volunteering at the EPJC when she was sixteen and was at the time I arrived a full-time staff member. This talented group was composed of a range of different women: some with college educations, even from Ivy League schools, working-class Chicanas and *mexicanas*, and young women fresh out of high school. I cannot emphasize enough how extremely rare it was to find a group of this kind in San Antonio: radical left Tejanas, *mexicanas*, and Chicanas of different ages, classes, and histories dedicated to working together in the name of social justice in the ultraconservative red state of Texas.

To activate its vision of social change, the EPJC organized a variety of cultural programs and events that promoted and articulated people's convictions about the systems of oppression in the city and across the world. Culturally grounded activist and artistic actions provided some of the best, most moving ways to describe the forces at work in people's lives and cultures. In effect, this cultural work redressed the effects of tourism, classism, and racism that permeated our city. Our cultural events were oppositional and resistant, creative, incisive, and always opening outward, toward inclusiveness. Typical activities included organizing art exhibits by local and national artists, featuring local craftspeople as well as master artisans from Mexico, helping to organize public art actions for local events such as community marches and protests, hosting theater events, and programming a great many music concerts. Alongside these cultural activities, the staff spent long hours helping to better inform our San Antonio Tejana/o community by arming them with knowledge that they might not find elsewhere: we presented authors, intellectuals, and activists of all kinds, and created educational and cultural events such as alternative film and arts festivals, usually featuring independent films and filmmakers and progressive artists who would otherwise never be seen or heard in the city. Along with these efforts we organized community workshops and *pláticas* to discuss and learn about the complexities of local, national, and international issues in order to find the linkages between our locally specific concerns and their global corollaries. We also worked extensively with young people; this was one of Virginia's primary projects at the EPJC.

We used a collective approach to administrative and maintenance tasks for the organization. The staff maintained and repaired the EPJC's very old building, organized its vast archives, prepared our space for rentals, kept paperwork orderly, produced a monthly publication, produced press releases for events and actions, wrote numerous grants for our programming, maintained data about our community, monitored local issues, gathered together and coordinated meetings . . . and cleaned and organized . . . we were always trying to clean and organize, on so many literal and political levels. In total, the Center pursued an ambitious, year-round, multidisciplinary, community-based agenda.

To accomplish this work, the EPJC sought to organize itself structurally as a reflection of the world it would like to see by working ardently to move activist and feminist theory into organizational practice. As a staff, we shared tasks and eschewed titles and thus hierarchy. In the morning you might be cleaning a toilet, in the afternoon holding a meeting with a city council member, followed by an evening setting up an art exhibit or preparing our performance space for a concert. In actuality, this type of horizontal structure was exceedingly difficult to maintain; for example, funding agencies required organizations to clearly identify the person who was "in charge." Despite ethos, this forces organizations to construct hierarchies, so eventually titles emerge and with them further ramifications connected to power.

In its best moments, this type of feminist philosophy in action was a powerful thing to behold, and it was deeply gratifying. At its worst, a structure of this kind took a heavy toll on the staff as we tried to find our way in the dream, sometimes nightmare, of a truly egalitarian working structure within a societal matrix that begged otherwise. The important fact was that we persevered nonetheless: each day we attempted to manifest our feminist philosophy yet again.

The creation of *The Panza Monologues* arose from the time Virginia and I spent working as community activists and cultural workers within this radically left, feminist, queer-friendly, Chicana/o nonprofit cultural organization in San Antonio. There never seemed to be enough daylight to complete our work; we continued on into the night, quickly melding any social or personal life we might have maintained into the work of our social justice projects. And even in this constancy of projects, ideas, and actions, there were always unplanned eruptions that demanded urgent attention and swift refiguring of the best-laid plans: a woman would arrive seeking help for sexual harassment, a crucial school board vote needed support, city council actions needed response, elections, bond decisions, worker violations, workers organizing, environmental endangerment, or the constant machinations of gentrification. By 2002, over the course of its nearly twenty-year history, the Center had established itself as a locus of social justice in San Antonio that offered community members practical and theoretical assistance or functioned as a harbor for social injustice; it hummed with a steady inrush of people in need of help or support. There was always something to address, and as a staff we monitored our city's currents in a heightened state of awareness and readiness. As we watched a constant barrage of social issues crosscut in the Center, in terms of thinking about art and social change, it was an immensely rich conceptual environment.

However, you can push along in this highly primed, ever vigilant state of engagement for only so long before a form of erosion begins to take hold. Maintaining hyper-readiness to combat injustices and oppression as a lifestyle burns through you, hollows you out even as you hope to give more. Because the injustices you engage are often intertwined and seemingly endless, you often have no sense of a horizon—the place *over there* where you meet your goals, the place where you could possibly rest or reassess. It seems you are caught on a treadmill of hope—always running toward the future you desire, never arriving. When this condition suffuses your life, it can be a source of exhilaration in facing the struggles at hand or, for a large majority of us, a condition that causes you to fill yourself with less wrenching diversions, more palpable ends, like the satisfaction of Bill Miller Bar-B-Q's fried chicken.

"Sin la tortilla y el frijol no hay revolucion"

In the late afternoons, when the workday had grown longer and our blood sugar lower, the staff usually found a break moment and a snack, right across the street at Bill Miller Bar-B-Q restaurant. In Texas, Bill Miller Bar-B-Q is not just a restaurant; it's a venerated cultural institution in its own right.[2] This San Antonio–based barbecue restaurant chain—where the long, tender slices of brisket drenched in a tangy red sauce flow as easily as its gallon tubs of cold sweet tea—was a staple "go to" place for staff . . . well, because it was *right next door*. Bill Miller's has made an art of barbecue's transformation into fast-food convenience, with prices to match. Their drive-thru service is usually quicker than any other fast-food chain around, and the cafeteria-style layout inside is not only exceedingly quick, but you also enjoy the pleasure of gazing at your meal as employees carve up their smoky meats right before your eyes. Bill Miller's is ubiquitous in San Antonio, always situated on the choicest parcels of land at key intersections throughout the city. Texas barbecue, always right there, waiting.

It was all too easy: we could run across the street, grab our "snack," and return in usually five to seven minutes. With this type of unfettered access, we could make a Bill Miller's run and come back to eat, talk, eat, laugh, scheme, think, organize . . . and tell stories in between. In brief moments of respite such as these during days that often stretched into eighteen-hour hauls for weeks at a time, these were the types of moments when we bonded as *comadres*, as cultural workers in an ardently feminist refuge deep in the heart of Texas. Here, amid the food and goodwill we shared ourselves as we planned our takeover of the world and all the good that might come of it. Seated together at a large table in the center of our office where we laid out our various snacks, we turned over the political issues at hand in discussions that jumped between insight, analysis, commentary, jokes, and stories. Activists have to have time not only to think, plan, and do but also to dream and divert: vision is what keeps you going.

As we knew, sharing food creates community; we served food at almost every community event.[3] Dreams and visions fuel fortitude, but even so, you still have to eat.

Mapping Our *Panzas*

In the early 2000s, a plentiful, endless supply of cheap food sources surrounded our workplace on San Pedro Avenue. These types of restaurants should not have been part of our daily diet. But they were. Staff members frequented them regularly, almost daily. There are, of course, outstanding culinary experiences throughout San Antonio. Unfortunately, these high-end restaurants were not in our immediate area, situated as we were outside of downtown proper and away from the more developed boutique neighborhoods dotting the city. Besides, who among us—earning activist, nonprofit wages and salaries—could've afforded those prices for lunch every day?

San Pedro Avenue is one of several main arteries that stretch across San Antonio. It originates on the far north end of downtown and shoots up to the northern reaches of the city, eventually intersecting "The Loop" (a connection of interstates that encircle the city's core), before the "avenue" cuts north into the Texas Hill Country and terminates in North Texas. Our workplace was located at the origin of the street, which commences immediately outside of downtown proper. At the time we worked in the area, this portion of San Pedro's route was economically depressed and somewhat blighted—neither particularly vigorous nor wholly abandoned.[4] Although a few miles away San Pedro brushes against the city's posh North Star Mall, our end of San Pedro was lined by far less luxurious attractions: empty, unkempt buildings, a drive-thru liquor store, social service outlets for the city and other nonprofits, auto garages, and the main city bus terminal. Farther on, the area was home to San Antonio College's small campus, an adjunct branch of the city library situated in San Pedro Springs Park (the original site of seventeenth-century settlement by Spanish colonizers), and all along this part of our street were many, many fast-food restaurants.

There was Bill Miller next door but also Weinerschnitzel up the street toward downtown, Jack in the Box at the corner of Elmira and San Pedro right underneath I-35, Wendy's, McDonald's, Sonic Drive-In, Luby's Cafeteria (another landmark Texas restaurant chain) up three blocks and one block over on Euclid, along with a smattering of different fast-food type, locally owned Tex-Mex places that served steaming breakfast tacos dripping with eggs and *chorizo* as well as *platos* of chicken enchiladas *suizas* at lunch. In back of our building, surrounding the college campus, there were pizza joints, sandwich shops that randomly appeared and disappeared over the years, a Vietnamese restaurant, and one lone Subway tucked away in a strip mall near Myrtle Street on the far eastern side of San Antonio College's campus.

As smart women, we could have made better choices all around, but the intense pressure of time, geography, economics, and the structure of our working day often derailed our best intentions. Often we didn't have more than thirty minutes for lunch, so convenience became an important deciding factor. The fact that this bounty of fast food cost relatively little also didn't help. A more decisive factor was that we worked long days and often weekends too—which frequently stymied efforts to pack lunch and dinner, much less find the time (or interest) to shop for groceries. Also, the nearest grocery store where we could find fresh fruit or vegetable alternatives during the workday involved at least a thirty-minute round-trip. (There were no fresh food access points in our immediate area.) In our work place, there was also an implicit notion of how and where to spend our time and energies as cultural workers, a sense that every day, every moment could not be wasted. This urgency to do more played a large role in our psychic relationship to the quality of our diets—often inhibiting any action toward more attentive self-care because it could be read as a bit too self-interested. Self-interest, too strongly expressed, is an implicit community activist no-no. In the end all these contributing factors did not help the health or girth of our *panzas*.

The majority of the women of color working in the Center were in some measure overweight or obese. As we say in the play, "San Antonio is the *panza* capital of the world! Home of Chicana heavyweights!" We are sincere when we say this—both figuratively and literally. Moreover, in the spring and summer of 2003, as our local newspaper reported, San Antonio had achieved the distinction as the top U.S. "unfit city": "S.A. ranks as nation's fattest city on fed list . . . study shows 31.1% of Alamo City residents are obese."[5]

As we gazed down our center's street lined only with fast-food options and thought about the composition of the city's working-class neighborhoods, usually Mexican American or African American residents (where fast-food corporations flourished), none of us were surprised by this unflattering achievement. Alarming statistics continued to flood our newspaper's pages:

- "More than 30% of Hispanic children across the country are over-weight, compared with 25% of Anglo children."
- "Living in sprawl can increase your spread—those in compact counties weigh up to 6 pounds less."
- "Among kids 12 to 19, 44% of Hispanics are overweight and 23% are obese. Nearly 40% of younger children are overweight and 24% are obese."

Abundant, therefore convenient, low-cost foods were not only serving our needs, but perhaps our needs were emblematic of those of a majority of Latina/o people. When does lifestyle stop becoming a choice and start becoming an adaptation to one's surroundings? We began drawing lines between our local girth and a local and national epidemic in Latina/o communities—mapping our *panzas* onto a much more prevalent problem than the "choices" offered by San Pedro Avenue. What we witnessed in microcosm among the women of our organization dramatized an epidemic of unhealthy body weight accumulating not only in South Texas, but across the nation.

It was in those late afternoon snack/break moments, when we talked and munched—obstinately consuming *both* culturally and mass-produced unhealthy foods—that we had the opportunity to sift these personal stories and feelings about our bodies through our political insights about the city or the clarion of local headlines. This inevitably led us to rich analysis, to collective theories, or to hilarious send-ups of our dilemmas and contradictions. These discussions were when the seeds of *The Panza Monologues* were planted, in this fertile form of unfettered "casual talk," part *chisme* and part dead serious insights exchanged among the politically astute women we had the good fortune to work with. Yes, we realized, we had *panzas*, lots of *panzas*, but other factors were also implicated in how they came to be. We each tried to break it down, sort it out: personally, systemically, racially, culturally, and historically.

"If our body breaks down, then how are we going to do all this work?"

What also became clear to us in these ruminations was that although we tirelessly advocated for the health and well-being of our community, our own lifestyle in the name of this hope was quite poor, and in fact we very much neglected our health because of efforts made on behalf of our community. In our lives as activists, we had grown physically larger—too large. All of us. We worked for our community at the expense of ourselves. In this, we now believe we followed in the long tradition of Chicanas who have worked very hard, usually behind the scenes, for their communities and in complete disregard of taking care of themselves. Sacrifice, they call it, for the sake of social justice, *la causa*, el Movimiento. But there wasn't something quite right about the enduring legacy of this equation. Why couldn't we care about both the health of our own bodies and those of our community? Why was this a contradictory tension? Why was the need for basic self-care viewed as *selfish*? As our *sabia* Petra Mata says in her monologue, "A Hunger for Justice" (see p. 55), "If our body breaks down, then how we are we going to do all this work?"

Drawing attention to our weight quite naturally led to a focus on our midsections—the thickest part of so many of us. Our *panzas*. The word *panza* soon came to the fore in our analyses and jibes and began to take on a life of its own in these conversations. As a playwright and worker bee–scholar in the activist hive, I hastily and secretly recorded particularly humorous and acrimonious moments from our *panza* riffs on my computer, taking down the choicest anecdotes, partly because they were very smart reflections, partly because I could feel something important was being articulated among us, something unmediated by dominant culture and something strongly, unapologetically Chicana feminist in its form. When I heard keen language or an idea/connection that was especially comedic or sharp, I would collect and save it for later . . . you just never know. Most of these *notitas* were about our rich reflections on our physical, political, and emotional health— as women, as Tejanas, as Chicanas, as San Antonio residents, as *panzona* activists and cultural workers.

The incomparable Virginia Grise proved one of the strongest storytellers among the staff. Bárbara Renaud González, who worked as a consultant for the EPJC at the time (and became a contributor to the play), was also an endless source of tales, observations, and thoughtful connections. And the woman was downright funny. When Bárbara stopped by on certain afternoons and let her thoughts roll, she served as a storytelling instigator of sorts. In those days La Bárbara—as we affectionately called her—didn't own a car, so when she arrived she would inevitably bring us her report from the street, direct from the trenches of San Antonio as one can only witness by moving around on mass transit in a city designed for cars. Bárbara was also *flaca, eskinny*. So she would inevitably lecture us, as *flacas* tend to do—even as she snatched a Bill Miller's fried potato wedge off of somebody's plate—about our bad choices and future actions. When *flacas* meet *panzonas* in discussions about the body, *watchale!* Thus when Virginia and Bárbara got together what ensued was a raucous, sometimes bawdy, and always engaging analysis of politics and culture, history, or proclamations about beauty. Our small office (eight or nine of us packed in there) became electrified, the charged banter between Virginia and Bárbara egging us on. The room soon became filled with riff after riff on *panzas* as well as insights, self-deprecation, and smart-aleck wisecracks. In this cacophony, some of the first one-liners that would later be developed as monologues for our play were articulated. I contributed to the exchanges, of course, but perhaps more important I also listened hard, took it all in, and wrote it all down.

As a theater artist, I knew that this type of animated discussion among us—multivoiced, thus a jumble that was alternately sad, funny, self-righteous, melancholy, insightful, theoretical, and all shot through with a Tejana/o cultural vernacular—could be shaped into some form of theatrical storytelling. Fresh from working with people of color narratives at New World Theater in Massachusetts, I believed that a performance of some type could seize the ideas of these moments and make something of the raucous and highly theatrical enactments occurring right there in our workplace. This was precisely what our Texas Mexican city needed onstage: our conversation's Tejana-Chicana perspective.

Both Virginia and I had backgrounds in theater and writing, but it is the intermixing of those backgrounds—as well as our shared feminist practice—that I believe enabled us to create a stronger *teatro* between the two of us. Virginia had worked with the poets and activists raul r. salinas and Sharon Bridgforth and participated as an ensemble member in producer Omi Osun Joni Jones and Bridgforth's company for the Austin Project (tAP)[6] beginning in 2003. She had also trained in street theater traditions—specifically, in Latin American street theater in San Antonio in coordination with protests and political actions. I arrived at our collaboration with a more formal (traditional) education: a BA in theater, an MFA in theater design, and then a playwright/director/dramaturg during my Ph.D. program in theater. I had also made my living as a working theater artist in professional venues. In our collaboration and over the years, we have tried to figure out how to bring the best of our individual practices to the service of our shared projects, even as these experiences continue to shift and grow. This has required an intense (i.e., not always smooth) collaboration between us. Collaboration isn't easy, nor should it be. The extraordinary things you can make from it usually need the tumult and catalyst of thoughtful friction.

Despite the fact that we were only in our workplace, only cavorting with ideas among friends and coworkers, in Virginia I saw the splendor of her as a performer for the stage. She had what I as a director call the elusive "it" factor, that ineffable, irresistible charisma that compels your attention—this, by the way, also made her a powerful activist. But perhaps more important for my theatrical plans, I quickly discerned that she possessed precise comic timing and a happy self-possession of her body. She knew how to deliver a quip, interject a pun, or put an exclamation point on someone else's thought—all with a shake of her hip. She also had an articulate and large sense of physicality when delivering her stories or her analysis; she acted it out for us—usually taking up the whole office to do so. She had a humorous physicality born of drawing from distinctly Texas Mexican cultural manners, gestures, and expressions. For example, the crux of both "International *Panza*" and "*Panza* Girl Manifesto" depend on the moment when she rolls up her shirt and exposes her *panza*. This is a brave act, but this is also *puro* Virginia of those office days. She would do this all the time, causing calamity—"Put your *panza* away, Vicki!"—all for the sake of punctuating her *panza* theories. As a director I knew I had to transpose these gestures of ferocity, playfulness, and vulnerability into the play's staging.

Virginia's storytelling style also knitted together Chicana/o, Anglo, and Texas Mexican symbols, situations, politics, history, and cultural hot points. She often code-switched not only between Spanish and English but also between Tejana/o, African American, and Anglo-American manners of deportment to construct a thick crosshatch of meaning. Through this type of play with vernacular, orality, and physicality, she created *experiences* through her storytelling style, which spoke between cultures, languages, and versions of history. She did this innately and spontaneously; it was her *manera de ser* (way of being, modus operandi). I may have felt like a Tejana; she felt like San Antonio. This, I knew, could not be taught in professional training programs for actors or theater and in fact is often dredged out of Latina/o actors in the "professionalization" of their programs. Her style was effervescence in motion, and as a theater director I made sure to move that aliveness from our office into our production.[7]

Making Theater 1

I believe Virginia and I slowly came to realize the cultural power of the *panza* as a vehicle for theater in these group conversations. Foregrounding *panza* allowed us to tell the deeper stories about our community, the here and now of San Antonio. Friends saw the connection between us as collaborators for a theater project sooner than we did, and they urged us to work together, to get busy and make something of these *panza* insights that were rolling off our tongues, causing us to double over in pain and laughter with their brilliant, violent ironies. The idea was attractive to us. We both wanted to make more art—especially theater that engaged our community. And for us at the time, working on a theater piece, on something more directly personal, balanced the intensity of our activist work (but never replaced or negated it). Introducing the necessary elements of fun, creativity, and revelry into our social change energy would, in the end, bolster our activist commitments even as this kind of creative project could capitalize on our political thinking. It was how we chose to devote our rare moments of free time, our own time. Whatever came of it, it was a risk we were willing to devote ourselves to: it would be serious *fun*—so simple a word, so vast an idea. One spring day we made the decision to work together to fashion some type of a performance piece.

To ensure that "something" would come from our effort, we pinpointed a date for the first workshop to show the forthcoming project—even if it existed as only a rough conception. In August 2003 the Latina-focused organization Mujeres Activas en Letras y Cambio Social (MALCS) had selected San Antonio as the site for its annual summer institute. MALCS's many activities support Chicana/Latina and Native American women's issues in community and academic settings by conferences, education, networking, publications, and mentorship. We eyed their approaching national meeting as a place to perform because it would provide us with a supportive environment and an ideal audience—other women of color.[8] We proposed a staged reading as a session for the institute. The deed had been done. A commitment made. Now the real work.

Feeling San Anto, Thinking *Panza*

Earlier in the spring of 2003, I had written a few personal observation columns for the *SA Current*, a San Antonio alternative weekly newspaper. For one of these columns, I had sent letters to two dozen Tejana-Chicanas, asking them to help me compose a list of the "top thirty Tejana women of Texas history." I circulated this call for help in order to compose an observation that responded to a *Texas Monthly* article titled "30 Texas Women" that had named their thirty most important women in Texas history.⁹ The prominent Texas magazine's profiles had included only three "Hispanic" women. Not surprisingly, there was an abundance of replies to my petition. The whole exercise of gathering women's thoughts in this manner demonstrated how with a few well-placed emails and letters we could readily gather perspectives and insights from a wide range of women to accomplish our ambitions for our play.

Collecting materials in this way drew on strategies from the traditions of documentary theater, notably contemporary techniques practiced in the work of women playwright/solo performers such as Anna Deavere Smith and Eve Ensler, who wrote *The Vagina Monologues*. We, of course, were both familiar with Ensler's solo performance success with *The Vagina Monologues*, but unlike Ensler's wider ethnographic reach, we wanted our work to be culturally specific. We didn't want to look outward for our stories but rather inward, to the *historia* held on the tongues of San Antonio Chicanas—something we believed was not in the public sphere (as the *Texas Monthly* article clearly demonstrated). As we state in the play's prologue, "Before you can get to the *chocha*," we had "a different score to settle." We had to explore the *panza*. As we had learned from our community work, for Latinas/Chicanas, sexuality, race, gender, and culture crosscut much differently, perhaps both more expansively and at the same time much more timidly, than the prominent focus on female genitalia in Ensler's work.

We sent letters and emails to many San Antonio women asking for their participation. We described the rough parameters of our *panza* performance project, included a set of questions they might address ("prompts"), and asked them to respond in writing. This request (plea, really) asked for a straightforward narrative but also encouraged creative submissions about their *panzas*. Women replied with great generosity. All the pieces they submitted were performed in at least one phase of the play's development before we arrived at the final sequence of the script, published here.

Therefore, *The Panza Monologues* became an assemblage of women's writing and voices that Virginia and I worked on side by side to shape into a solo performance. As women's pieces arrived, we would think about how a certain response contributed to the play's growing ideas and form. We also wrote our own individual monologues and other material for the play from our life experiences. As our conception grew, three broad tenets guided us. First, although San Antonio has one of the largest Mexican American populations in the United States, theatrical production by Mexican Americans in the past twenty years or so (since the heyday of the Guadalupe Cultural Center's programming in the 1980s) was far too infrequent. We wanted more theater and more new works about the contemporary struggles of our city and its people. We were also in search of new aesthetic forms and more work written by women.[10] Second, narratives about *panzas* had deep resonance in Texas Mexican American communities precisely because the term *panza* quickly springboarded discussions of body image, obesity, diabetes, identity, place, and history. And third, the invocation of the *panza*—as both metaphor and body part—invariably incited a collective identity among Texas Mexicans. When people of both sexes and a wide variety of genders talked to us about their *panzas*, they inevitably created linkages that exposed the interconnections of race, culture, socioeconomic history, material and political realities and adaptations, and their bodies. We began to realize that we had struck on something much bigger than our locale, our *chistes*, and ourselves.

We received pieces from women with a range of writing experience. Some of the pieces required very little editing or dramaturgical work. For example, María Salazar submitted her poem "Inside the *Panza*," which she had written years earlier in a workshop conducted by Cherríe Moraga called "Indígena as Scribe." María was especially prolific; she also crafted new work written specifically at our invitation, including "Sucking It In," "*Panza* to *Panza*," and "Praying" (see pp. 58, 70, and 67, respectively). On the other hand, some contributions were from first-time writers, the first women in their generations to write down a story—as both Virginia and I are. And some women, so intimidated by forces that had imparted to them that they *couldn't* write, let us record their stories as they spoke them to us. Virginia conducted an interview with the workers' rights activist Petra Mata that was shaped into "A Hunger for Justice" (p. 55). When originally asked to share her *panza* story, Petra responded, "I'm not sure what to say." She began slowly with the words, "I have always been *pansonsita . . .* " Two hours later, she had shared the story of her upbringing and background, which described the strength of the *mujeres* who had raised her and also recounted the strike she had led against Levi Strauss after the company closed its factory on the south side of San Antonio in 1990, leaving 1,150 mostly female workers without jobs and with unjust severance pay. These efforts to gather Tejana women's voices are similar to those described in the 1981 introduction to *This Bridge Called My Back*. "Most of the women appearing in this book are first-generation writers. Some of us do not see ourselves as writers, but pull the pen across the page anyway or speak with the power of poets."[11] Over twenty years later, the same circumstances persisted. Still, so much work remains to be done.

As our material came together, it became clear that our play should be presented as a solo work featuring Virginia. As opposed to creating a multiperson piece, this choice would make the project manageable. Our decision also would bring forward Virginia's compelling storytelling talent. I would bring to bear my strengths as a director and dramaturge to stage the play. We both continued to write pieces, gather work from women, and then think on all the monologues that would eventually form the performance.

A Collection of Good Stories

Performance work, acting, is always more evident in terms of theatrical contributions. This is understandable: the performer is the most highly visible artist. But the work of a director or dramaturg requires some elaboration to understand how these important roles factor into making theater work. And frankly, I take the time to explain these roles in more detail not only because it renders a more complete picture of our collaboration to develop *The Panza Monologues* but also because they are essential, *imperative* in fact, to the continued development of Chicana/Latina voices and participation in American theater. We need to produce more Chicana/o dramaturgs and directors—and these numbers should make sure of the development of women in equal proportions—for the future of our *teatro*.[12]

Dramaturgs perform a wide, ever-changing variety of tasks for theater and performance, which is part of the reason their role is often a mystery to an audience. Any number of books relate different ideas about a dramaturg's work, which can be difficult to define because every dramaturg works differently for a production depending on the work itself, its subject matter, its means of production, and a dramaturg's working relationship with directors, designers, and actors. For *The Panza Monologues*, I functioned as a production dramaturg—someone who works with writers and directors in an immediate, hands-on way to develop performance work by bringing (among a host of other things) a deep, historically centered, and keenly conscious artistic eye to bear on the three-dimensional nature of a work of theater (the staging). This includes careful attention to the script—its content, its structure, its language, and its theatrical possibilities. So to serve as a dramaturg takes a bit of training: life experience learning about how theater works (figuratively and technically), knowledge of how stories are told theatrically, learning how to pull apart (and also perhaps reformat or recalibrate) the material's themes and content to discern how best to stage ideas— in space, in bodies, through voices.

Pulling together materials to make a performance piece does not actually make a performance piece: it's just raw material. A collection of good stories doesn't make a play. In this sense, all the contributed pieces that we received were simply possibilities. As a dramaturg, I worked to find the cohesion a theatrical presentation made from this type of material would need, the arc of the journey for our audiences. I searched for through lines, metaphors, organizing ideas, places for expansion or filigree, places for transition, any opportunity that would transform the raw material of the stories into emotional, thematic, consonant, and political sense. I "dramaturged" the pieces into theatrical shape to find our performance.

In part, this grappling occurred on paper: each piece was tightened or edited or enhanced or rearranged or reformatted in particular ways that would bring forth the strongest theatrical version of the writing. We often held writing sessions over late-night dinners at my home (after my work "day") and spent almost two months arranging the script's order even as we added new ideas to discern its overall shape. I had to imagine the pieces not as written stories but as spoken work that Virginia would embody and enact. I had to imagine it off the page, see it in multiple dimensions.

But thoughts on paper cannot reveal all your dramaturgical needs. Some dramaturgy had to happen in the presence of an audience. We needed to listen to their emotional responses, places where they laughed or wiped at their eyes, places where they fidgeted with their purses. You have to pay attention to an audience's many responses even if it's only to mark where they got up and went to the bathroom or yawned. All of this is good dramaturgical information. It's all about a search for rhythm: moving the material and ideas around to create emotional cadences—story rhythms so compelling that audience members can't imagine getting up to go to the bathroom. However, my dramaturgical work was always in conversation with my thoughts about physically staging the play—about directing the work.

Taking on the task of a theater director involves formulating the overall vision of the show as a staged piece. Directing needs your emotional empathy and intelligence as well as your visual acuity. Your brain and your heart. You decide on the nature of a piece's energies, the textures and moods of its visual pictures, and the style of the action, as well as the "blocking," that is, the positioning of bodies, objects, and movement onstage. As a director, you are shaping the schematics of all the events on the stage, from atmospheric moods to bodies. In effect, a director cares about the overall experience of the story being told onstage for the audience.

In the outcome of most solo work, when a director and dramaturg have done their jobs well, the actor's performance in the event comes to the fore. This leads the audience to believe that the actor has fashioned everything they have viewed onstage, everything that is felt, conveyed, or seen, but this is rarely the case. The show is as it is (good or not so great) usually because of the creativity of the director and the collaboration with fellow theater artists.

Panza Positive Cultural Practices

Over the course of three months, Virginia and I worked hard as performer and director, respectively, to develop the first workshop production of *The Panza Monologues*. But the first public reading of the script at MALCS in August 2003 was both compelled and interrupted by unforeseen events that fundamentally changed how we thought about our work as artists, activists, and Chicanas. In the midst of writing and compiling *The Panza Monologues*, Virginia was abruptly fired from her position as a staff member at the Center. The dismissal was sudden, unparalleled in the organization's history, and devastating for all staff members to witness in a space that promoted itself as adamantly and radically woman-centered, a place that sought to create bridges and hope. Only in retrospect have we been able to fathom how devastating and important living through an event of this nature has been to our relationships with formal institutions of social change because the event caused a crisis of activist faith in each of us.

What we have learned from working at the EPJC is that our point of conflict in the manifestation of its feminist institutional ethos lies in how we envision the production of art in the stead of social activism. For our part, we believed that we were staff members who offered an analysis *as* artists who were then *activating* art in our organization's work. We also truly believed that we were working in a collective; we had no titles among us, and we took great pains to embody this idea in our working relationships both among staff and with the community. Over time, it became clear that we were, in fact, implicitly (and in some ways explicitly) functioning under a hierarchical model of leadership. This arrangement of power caused deep confusion and many misunderstandings.

Our Center strove to be a cultural crossroads for many different communities of people in San Antonio who were united by the shared vision of social justice and equality. Because of its public support of underclass people's struggles within the city, its advocacy of responsible urban development and environmental custodianship, its queer inclusivity, and its advocacy for people of color, women, and workers, the Center has always been met with hostility from San Antonio politicians, power brokers, and elites as well as rabidly conservative city residents. Yet the EPJC is not a political organization. It stands as a cultural organization that attends to the cultures and cultural production of peoples of color, women, queers, youth, and the poor. This stewardship necessitates interrogation of the sociopolitical, historical circumstances that surround and, indeed, shaped those lives—by both the Center and its participants. In a place like Texas, famous for drawing clear lines in the sand, which demand the construction of deep binaries, the effort to envision complexity, cross-purposes, linkages, matrixes, or webs is considered not only a waste of time and city funding (which the Center received for cultural programming, meeting all city criteria) but also fundamentally dangerous to the precarious position of the status quo.

As a result, the Center's working environment was one continually interjected with hostility and on occasion violence directed at our events (LGBTQ film festivals drew a special wave of ire) or at any form of our participation or efforts that contributed art to campaigns that called for transparency, justice, and social equality. It's almost impossible to describe how crushing the pressure is for Texas Mexicans to remain apolitical with their cultural production, to fall in step with the city's promenade of colorful (and underpaid)

Mariachis and other "ethnic" flourishes. In other words, to divorce art from politics or historical insight that might call into account how racism and classism inhabits San Antonio. Appearances count to tourists, tourists count to dollars, dollars drive city leaders' efforts to promote a specific, usually culturally and racially sanitized version of "Old San Antonio." Unrest and opposition disrupts this chain of power, homogenization, and commerce.

Yet this is part of the work done by social justice organizations across the country and around the world. We can only speak to our circumstances and the events in our own lives, but as we have observed, this type of continual alertness to hostility wears people down quickly and turns your organizational focus ever outward. Staff bands together more tightly in the face of adversity, as campaigns directed specifically against your organization are especially good in creating solidarity and a sense of shared purposefulness. This type of responsive, reactionary focus—an ever-readiness of sorts—leaves very little space to launch an internal critique to address working conditions that may deteriorate in the face of adversity (despite a well-articulated mission). However, organizations working to deploy the practices of social justice *must* be willing to be as excruciatingly and constructively critical of themselves as they are of forces met in the larger social sphere. In a way, this explains why Virginia was fired one May afternoon when she launched a particularly incisive and vehement critique of our organization's internal contradictions, the discrepancies between our ethos and our practice, and especially the treatment of staff.

I believe that her critique was a heated, highly passionate eruption of many tamped down frustrations. Yet she was not alone in her observations; many of the staff had buried similar critiques for far too long and out of fear of receiving scorn. No one should have to work under this type of fear—least of all in a feminist space. Virginia's heightened energy and intentions that day were mistaken for peevishness, rather than the long-delayed, compounded exasperation they really were.

Over the years, when we have discussed these circumstances with other feminist activist workers connected to nonprofit or social justice organizations, we have learned that this paradox between feminist and progressive theory and practice exists elsewhere, many elsewheres. We've also experienced the same set of inconsistencies in other organizations that we have worked for or participated in. In conversation with our activist peers, through their stories, we have heard time and again the outlines of the basic shape of our own trying circumstances. We believe nonprofit, social justice workers are slowly naming the problem of institutional contradictions between intention and practice (even as there is intense pressure to remain silent), and thus we believe a growing critique of this type of ironic circumstance has begun to emerge. This is an important development because people have yet to speak fully of their contradictory (often demoralizing) activist experiences. Instead of speaking against an organization, and thus possibly diminishing or harming its standing, many strong activists are simply leaving the ranks of formal nonprofit institutions—burned out by the stress of contradictions such as these, or earning merely a "living wage," or simply daunted by an endless list of wrongs to right and too little affirmation or recognition for their efforts—their sacrifice. Formal studies of "nonprofit burnout" from the past ten years or so invariably substantiate our experiential knowledge of the problem and strongly advocate for systemic change in nonprofit organizations in order to retain good people with good intentions. We have come to the same conclusion.

As individuals, we each arrived at our positions at the Center with a stalwart commitment to social justice. Virginia's dismissal didn't change those principles; she left with the same commitment. I remained on the staff after her departure, but a year and a half later, right before Christmas 2004, I and a number of other staff members were laid off due to the Center's lack of funding for our salaries or hourly wages. Most of the employees who witnessed Virginia's firing were let go eventually.

Each in our own way, we had to slowly let go of one dream and begin conceiving of others. Virginia and I have never stopped working in the name of social justice or as artists. Instead we have taken the lessons and tools of that time and have been trying ever since to create what we now call *panza* positive cultural practices. This has been our transformation.

The community that was created around the table in our small office, however, did not disappear from our lives. While Virginia's firing shocked both staff and the immediate supporters of the EPJC, many allies rallied behind the forthcoming creation of *The Panza Monologues* and provided much-needed moral and financial support to help make our vision a reality. In the months that followed her dismissal, Virginia wrote her pieces for *The Panza Monologues* on borrowed food stamps and in her "restaurant office" at Café Latino, whose owner, Jessica Cerda, and the visual artist (then employee) David Zamora Casas fed her with many bowls of free *fideo*.[13] Virginia's "unemployment blues" would last throughout the summer as she regrouped and continued to work on our play.

New England Perspective

In the early summer of 2003, the Eugene O'Neill Theater Center's Annual Playwright's Conference selected my play *Cascarones* for development.[14] The conference, held in Waterford, Connecticut, offers playwrights a professional cast, director, and "on-call" dramaturg to help think through their scripts and a roughly staged workshop production of their plays. Scripts are selected from a national pool of submissions every year, and the purpose of the conference is to nurture and develop new work by playwrights. My time at this apex of U.S. American theater afforded me an unparalleled view of theater making from a highly privileged vantage point. Yet watching my play about a working-class Tejana/o family take the stage at the O'Neill—before a wealthy audience composed mostly of white, older New Englanders—only served to show me how removed Texas Mexican stories are, not only from that particular reality, but also from the American imaginary in general. As a playwright, I watched closely and thought about the hard work we have to "perform" as Latina/o playwrights in order to make our work resonate. And I asked myself, resonate for whom and to what end?

Panza Boot Camp

Although we were separated during my residency that summer, Virginia and I continued to work on *The Panza Monologues* by exchanging drafts and thoughts via email. I returned to San Antonio only a week before our first staged reading, in August 2003. In the compression of my living room and our seven days, our rehearsals were not only intense sessions to ready the play for staging but also dense conversations where we processed different theoretical and political questions about what it meant to be both artist and activist, what it meant to work as a Chicana and theater artist.

With only a week remaining to get our piece on its feet, the effort tested our stamina, focus, and abilities. Solo work demands endurance and technique from an actor/performer to accomplish the feat of capturing and holding an audience's imagination for seventy or so unbroken minutes alone onstage. It's not simply standing and speaking. There's a need for working knowledge about how theatricality functions in even the simplest moments of the performance. Virginia had worked more steadily as a performer, not as an actor, and never in a piece that required such physical stamina. Theatrical solo work is a unique mode of performance that demanded a new set of strengths from her, a different kind of performance knowledge that had to do with thinking about acting, creating character, and an overall theatrical awareness and concern for her actions onstage and her relationship to an audience. As we rehearsed that week, I helped Virginia recalibrate her *manera de ser* for the work of solo performance.

In my time away, Virginia had secured work as a public school teacher in bilingual education (after college she had also been a public school teacher), but for our reading she had to return to the Center one last time. We had suggested the EPJC as the site for our staged reading to MALCS, and this commitment remained intact despite our new circumstances. The return proved to be both uncomfortable and bittersweet for all concerned. Even though we were proud of our efforts for the staged reading, the reading made it clear that this particular era of our activism was over. On the other hand, our audience's response to the first staged reading of *The Panza Monologues* was wholly generous and immensely gratifying.

With the deadline of our MALCS performance met, we continued to refine the work dramaturgically. Watching reactions from our MALCS audience proved that we couldn't string some of the tougher monologues together ("Praying," "*El Vientre*"); it was too hard on everyone, including Virginia onstage. This is one of the important lessons learned from workshopping our piece. After this initial performance, we knew that we needed to trim the work, and we needed a frontispiece of some sort to make for a better start to the play overall, so I wrote our "Prologue." I specifically wrote it in direct address and asked for our audience's voices: "Say it with me, here we go: *¡PAN-ZA!*" It's a strategic invitation that requires active participation as response—a request to join in a collective aliveness.

As we moved forward with observations and lessons, the next steps for the play's development needed to address Virginia's knowledge and ability as a performer. Solo work needed tremendous amounts of her physical and emotional strength and endurance and would be made better in total by further training for the stage. We commenced what we jokingly called "Theater Boot Camp"—my version of acting training. This involved building on Virginia's performance strengths from street theater, performance art, and other types of activities such as giving protest speeches, speaking at press conferences, and teaching high school. But it also involved some "basic training" for the more formal processes of theatrical enactments—how to stand onstage, how to develop a gestural vocabulary, when to be still, how to "find your light," precision in physicality altogether, as well as attention to creating portraits or impressions for different monologues, developing her vocal strength and volume, learning how to move in a proscenium setting or on a narrow platform in a community college cafeteria. Women have always commented on how very physical Virginia is onstage; this was the result of our hard work at "Theater Boot Camp."

We soon learned we had to, in fact, return to our bodies to help build her physical strength for performing—our first staged reading had really wiped her out. We had *panzas*, but they weren't helping to tell the *panza* story. The need for physical conditioning became imperative. In an unprecedented move, we joined the downtown YMCA and went every single day, whirling on ellipticals, reciting lines. Memorization became another hurdle to overcome at boot camp. As fall progressed to winter, time at the gym not only developed much-needed physical endurance; it also instigated many conversations between us about the show's evolving shape and our next steps . . . as well as the changing shapes of our bodies (don't worry, we still weren't *flaca*, but we were in much better, and leaner, physical health).

"What do you need?": ALLGO

Our first reading provided us with a clearer picture of the potential of the materials we had written and gathered. Now we desired a fully staged premiere of the work in San Antonio. As we strategized to achieve this goal, we continued to refine the aesthetic components of our work. We presented revised staged readings of the whole play during Women's History Month at both the University of Texas at San Antonio and Northwest Vista College (San Antonio). During this time, Virginia often received invitations to read her poetry and writing at events in a wide variety of venues. With these lively audiences, she would also test new stylizations or edits of a monologue. Jumping into new spaces with new material steadily built up her growing performance skills and also taught us how to be extremely flexible and mobile.

In the spring of 2004 Resistencia Bookstore in Austin invited Virginia to give a reading, and she performed "The International *Panza*." Sharon Bridgforth, who has continued to be a supporter and ally of Virginia's creative work, was in the audience. Sharon worked as the artistic director of ALLGO, the Austin Latino/Latina Lesbian, Gay, Bisexual & Transgender Organization. Founded in 1985, ALLGO functioned as a community-based, nonprofit organization that focused on improving the lives of Austin's LGBT people of color communities through its civil rights activism, through proactive health and social services programs, and by promoting and fostering queer people of color's artistic voices and cultural production.[15] Similar to the work of the EPJC in San Antonio, ALLGO's mission underscored an abiding commitment to engendering social change. In her capacity as ALLGO's artistic director, Sharon invited us to stage the world premiere of *The Panza Monologues* in Austin, fully produced and coordinated by ALLGO. To this day, both Virginia and I find it extremely important (as well as a point of honor) that our woman-centered work was first picked up as a "show" by a radically queer, people of color–centered space, a nonprofit political-cultural organization, as opposed to a more traditional *theater* space or company. Yet again, we believe this invitation demonstrates that for the majority of people of color artists in theater, the paths for our work's development do not always follow the models of traditional American theater and most often works such as our own find their best allies in organizations and venues that directly open out or have dug deep into people of color communities through self-created spaces—the same spaces and people so many theater companies want to garner as new audiences.

Sharon Bridgforth is an award-winning, nationally recognized writer who was, in effect, secured by ALLGO as an artistic director in order to forward its vision of "a just and equitable society that celebrates and nurtures vibrant people of color queer cultures." With her artistic knowledge and practice and through her curatorial, educational, and presenting activities, Sharon's cultural programming efforts for ALLGO complemented and expanded on work done by its social change programming and advocacy.[16] When Sharon approached us to hold our world premiere at ALLGO, she asked a fundamental question: "What do you need?" This was an astonishing question, because its breadth looked not only to the care of presenting the play for ALLGO's community but also to our needs as artists. Furthermore, a production with ALLGO created an opportunity for us to work with someone of Sharon's caliber, a pivotal theater artist, as well as an opportunity to stage the play at a high aesthetic level, something deeply important to both Sharon and us. We, like Sharon, are searching for the power of new aesthetics.

At ALLGO we found tremendous care for our rehearsals as we moved through tech week and into production.[17] It was a small but important gesture: at every rehearsal, Sharon provided food for everyone—good, healthy, nutritious snacks and meals laid out on a table. (No Bill Miller in sight.) She also gathered together an extraordinary backstage crew—composed of a majority of women of color and queer women who were capable, organized, and extremely attentive collaborators. Some were old hands at theater; others we trained on the spot; all were thoroughly committed to the show. Our run consisted of packed, vocal audiences composed in large part of women, yet many men were in attendance too. All were mostly people of color to whom we presented a finely tuned, exuberant version of the play.

In addition to the world premiere of *The Panza Monologues* at ALLGO, Virginia and I had decided that what we needed was the possibility of publishing the play. ALLGO invited Jackie Cuevas and Jennifer Margulies's Evelyn Street Press (a small feminist press founded by queer women) to the project, and they partnered with ALLGO to publish the play's first edition in print—a slim, beautiful volume of all our efforts up to that time.

Despite these important developmental milestones, *The Panza Monologues* has never received a full production, a *premiere* in San Antonio, the city for which it was written and created. It has played to a number of closed, invitation-only events or special readings in the city, and it has even received a staged reading by a collective of University of Texas at San Antonio students and faculty in 2007. We did enter into negotiations with the Guadalupe Cultural Arts Center,[18] but those plans fell apart when the organization's president felt that the project (again, a theater project by Chicanas from San Antonio, written about San Antonio offered to a Latina/o cultural center—*qué, qué?*) did not merit space in its budget allocations. We also suspected that the work was too adamantly woman-centered for this particular president's leadership plans at the time. Later, the Guadalupe's president was removed from office (forced to step down), and he along with several board members were sued for sexual harassment and racial discrimination by a former Chicana employee; the suit was eventually settled out of court. This is why sometimes we gotta take our work into our own hands.

We have toured the show by invitation to Phoenix, Boulder, and Los Angeles, as well as up to northern Texas. We have also done additional readings of pieces from the play in various cities and venues across the United States. Each engagement helped us to refine its structure, content, and timing, bit by bit, in order to find its final form. And as we prepared for each opportunity, we rehearsed in the spaces that we could find—namely, my living rooms or backyards where we could really lay out our setting and have room to work. We have subsequently dubbed our production company Backyard Productions because of the fact that in those first years of *The Panza Monologues'* inception, we always ended up in my backyard to rehearse (even in our preparations for our premiere in Austin), portaging the small platform we use from one clear expanse of lawn to another. The irony was that we knew theaters across San Antonio sat empty, cool, and dark even as we ran through the monologues to the accompaniment of cicadas sawing away on those hot, sticky days.

We presented our performances in this rough-and-ready manner on and off for five years, but putting on the show in these sporadic spurts, usually for engagements that lasted just a few nights, is a costly endeavor in terms of both time and money. Again, we weren't usually invited by theaters.[19] Instead, other Chicanas and women of color across the country, who had either got their hands on a copy of the script or the first edition of the book or heard about the show by word of mouth, usually initiated our opportunities. In the years that passed, we moved on to other projects. We could no longer pull the piece together efficiently, and what we took in as compensation could not cover the costs of staging the performance. We made the decision to mount the show only if very specific parameters were in place: a good, fully working theater space, a crew to help run the show, strong administrative support, and a site or city that spoke to us. Slowly but surely, we came to consider the show semiretired.

From *Cuentos* to DVD

The story of *The Panza Monologues'* genesis could conclude with its premiere in Austin, or its city-to-city incarnations, or its various productions by groups of determined women. Yet our story with the play takes one more significant turn. While the development of the play revealed many personal and artistic challenges, some of the most important lessons we have learned about the conditions facing theater artists arrived with our effort to compose a more permanent document of the play in performance, something we have come to call a "performance DVD." Relating this supplementary journey enables us to illustrate the import of allies, the goodwill of communities, and the challenges of working outside of more established or institutionalized theater-making circuits: circumstances that not only we but also a vast majority of people of color or women theater artists face. As well, this final story allows us to articulate our concerns and actions about the dearth of theater in, by, and for Latina/o communities throughout the United States.

The retirement of our play compelled our thoughts to create some record of the piece that would be more permanent, something that captured our years of effort, something that could respond to different requests we had to bring the show to new venues, and something that would allow theater to reach more *gente* than touring a play city-to-city ever could. Moreover, as the new millennium aged, we were alarmed by the rising epidemic of obesity and diabetes, which had only grown worse among Latina/os.

We knew from our many readings and performances that *The Panza Monologues* struck a chord in people; its resonance was palpable. We had always played the show to a Latina/o majority audience (another rarity for mainstream American theater), and we could see that it helped to initiate important dialogues within these communities. But live theater is a time-dependent event—you have to catch it when it appears, and then just as quickly, it vanishes. It's also difficult to attend theater from a monetary perspective: you have to be able to afford to take yourself, your *novia/o*, your *abuela*, *las* girlfriends, your *tía, primo* . . . *tú sabes* . . . and as low as we tried to keep ticket prices, the price of a ticket still remained out of some people's reach. How then could we circulate this play more widely and effectively without either touring the show here and there in perpetuity or continuing to accrue the costs attached to producing live theater—even as new offers to perform it came in? How, given our severe financial, institutional, and artistic restrictions, could we solve the problem of making theater more accessible for Latina/o communities? How could we reach audiences we had yet to even consider or imagine?

With the advances of technology in mind, we started to investigate the possibility of using new media in order to circulate the show and were attracted to the idea of creating a recorded performance of the play. Here, we were inspired by and looked to precedents such as Margaret Cho's and John Leguizamo's concert films, the work of Anna Deavere Smith on video, and of course the wildly popular recorded performance of Ensler's *The Vagina Monologues*. The admirable production values of these stellar examples served as our motivation and benchmark.

In conceptualizing the play recorded for DVD, we believed a taped distribution of this kind offered the most portable, perdurable, and accessible solution to the task of circulating theater to Latina/o communities. More specifically, what we sought to capture in our recording was some semblance of a theatergoing experience. Our performance DVD sought to represent the multiple interactions you experience at a live theater event. The goal was not to convert the play into a movie version of itself, as many plays that make their way onto film or recorded media attempt to do—trimming away the roots of their theatrical origins. Instead, we wanted our DVD's viewer to be positioned as an audience member, seemingly seated among the live audience watching the play in real time. We hoped viewers could feel as if "they were there"—in community, watching, hearing, and participating in the vibrant response of the audience, and watching Virginia respond to them in that unique relationship that occurs between a live performer and his or her audience. We hoped that somehow a DVD experience would capture the stimulating energy of *a play* in performance, not supplement or erase it. With these intentions in mind, making the DVD would prove both one of the most exhilarating and confounding projects in our play's production history.

In July 2006, Virginia left San Antonio to begin her studies at the California Institute of the Arts Writing for Performance MFA program. In 2007, although I fervently wanted to remain in San Antonio, I too was lured away and finally committed myself to the academy by accepting a position at Florida State University. Undaunted by the separation of an entire continent, we began planning our project with the goal to meet in San Antonio in the summer of 2008 and film the play over three days of live performances.

A key element to accomplishing our performance DVD was funding, not only for the material needs of the project, but also for our desire to compensate the various collaborators we would call upon. We intended to offer every person working on our project fair compensation for his or her efforts and talents, which we did. From Florida State, I secured university grants as seed money. I also wrote grant proposals to foundations. Some applications reaped monies; others did not. Despite the possibility of disappointment, you have to continue to put forward your project and to keep a firm hold on its merits. These were the years before the advent of popular online fund-raising tools such as Kickstarter or USA Projects, funding streams that now seem de rigueur for self-producing arts projects. Therefore, we relied on raising funds by petitioning foundations. We were grateful to receive support from the Alice Kleberg Reynolds Foundation, a Texas-based philanthropic organization that funds Texas artists. We also drew heftily from our personal funds as well. As our funding grew, we booked a San Antonio Latina/o arts organization's newly built, well-equipped theater space for June 2008 and also secured a well-respected Tejano filmmaker to record our enterprise. We wanted an accomplished artist behind the camera. Moreover, filming the show would serve as our San Antonio premiere for the play (finally).

In every other production of *The Panza Monologues* to that date, we had selected recorded music to serve as a "soundbed" throughout the piece. Music helped to stitch together the show's many transitions and created a mood for each monologue. A selective choice of music also helped immure the piece in a *Tejana/o* sense of place. However, as we drew together ideas for making a more perdurable record of the play, we decided to enlist our good friend and musician Alexandro Hérnandez Gutiérrez to score the show with original music.

We had first worked with Alexandro (also a Tejano from South Texas— who was pursuing his doctorate in ethnomusicology at UCLA) as a musician for a theater project we developed in 2007 after *The Panza Monologues*. He was not only a consummate musician, equipped with an expansive knowledge of Mexican folk music traditions, but he had also demonstrated his artistic commitment to working within a feminist ethos. As we've explained in our "*Introducción*," we strive to implement feminist practices in our artistic work. By introducing Alexandro into the equation of *The Panza Monologues,* we did not want to gain original music for the play at the expense of laying aside our feminism. In other words, we knew that if we invited Alexandro to collaborate we would not have to fight with machismo, misogyny, a doubtful attitude, or belittlement or battle against sexist subordination of any type—especially in terms of our leadership and aesthetic choices. The bonus was that as a musician Alexandro understood inherently the powerful role music could play in live theater. His work to score *The Panza Monologues* has been a tremendous evolution for the play.

The plan was that all three of us would converge on San Antonio in May 2008, rehearse to incorporate live music, make good use of our many supporters in the city to fill in help with technical elements such as lighting and marketing, and then tape performances before a live Tejana/o audience in June. That was the plan.

Then things changed.

Nuestra Señora de los Ángeles

Making a piece of live theater takes equal parts meticulous, indeed obsessive, planning and constant openness to and patience with the arrival of shifting circumstances. But the series of events that led up to our taping dashed our best-laid plans on almost every count even as their unpredictability opened up unimagined opportunities.

Working from Los Angeles and Tallahassee, we planned and secured our needs. But when checking in to ensure our taping venue, we learned that our San Antonio space had scheduled another gig on our promised dates. Essentially, they had bumped us out of their theater. Moreover, the organization didn't have any other free slots available on its summer schedule. Summer was the *only* time we could gather all our people and resources for the project. We learned about this development in late April 2008, about a month and a half before we were set to meet in San Antonio and begin rehearsals for taping. I still believe it would have been easier to address this situation—find another theater, amend our schedule, or shift somehow—had we learned about a crucial development such as this at the beginning of March 2008. This would have (possibly) given us more time to work ourselves into another organization's theater space. Although we had booked the space at the beginning of February, we had not been contacted about the development in their calendar—a testament not only to our detailed attempts to put everything in place but also to this particular organization's disorganization. Perhaps we had planned *too* early? Yet this obstacle is indicative of attempting to create artistic work in San Anto in so many ways.

Over the phone and a continent apart, we scrambled to secure a theater space in San Antonio that had (1) technical equipment such as a lighting board, lighting instruments, and sound equipment; (2) an adequate stage space, that is, a formal playing area; and (3) a location in the city that wasn't prohibitive for our community. Specifically, we wanted a location near Tejana/o communities. Because the majority of San Antonio's Mexican American population resides on the south or west side, we needed a site amenable to these communities. As we knew all too well from our time as presenters/artists/organizers for the EPJC, a location on the north side would deter most Mexican American audience members, many of whom were first-time theatergoers.

Our search for a viable alternative encompassed an exhaustive series of phone calls, dead-end inquires, and various speculations that in the end turned up nothing. Appropriate theater spaces were either already booked for the summer, in challenging locations, or too costly to rent. May was simply too late in the calendar year to find open slots in summer schedules.

For a city of San Antonio's size there are very few well-run, professionally equipped theaters, much less theater spaces that are accessible to independent artists (i.e., not attached to companies or that don't require sky-high rental fees), especially to Mexican American theater artists. But with time in the balance, we were willing to make *almost* anything work as we even considered bars and backyards that might do the trick. Finally, faced with no possible venues in the city and with the days counting down, our prospects turned extremely grim.

Nuestra Señora de los Ángeles came to our rescue in this eleventh hour when San Antonio de Padua couldn't help us find our lost space. At Cal Arts, Virginia had worked with East Los Angeles's Plaza de la Raza's Youth Theatre Project, a program of Cal Arts' Community Arts Partnership. With our options exhausted in San Antonio, she suggested the radical idea of shifting the project to Los Angeles. Based on her connections, we could ask to rent Plaza's facilities. Although a geographic switch of this kind would be difficult, it would satisfy nearly all of our requirements. We'd have access to a theater space that would work adequately for staging and recording. We'd have access to rehearsal facilities at Cal Arts. We'd be closer to Alexandro. And in East Los Angeles we'd still have the ability to gather an audience populated by *gente*. While we had sent out feelers in San Antonio for two solid weeks with no results, all it took to secure renting Plaza was one five-minute phone call. It was decided: we wouldn't tape in San Antonio; we would move to Los Angeles. Plaza agreed to rent their theater to us in early August for a "one night only" performance (we had originally wanted three nights in San Anto). We quickly rearranged our lives, plans, and people, thankful but shaken. In mid-July I joined Virginia in L.A. to begin rehearsals and coordinate finer details.

Over the course of the summer, once we switched our filming location to California, Alexandro had done an extraordinary thing. With access to top tier Mexican American folk musicians in Los Angeles, he had gathered together three other musicians to create a virtuosic quartet. As a director, I placed them onstage to showcase their talents and create a sort of backup band for Virginia's performance. Looking back on this particular development from the long view of hindsight, we cannot envision how we would ever again return to recorded music for a performance. Again, working from our steadfast goals to foster women, Alexandro had made sure that the musicians he invited included an even number of women and men. These good people and their jubilant spirits provided a much-needed salve for the wounds incurred by rapidly changing circumstances, such as the next challenge ahead of us: the loss of our filmmaker.

With the shuffling circumstances of our change in time schedule and the move to a new city, the many elements of our project had to be juggled rapidly and with a keen eye for all the moving pieces. Amid the chaos of July, our filmmaker had to bow out unexpectedly. The most important linchpin for our film project had been pulled.

If you spend any amount of time in L.A., it soon becomes apparent that there are many Tejana/o transplants finding home there, among them our friend Mirasol Riojas, who at the time was a graduate student in film history at UCLA. In our desperate search for a filmmaker, we pulled on Mirasol as a resource, and she placed a call to an acquaintance. Thus five days out from taping, we gained our new filmmaker, Roberto Oregel. Miraculously, not only did we manage to secure a new collaborator at this very late date, but he was also a Chicano filmmaker. At least we were in the right town to address this particular calamity. What we didn't know at the time and learned only when we began working with him was that Roberto was also a tremendously gracious, thoughtful, and giving artist. As she had done earlier that spring, Nuestra Señora de los Ángeles had come to our rescue again.

On 2 August 2008, we welcomed an overflow audience of over two hundred people to Plaza de la Raza's Margo Albert Theater on Los Angeles's East Side for the taping of a fully staged production of *The Panza Monologues*. The line of audience members waiting to come in stretched around the building like a necklace, and as we heard from friends and allies serving as ushers, people tried to sneak in through every available door once the theater reached its capacity. With the camera rolling, the Margo Albert Theater shimmered with energy as our L.A. audience responded to the performance with their hungry attention, laughter, and ample shout-outs of recognition and affirmation.

No one in Los Angeles would have heard about the free invitation to participate as our film audience in the summer of 2008 without the tireless efforts of la Chingona de Publicity, Karla Legaspy. Her marketing strategy consisted of putting the word out all over the streets, clubs, and *nichos* of L.A., filling the city with handbills, flyers, and irresistible charisma. This was how she delivered our standing-room-only crowd at Plaza. Abel Salas (another Tejano transplant in L.A.) worked on getting the word out too and helped with many technical needs backstage. Marissa Ramirez, our very first technical aide extraordinaire, flew in from San Antonio to assist. In addition, numerous volunteers who seemingly appeared from the ether aided us. Mirasol Riojas labored to piece together the many angles Roberto had shot, and by the summer of 2009, she had edited our footage into a seamless video for replication.

Making theater demonstrates the power of community and humbles you with its possibilities, unexpected joys, and, in our case, cultural edification. Even for a solo piece, it takes a group of dedicated collaborators or allies, willing to stand side by side with you, putting their hands and hearts into the mix if you are to accomplish the feat. In essence, what you see in front of the camera on our performance DVD in no way accounts for the multitude of hands behind it or the challenges surmounted to produce it.

With our performance DVD and the first edition of the script in circulation, the play has begun to find a life of its own, one separate from us. We have recently noted an increase in groups of Chicanas and their allies in university settings who have taken up the task to produce their version of *The Panza Monologues* as a theater event or organize screenings of the DVD. Although the first edition of the script is out of print, *las mujeres* have found copies and produced collective shows. Some of these collective productions have been staged at schools in California, Oregon, Texas, and Colorado. And, we have heard rumors about productions presented in other places. We continue to sell copies of the DVD at *Panza* Parties or through the modern survival mechanism of our Internet sites. We continue to think about the role of theater and theater artists in our contemporary era. The lessons we have gathered along the way are many. We hope that with the availability of this second edition of *The Panza Monologues* even more *mujeres* will have the opportunity to hear the stories our play relates. They are important. *Son importantes y nos importan.*

It all began with *cuentos, chisme, chistes,* and the intimacy of *mujeres* talking. It was never meant to be repeated, but like any juicy, good story—it was.

IRMA MAYORGA
with remembrances & thoughts by Virginia Grise

DOS/TWO

SCRIPT OF
THE PANZA MONOLOGUES

THE PANZA MONOLOGUES

PROLOGUE

An altar lit by strings of lights sits upstage center. An ensemble of four musicians, two women and two men—Los Flacasos—are seated upstage left. The women are dressed bien *classy and the men sport "pachuco chic" long-sleeved black shirts, pants, smart ties, tight fedoras, and badass Stacy Adams two-toned wing tip shoes.*

Los Flacasos begin playing a son jarocho, *"El Cascabel."*

Lights rise to reveal the stage. A wooden stool sits in front of the altar.

The altar is decorated with great detail. It consists of two levels: a 4' x 6' platform about 18" high with a smaller 14" cube centered on top. Colorful skirting conceals the platform's legs. Roughly, these two pieces form the shape of a pyramid.

Decorations and meaningful obsequios *have been placed on the altar, including electric candles, pictures of the playwrights as young girls in various outfits that show their bare* panzas, *family photographs, a basket of confetti, pliers, a shopping bag, cut flowers in vases, scarves, piles of books by women of color feminist writers such as Cherríe Moraga, Gloria Anzaldúa, June Jordan, Audre Lorde, and Sharon Bridgforth and others as well as plays that serve as inspiration. There are also pieces of cut fruit and dried chiles in bowls, cans of beans, boxes of fideo, and other assorted favorite prepackaged foods, a small United Farm Workers' flag, two empty tin cans connected by string, a large palm plant, a pillow, a fedora, a plastic image of the Virgen de Guadalupe that lights up, a Styrofoam cooler with the state of Texas stamped on it, and a black feather boa. Most items gathered were from our homes. Strings of multicolored lights are threaded between all the objects.*

At stage right, a closed folding chair leans against the altar, and at stage left stands an ironing board and iron.

Behind the altar hangs a large screen decorated with brightly colored ribbons on each side. When each monologue begins, the title of the monologue is always projected on the screen.

As the music builds, Vicki enters and sits on the stool. She pauses a moment to take in the audience and then begins.

There once was this play. This really quite interesting play.
It was this play about women. Well, not just anything about women,
but about them in a specific way.

It described all these women from different places, different
groups, different races, different ages, with different boyfriends
and girlfriends and lovers who were both boys and girls.

And it told stories.

Stories about these women that united them
through one particular thing.
The play was about *(beat)* their vaginas.
But vagina is not what I call it. I call it my *chocha*.

Translation.
Recoding.

Sometimes translation makes all the difference in the world.

Just listen:

(said low) Vagina.
(said lyrically) Chocha.
(said low) Vagina.
(said lyrically) Chocha.

One has music.
The other sounds like sandpaper.

But what this woman's play said once again—as so many great
women have said over and over—is that we are in a war. A war for
our own bodies. And, in the war of our bodies, it became clear
to me that before you can get to the battle of the *chocha*, we have
another score to settle, another place on our beautiful bodies

to baptize,
actualize,

a place that had been

demonized,
sterilized,
starved,
stuffed,
covered over.

In fact, we have been encouraged, or commanded, or scared
into actually getting rid of it. Before I can talk about the *chocha*,
I need to tell the story of us—

Whose us?

We are the ones who carry the sun in our skin, brown like
almonds or *café con leche, color de la tierra.*

Tú sabes, the "us" that uses the word *chocha, ¡Panocha!*

But you see—the story of us is not just *chocha* it's . . .

Panza
¡Sí! ¡Panza!

Now you know what I'm talking about, don't you?
Don't you? Come on. *Ándale.*

> *waits for recognition from her audience*

Say it with me, here we go:

urges the audience to join her—and they always do!

¡PAN-ZA!
¡Brava, brava, bravissima!

Now, raise your hand if you've thought about your *panza* today!
Cuz I know that when I talked to my homegirls, they weren't all spilling
over stories about their *chocha*. There we would be—with big plates of
fideo, or *pan dulce*, or *menudo*, or *tripas*, Sea Island, El Camarón Pelado,
China Sea Buffet, or Luby's—and we'd all be telling the stories of
our *panzas*.

And I thought, we gots to hear the story of the *panza*. And so I listened,
with my heart in my hands, I listened as women told me about the life
of their *panzas*. *Panzas* were crying out everywhere: "Tell my story!"

Shift in mood, the telling of a secret, something special.

Now someone's *panza* story is a sacred story, and to share it with someone else is to tell them about the condition of your life. Cuz the *panza*, it
does have an ego. Every time your *panza* pooches out from behind that
long sweater you try to put on or when you're walking by a piece of glass,
turn, look, and it's flashing its big *panza* "I'm here" *lonja* roll back at you.
That's it—that's its ego.

Cuz society has told it again and again—"You're bad. Bad *panza*. Go
away." The *panza*, it knows, in its own way. It knows, about us, about
you. But the *panza* also knows that it ain't alone there in the middle of
us. That it needs the legs to walk, the arms to carry it, the mouth to feed
it, and the heart to excite it.

And when you listen to the *panzas* of all the *mujeres* out there, you can
hear the world according to women. That's the power of a *panza* story.

Well, *that* woman, she called *her* play *The Vagina Monologues*. And for
her play, she sat on a stool, kind of like this, like me here. She got paid
to go all over the world collecting stories about the *chocha*, and she didn't

even get dressed for her performance—she wore a slip. And she spoke her stories from her stool. But the *panza* is the heart of *ritmo*, movement.

Music builds.
She begins swiveling, tapping her pata pies, *and moving her arms.*

So, I can't sit here anymore.

She rises.

My *panza*'s got to move!

And in honor of all those women who let me borrow their stories, I share them with you cuz they're not just her stories

points to a woman in the audience

or her stories

points to another woman in the audience

or my stories anymore. They are us. They are our stories.
I present to you . . . *The Panza Monologues.*

A new slide is projected on the screen: The Panza Monologues.

Slide fades out, lights transition.

She dances to stage left side of the altar, taking the stool with her.

HISTORIA

Music rises and underscores throughout. Vicki stands center stage.

In the beginning . . .
    cuz every people needs a story that starts that way.

In the beginning . . .
    was the sound like the universe exploding.

It came,
        took form,
                gave life.

In the beginning . . .
    when there wasn't just one god, but many gods.

Las diosas dijeron:

"Give me *panza* . . .
    large and round.

Give me *panza* . . .
    to keep me warm.
Give me *panza* . . .
    my body's own drum,

> *Stands with her feet apart, places her hands firmly on her panza, and shakes her hips to Los Flacasos' funky riff.*

music making sensation."

> *Moves to the altar as she speaks and picks up the basket of confetti. She showers confetti around the stage as she speaks.*

Las diosas dijeron:
    "Let there be *panza*!"
        And so it was.

La panza—esta parte tan importante de nuestro cuerpo.

Allí va todo—
> *los ovarios,*
>> *la matriz,*
>>> *el vientre.*

Las diosas
> prayed,
>> lit *velas,*
>>> asked the moon.

"Watch over our creation. You, who controls the waves, will control woman—her bloods, *cada factor, cada molinito de su cuerpo.*"

Las diosas imagined *un mundo donde la gente no tendrá que sufrir hambres.*

"You will learn your *abuelita's remedios—aceite de olivo calientito, un tecito de canela o manzanilla. Curarás con tus propios manos.*"

Las diosas dijeron:
"Let there be *panza!*"
> And so it was.

She turns quickly to face stage right.

¡Que vivan las lonjas!

LOS FLACASOS
> *¡Que vivan!*

VICKI
> So it was written on the bodies of women.

She turns quickly to face upstage.

¡Que vivan las chichis!

LOS FLACASOS
> *¡Que vivan!*

VICKI

So it was written on the hearts of *panzoncitas.*

¡Que viva la panza!

LOS FLACASOS

¡Que viva!

She slowly rotates to face audience, extending her arm and pointing at them.

VICKI

So it was written on the bodies of Chicana heavyweights
all across Aztlán.

Live your life
without shame

LOS FLACASOS

¡Que viva la panza!
¡Que viva la panza!
¡Que viva la panza!

VICKI

So it was written.

*Lights shift. She picks up the "telephone" made of two tin cans and
string from the altar and sets folding chair downstage left.*

Historia by I. Mayorga © 2005. Courtesy of I. Mayorga. Virginia Grise in *The Panza Monologues*, presented at Plaza de la Raza in Los Angeles for a special one-night performance on August 2, 2008.

INSIDE THE PANZA

New music rises and underscores throughout the following cuento.

When I was a kid
I would watch TV with my mom and dad.
Sometimes, I would rest my head on their *panzas.*
As my ear pressed against their full bellies,
I would hear water sounds, creeks, gurgles, and swooshes.
To me, it sounded like a river gushing through my *papi's panza*
To me, it sounded like an ocean way out deep in my *mamí's panza*

And in my head
I could see whole worlds inside their *panzas*
I would imagine canyons and mountains in their *panzas*
I would imagine little people running around in their *panzas*
And then my head would picture
Their whole body as vessels for whole worlds
In their legs, I could picture Japanese people farming their own land
And on the backs, I could see animals like turtles and rhinos running
   all around
On the shoulders, I pictured cowboys and Indians shooting it out just
   like the John Wayne
And Lone Ranger movies I watched with my dad on Saturday afternoons

But the *panza* was a special place, cuz that's where all the water was
And that's where all the people were
So I would be careful not to crush *la panza,* because that's where all
   the little people lived

Then one day, I was laying on the couch with my mom and dad,
   watching TV
And I heard a gurgle sound inside my *panza*

*She places one tin can "telephone" on her ear and one
on her panza. She "listens" to her panza as she speaks.*

Was it a river? A pond? A lake?
Did I have little people living inside me too?
I must have worlds inside me
I must take care of the little people inside my *panza*
So for weeks I was careful at play
I was careful when I slept
Careful not to crush *la panza,*
because that's where all the little people lived

And from that day on, I knew
the *panza* was the most important part of the body,
because people lived inside the *panza,*

including me!

She continues, "listening" to her panza as music fades. She slowly
offers her "earpiece" can out to the audience so they can hear too.

Lights dim. Music transitions. She places cans on altar,
strikes folding chair, and sets up stool stage right.

She picks up shopping bag from the altar and places it on
floor beside her stool. The shopping bag holds a pair of red,
higher than high-heeled shoes or tacones.
She sits on her stool.

FROM CHA-CHA TO PANZA

New music rises and underscores throughout the following cuento.

(*seductively*) I wasn't always big. I use to be cha-cha thin, tall and skinny like my gringo daddy, and I would wear *tacones*, black with straps that reached across my ankles, boots that stopped short of my knees, diamonds across my feet.

Tacones.

Upper leather, suede, alligator, snake, all leather and in different colors: brown, red, cork, beige, black, blue even. *Tacones* that matched the dresses I wore, dresses that always fit my body, showed shape, whether they were long with a slit on the side, in the front, in the back—separating my *piernas*, or short—showing my thighs.

Me and my *tacones*.

> Stands, pulls the tacones *out of the shopping bag and holds them up*
> *for the audience to admire.*

And they weren't *puta* shoes.
Girl, they were classy.

Tacones made me feel taller, stronger, more sure of myself. Not submissive or antifeminist but like the Virgen in a Yolanda López painting, karate kicking her way out of blue veil with gold stars, stepping on the head of an angel with her *tacones. Pues yo también.* I throw punches for my *raza* and I can do it with my *tacones* on too, just like the old skool *cholas* used to do.

> Sits on the stool and begins to put her tacones on.

And the men, the men were scared of me when I walked into the cantina—made up, hair swept, red lipstick and *tacones*. You see, men like fuckin but they don't like bein fucked, and when I walked in I wuz

the one doin the choosin. I didn't sit back in dark corners waitin for
someone to ask me to dance.

I asked you.

Locked eyes and said, "You will dance this polka with me," sometimes
without even sayin nuthin. Other times I'd say, "Fuck all of y'all" and
take the dance floor at Daddy O's all by myself.

> *Music erupts into full-blown conjunto.*
> *She dances across the stage, swirls, turns.*
> *Music lowers, she remains standing.*

And they all watched.

Old skool *vatos*, young *cholos*, graduate students—trying to remember
their hometown *barrios* in a bar east of the freeway, forgetting in
between too many beers. Hell, even the *cholas* were lookin. Some,
worried I'd take away their man. Others, others just wanted to dance
wid me.

Be free.
Be free like me.

They say a bar is a man's space, but I owned that motha fucker. I walked
in with my go-go juice in blue bottle cuz my dad once told me, "Beer
makes you fat Virginia," so I drank vodka on the rocks, learned how to
play pool, "Call your shots cuz I'm not fuckin around." And I learned
more about community politics, who owns who, who runs what, than
I could of ever learned workin at a cultural center.

I claimed power through my pussy,
and I didn't even have to let any one in.

I just had to let em all know I knew I had one and that I controlled
my own *chocha*. Yeah, I owned that motha fuckin bar, till the city tore
it down after li'l Danny got cut.

> *She sits.*

I use to be cha-cha thin. Proud of my calves, well defined, calves that didn't look like my mother's calves. My mom's calves were more like tree trunks. Her whole body was one huge *bloque*. My mother gave us everything, everything, but I never remember her having anything. Instead of *tacones*, she wore *chanclas*. She use to threaten us with her *chancla*, and it didn't matter if she was big and old, she could still bend over, take off her shoe, grab us by the arm, and *meternos un chingaso*, real quick like—good ol' fashion *chancla* discipline.

My mother used to say that my father wanted boys. We were three girls. She never said what it was she wanted. That was her way I guess. I'm not sure if my mom ever really loved my dad, but I grew up thinkin that women that fell in love were weak.

I never thought my mom was pretty, even when she was younger, and I never wanted to look like her, but slowly the image of my mother crept into my own body. Slowly after too many two o'clock after closin time tacos, candy bars and coke for breakfast, they started callin me *dis* (short for *gordis*) instead of La Vicki.

Cha-cha became *panza*
and not little *panzita* even.

The whole body grew and you know—it's not easy balancin this much woman on an itty, bitty heel. I no longer walk real straight and tall. Hell, I look more like a weeble, wobble—all my weight on a heel as wide as my pointing finger, with my foot arched in the middle. I feel the weight of my *panza* all the way in the ball of my foot. And when your *panza* gets bigger, so do your feet—and those thin, sexy straps that use to hold your feet in, well they aint that sexy anymore. You've got these little *lonjitas* hangin off the side of your shoe, and it causes your feet to swell. It's like they're chokin, pulsatin, gaspin for air as they struggle to balance all of you on a *tacón*. And to tell you the truth, I don't really feel so strong, so sure of myself anymore. Shit, I'm scared I'll fall when I'm dancin and the people that are lookin at me now are starin because they're scared if I go too low, I might not be able to get back up. They're worried I'll hurt someone out there.

From Cha-Cha to Panza, The Panza Monologues DVD still © 2012. Courtesy of the authors. Virginia Grise in *The Panza Monologues*, presented at Plaza de la Raza in Los Angeles for a special one-night performance on August 2, 2008.

There's somethin classy about cha-cha.
Medias and *tacones.*

But when cha-cha becomes *panza,* and you think you can still pull
the same shit you could when you were 21, you just look kinda silly.
You lose your *tacón* super powers and your magic slippers—well,
they really were just *puta* shoes. Your dress clings tightly to *lonjas,*
and you can't lock eyes with anyone anymore and talk to them without
speaking cuz now they only look at your huge *chichis,* and, well,
chichis just aren't as powerful as *chocha.* I don't know why.

Who makes these rules?

Music rises. Lights dim.

*During the transition, Vicki sits on the stage right edge of the
altar, takes off her* tacones, *places them in the shopping bag,
and sets this back on the altar. She remains seated.*

A HUNGER FOR JUSTICE

*New music rises and underscores throughout the following.
"A Hunger for Justice" video commences. Vicki remains seated on
the altar for the video's narration. Projected on the screen, the video
displays a series of old black-and-white photographs of Mexican American
families in South Texas from the early twentieth century. Images used
in the video were gathered from the U.S. Library of Congress
digital photo collections. An "older mexicana" voice-over plays on the
house speakers—forming a narration underneath the images.*

VOICE-OVER

I have always been *pan-son-cita* not *pan-zona*, right. We come from fat
people, from big people. *Yo siempre fui gruesa desde chiquita. Venimos
de otros tejidos de herencia.* My maternal grandmother was a short lady,
dark *con facciones toscas.* My grandmother was a fighter, a worker, a
strong woman because sometimes the world makes you that way.

Yo nací en un pueblo en México, *un pueblito que se llama* Bustamante,
Nuevo León. I was born there, and I was raised in Nuevo Laredo,
Tamaulipas. I was raised mostly with my grandparents. My mother
died when I was five. We were four boys and two women, but my
little sister died, so I was the only one left.

We lived on a ranch. *En el rancho, en aquellos tiempos, la vida era muy
diferente pero éramos felices, éramos bien felices.* We didn't live with all the
pressures we have now. *Me acuerdo que mi abuela se levantaba bien temprano. Cocíamos el maíz, este, lo molíamos en el molino de mano, este. O si
no, lo quebrajaba en el metate. Hacía las tortillas sobre leña.* You know. *Esto
era divino. Esta era nuestra cultura. Estos eran nuestros valores de saber valorar lo que teníamos y apreciarlo.* That was our culture. Those were our
values. We valued things. We appreciated it. *Entonces, era una vida bien
bonita, bien bonita porque teníamos lo básico.*

I remember we had chickens, pigs, goats. When we killed the chick-
en, we would have a party because not every day could we have meat in
our soup. We would make *mole* or soup, and it was a wonderful day. I
would like to go back to those times because in that harmony we lived,

we didn't have so much pressure. You've gotta do this. Run here. Do that. You know, with what we are living with now. People did things in time.

Lights rise. Video fades out.

Vicki enters carrying the ironing board and iron to center stage and begins pressing a shirt. She continues in the persona of the older mexicana *woman from the voice-over.*

But the reality of living is getting food to your *panza.* I used to work at the Levi's jeans factory. But then they laid us off, hundreds and hundreds of us have lost our jobs. We had to do something—use our minds. During times like that, we work with our mind more than any other part of the body. Overnight, we became organizers. We were connecting the movement, the struggle, with the economy, with the systems. *Entonces,* why not center the body with everything we do?

Pensábamos que íbamos a sufrir hambres. When we worked, we had a good salary. Each week we had a check, a check we could go to the store with and buy 100, 200 dollars worth of food. After the plant closed, we would go to the store, and we could only get what we thought we *might* eat and sometimes not even that. When the plant shut down, what experienced the majority of the pain was the *panza* because there wasn't going to be nutrition, and we had a hunger for justice.

A lot of us lost weight because the suffering is reflected in all the parts of your body. So if you are suffering—so is your *panza.* Why? Because that is your *compañera* for life inside of you and it is hurting. It feels used. So if you are hurting in the heart, your spiritual self, I think the *panza* is hurting too. It's hard to identify, but the *panza tiene un motorcito* that connects it to everything. It must—right?

If you look at the *panza,* it's like half body from the *panza* up and half from the *panza* down. Sometimes we do not include it in our work and our mind goes elsewhere, and it's not important to us. We don't pay attention to our bodies. We have to pay attention and do things for our bodies. Why can we do things for our family, for the organization, but for us—when do we do for us? If we start with the *panza* that's good because the *panza* is a room where everything comes from. The *panza* is the only place where the baby grows, the place where you give birth. What allows for the *panza* to grow so much? And there are some women who do not just have one but two, three, four, five, six babies. Can you imagine? How important! I think if your head got that big you would die. Your arms, your legs only get that big if you are sick. What an important part of your body to give you all that *flexibilidad*.

I think our *panza* has a heart that in extension suffers—suffers from our not taking care of it. So, if the *panza* is one of the most important parts of our bodies, it's important that we think about it and tie it to everything we do. If our body breaks down, then how are we going to do all this work?

Lights dim. Transition music rises. Vicki returns ironing board to the altar and sits on the altar's edge.

SUCKING IT IN

*The following monologue is narrated through a
voice-over by Vicki while she enacts its story.*

VOICE-OVER

It happens; every now and then I have to pull them out.

She rises, frantic.

I search and search for them. I look for them everywhere: the junk
drawer, the toolbox, the trunk.

*She pulls pliers out from preset hidden spot on the altar—
holds them up triumphantly.*

Finally, I find them . . . the pliers.

I use them, especially when I put on my tiiiiight jeans.

She mimes putting on jeans.

Like everyone else, I put one leg in first, then the other. I hoist the denim
over my flat butt; I pull the jeans around my hips, coming full circle to
the front of my body.

Well, almost full circle.

*She struggles to "pull jeans on" over her tummy and hip area.
The overall effect is a violent struggle.*

The jeans will not close. I tug and pull the ends together, trying to
make them meet.

twists and turns

I suck in my tummy, I exhale, pulling and pulling, doing all I can to
bring the ends to the center of my *panza*.

(breathy and with exertion) I am so close to bringing that damn copper button into its little slit.

I'm . . . so . . . close!

The button slips out of my fingers. I stretch the ends, and by some miracle, I finally sneak that tiny copper circle into its spot.

(breathless) Almost there . . .

I look down, and I see a piece of my *panza* peeking out of the zipper.

mimes the following with precision

I must get the zipper to close.

I tuck the peeking *panza* inside my jeans. I grab the zipper and hope I can get it to the top. My *panza* is determined to stick out, determined to say . . .

"Hello world, here I am!!!"

So, I try and try to find the strength to zip up my pants.

The jeans . . . will . . . fit.
I know it.

I just gotta . . . tuck in my *panza* and find the strength to quickly zip up the jeans.

I see the pliers.

They are right where I left them—on top of the dresser.

stumbles/walks over to the altar where she has left the pliers

They look a bit out of place on the dresser, but there they are ready
for use.

grabs pliers and holds them up

I wrap my hand around the rubber-covered handles, lie down on
my bed, exhale,

lies down center stage on her back and struggles with pliers and zipper

I take pliers to zipper, and with one quick pull close the zipper.

Lies still. Then pumps her fists into the air with victory.

My little *panza* is now hidden behind the zipper. I wiggle around a bit;
the denim has stretched, my *panza* is settled.

*Slowly and stiffly, she rises into a standing position and mimes checking herself
out in a "mirror" as voice-over indicates.*

Taking a quick look in the mirror, I smooth out the jeans.

Everything looks good.

Thanks to my *panza* pliers.

*She holds up pliers victoriously. Transition music rises. Lights dim.
She places pliers on altar and moves folding chair downstage right.*

MY SISTER'S PANZA

Music rises. Lights rise. Vicki is seated on the chair and holds a small red book, which she "reads" from.

My sister lost her *panza*, lost it because of her husband. It left because he left her. It was bound to happen. You see, it sounds almost too good to be true, but they met and married through a personals ad. One of those corny "I'll never do that" ads that you only *think* you'd never do.

She did it. She threw her hat into the fire and picked an ad out one day, something that made her laugh.

They decided to meet at the Tiki Room, this fake Polynesian-style bar, complete with a band playing on a pontoon on a lake right in the middle of the room, right inside San Francisco's ritzy Fairmount Hotel. 'Cause if you're going to be corny enough to answer one of *those* ads, you gotta go all the way.

Within three weeks after that first date, he had tattooed a big red heart on his bicep with her name right in the middle of that red ink heart.

My sister still had her *panza* then. That's what amazed her. This guy loved her, really loved her—big, beautiful *panza* and all. Loved her enough to scratch his love onto his body, forever. Isn't that love? Saying you're "forever"?

She pulls out a paper chain of red hearts from the book. They hang over its edges onto the floor.

She'd had that *panza* since she was seven when she was all heat and baby fat. When we would run out to greet ice cream men calling us with their bells. Seven, when she slowly became more and more thirsty each day, itching for water at every moment, and then she'd pee hot streams of burnt yellow, every thirty minutes. Until finally, *mami* took her in to see the doctor man.

The doctor, he looked her over, up and down, and bled her, putting her gushing life force into vials for the lab.

The tests came back and there it was: sugar, sugar running *como* syrup in her urine, turning it golden sunset yellow, poisoning her pancreas. Poor little pancreas that couldn't keep up with her *panza* as it grew bigger and more round.

The doctor told us: it was diabetes.

"What's that?" Our *mexicana* mother didn't know what he meant when he said we had too much of us around to love. She said, "That's the way kids are supposed to be." But, to save us, we had to change— everything. All our *comidas* had to change, now, today, this minute! No more *tortillas de harina* smeared with butter, no more *Barbacoa* Sundays, or *Arroz con Pollo* Fridays. No more *capirotada* piled five layers high. No more ice cream man bells.

But worst of all, they made *mamí* go to a nutritionist to learn how to cook out her love. They were teaching her how to lose the savings of our *panza* banks. Our *panzas*, they are what told her that her kids were never "over her dead body" gonna starve. Even if we sometimes did. Mamí was crushed, broken. What had she done to her baby's pancreas? She didn't know, but she learned to poke my sister with life-giving shots to keep her *bebita* alive.

So when my sister met her future husband in the Tiki Room, the man who loved her even with the *panza* she'd tried to lose for twenty years, she took him and loved him to death right back. They moved in together three weeks later, and in a year, they married.

Pause. Music rises.

Two years later, it seemed he'd grown tired of his *panza* happy wife. Found himself a thin little blonde who worked the next cubicle over where he worked as a temp while he tried to write the next Great American Novel. Worked a temp job because

"Serious writers shouldn't have other jobs, their job is to write."

And then he'd recite his long list of starving artist strugglers. That's what he told her each time she tallied up their stack of bills, and he couldn't come up with the cold, hard Great American Novel cash to pay even one.

She pulls out a paper chain of dollar bills from the book. They hang over its edges onto the floor. Now the paper hearts, the long white ribbons, and the money flow out of the book and onto the floor.

But that's real love, right? Forever, tattoo heart love should be forgiving love, right?

He moved in with the cubicle blonde. The next day he told my sister, the tattoo wasn't forever.

I think it was that moment, that moment of fury and disgust, that her *panza* began to shrink, pulled into her by the gravity of her collapsing heart.

She stopped eating, stopped the *panza*, stopped feeding it the happiness it needed.

Stopped eating stretched from a week into a month, but he never came back to their apartment to move his stuff, just left it behind.

Stopped eating for two months, when she begged him for help to pay the Visa that he'd charged his hotel affair afternoons on, but he didn't.

Stopped eating during month three, when she screamed at him on the phone and telling him one more time, this was as civil as she was going to get about the divorce as her heart pulled and pulled her *panza* inward, but he didn't.

Stopped eating until every roll of her *panza* was gone. She measured her blood sugar to find sky-high readings of sugar, sugar, sugar. And I know, as she slid the needle of her insulin shot under her skin, she wondered how much would it take to take away the *panza* pain for good?

One day, she turned sideways, and you'd never know she'd even had a *panza* 'cause the sorrow of her hip bones pushed up against new, size 6 dresses she had to buy instead of 14's. And where her *panza* had been, only a hollow bowl of smooth skin.

I wonder if the doctor would think she'd done enough to help control the sugar sweetness of her diabetes now?

Music swells. She rises and places chair and book stage left. Lights shift.

NOTICIAS

Laura Cambrón, one of the Flacasos, moves center stage.
She begins to dance a traditional zapateado—a percussive dance,
the heartbeat of Mexican son. She pounds out rhythms with her feet
on a wooden tarima (platform) that echo throughout the theater.
The other Flacasos join her center stage, playing as she dances.

Behind them, on screen . . .

Rotation of multiple slides commences.

Each slide contains a headline or health fact gathered from our hometown
paper, the San Antonio Express-News, about the health conditions of
Mexican Americans in San Antonio—named one of America's "Fattest Cities."

Vicki remains seated at the altar throughout.

SLIDE:
Panza facts gathered from our hometown newspaper, the *San Antonio Express-News*

SLIDE:
"S.A. ranks as nation's fattest city on fed list . . . study shows 31.1% of Alamo City residents are obese."

SLIDE:
"More than 30% of Hispanic children across the country are overweight, compared with 25% of Anglo children."

SLIDE:
"The average restaurant plate has grown from 10" to 12" in diameter."

SLIDE:
"The number of obese or overweight Texans has increased by 10% in the last decade."

SLIDE:
"Texas schools generate about $54 million a year from vending machine contracts."

SLIDE:

"We know that the highest increase in obesity has been observed among Hispanics and African-Americans."

SLIDE:

"The food industry produces roughly 3,800 calories a day for every man, woman, and child in America . . . twice what they need."

SLIDE:

"Living in sprawl can increase your spread—those in compact counties weigh up to 6 pounds less."

SLIDE:

"15.7% of border residents suffer from Type 2 diabetes, compared with a national average of 13.9% in the United States and 14.9% in Mexico."

SLIDE:

"Among kids 12 to 19, 44% of Hispanics are overweight and 23% are obese. Nearly 40% of younger children are overweight and 24% are obese."

SLIDE:

"In 2000, more than half of Texas Hispanics had less than a high school education. Less than 9% had a college degree, and the income for Hispanics . . . was two-thirds what it was for Anglos."

SLIDE:

"One in two Hispanic females born in the United States in 2000 will develop diabetes if current trends continue, according to the Centers for Disease Control and Prevention."

Laura's zapateado ends. Los Flacasos return to their seating area. Lights shift.

PRAYING

New music rises and underscores throughout.
Vicki rises and stands directly in front of the altar.

Sitting in the backseat of the car
All I could do was pray

Cuz if I tried to talk to him
(whispered) We would all be dead

I held my sister's hand
She was very scared

If I talked to him
We would all be dead

He would turn around

She mimes reacting to a slap across her face that she "fakes"
by clapping her hands together as she quickly turns her head.

Hit me in the head
The car would swerve
In my eight-year-old brain
I could picture the car
Crashing into the rows of trees
And we would all be dead

She takes a pillow from the altar and holds it over her panza.

I sat in the back
Praying
All I could do was
Watch him
Hit my mother's *panza*

smacks pillow with her fist

He slugged it

smacks pillow with her fist

He hit her *panza*

smacks pillow with her fist

Hard

smacks pillow with her fist

All I could do was pray
Cuz if I talked to him
(*whispered*) We would all be dead.

Places pillow on the ground and kneels on it. Clasps her hands in prayer.

And I prayed
"Please god
Please god
Don't let my mommy die
Make daddy stop hitting mommy's *panza*
Make him stop
Please make him stop"
I prayed and prayed
I prayed and prayed

Make him stop god
Make my daddy stop

And then I got really scared
My mommy slumped over

Was she dead?
Did she die on me?

He kept hitting her
Screaming at her
He kept hitting her *panza*

I whispered to my mommy from the backseat of the car
"Mommy, are you OK?"
And daddy swerved the car
"Shut up!
¡Cállate el hocico!"

And I sat back

"Please god, make him stop
Don't you know?
There's a baby in her
I wanna see my baby brother live"
Was my baby brother dead too?

"Oh please god,
Please, please, please
Make him stop"

(whispered) If I talked to him
We would all be dead.

Music swells, lights dim. Vicki places the pillow back on the altar.

PANZA TO PANZA

Music underscores throughout.
Vicki places folding chair downstage left. She grabs a fedora,
puts it on, and enters with the swagger of a Chicana macha.
She sits on the chair. Legs wide and attitude large.

I must say
I love her *panza*
It's full and round
Perfect in all its roundness
I love kissing her *panza*
It's so perfect in all her fullness

And at night
When we are lying there
Her *panza*
Rests perfectly in the curve of my back
It's like we are pieces of a jigsaw puzzle
Fitting perfectly as we lie on our sides
She holds me, whispering,
"I got your back, girl"
Her lovely *panza* has my back

And when I hold her
My arm stretches across her perfect *panza*
It's so full
I love her *panza*

But my favorite part
Is when we first go to bed
I'll face her on my side
She will face me on her side
We will chat of the day
Panza to *panza*

I will kiss her good night
And all the while

There we are
Panza to *panza*

Perfect in all our roundness
Perfect in all our fullness

Panza to *panza*

Music fades out.

THE INTERNATIONAL PANZA

*Vicki rises from chair, moves center stage, and shouts suddenly as
slide shifts to the title "The International Panza."*

The International *Panza*!

"¡México! ¡México! ¡México!"

The *cubanos* shouted in the streets as we walked by, like sports
announcers.

"¡México! ¡México! ¡México!"

They recognized us by our nationality before we even spoke.
Confused *cuando yo metí la palabra.*

"Oiga, tú no eres de México."

And I tried to explain to them . . .

Chicana

points to herself

Aztlán

raises one fist in the air, revolutionary style

Broken Treaties

crosses her arms in front of her, both fists clenched

Border Crossing

moves her arms, still crossed, from center to the right of her in an arc

The Mexican-American War

uses her hands to create two guns, points them at the audience

La Migra

flips her guns sideways, gangsta style

The Treaty of Guadalupe

gestures the ripping of paper

San Antonio!

*Raises both hands in the air, exasperated. Runs stage left,
explaining the rest of the story to an audience member.*

You see, my mom's *mexicana*
but her father was Chinese.
And my father?
Well, he's white.

"So that makes you what?" he asks.

The *mexicanas* try to help, explaining that I am one of them, sort of, but
then again I'm not.

The *cubano* seems to understand, "Oh, like the *gusanos*, you mean?"
"No, not at all," the *mexicanas* say. "*She* didn't have a choice."

You see, Tejas was once part of Mexico, but overnight brothers became
enemies, *paisanos* outsiders, and invaders *rightful* owners of a land they
stole from the Mexicans, who stole the land from the Indians.

"She's a Tejana."

"*¿Americana?*"

The *mexicanas* try again. This time breakin it down into its syllables.

"Chi-ca-na."

And I decide not to tell them that I was really born in Georgia because my father was in the military but I moved to Tejas when I was three, and I've never lived anywhere else and San Antonio is my home.

sits on altar, center

I decide not to tell them that my mother's family is not *chichimeca*, that the border didn't cross her, she crossed it and no, not during the Revolution of 1910 but in the 1960s. That she married a *gringo* so she could go to the u.s. of a's.

My father was from a farming town, Goshen, Indiana. My real name is Virginia, Virginia May. Not Victoria, Vicki, Kike, or *(spoken in Spanish)* *Virginia* even. My ways are a lot less *rasquache* and a whole lot more trailer trash. My grandmother's last name was Cortez for god's sake. I decide *not* to tell them that the blood of the conqueror takes up more space than anything else inside my body but no,

I am not an *americana.*

The u.s. of a's did not want me

güera
    alta
        y gorda

any more than it wanted my mother

prieta
    baja
        y gorda

I don't explain to the *cubano* or the *mexicanas* why my Spanish is broken. That the reason I speak *pocha* has as much to do with assimilation as it does with oppression. That Spanish is also the language of the colonizers.

This they already know.

And just when I decide NOT to tell them all of that the *cubano* looks at me and says . . .

"México is in your face. *Tu gente sí era mexicana. Lo ves en tu cara.*"

I ask, "How did you know? Even before we spoke. How did you know to call them by their country of birth, me by my country of memory, us by the *tierra of nuestros antepasados?* How did you know that we were México?"

"*Es que la cara de México está más gorda, más redonda.* The face of Mexico is much fatter, more round."

I want to protest, but first I take a second to look at my *compañeras*— all *flacas,* not *gordas* like me, and it's true! All our faces are round even when our *panzas* aren't. Our faces are round like the *luna,* who doesn't show her face in Cuba during the winter months. Our faces round like the *tortilla, pan* the *cubanos* do not eat. All of us—big, fat *olmeca* heads, not like the faces of other Latinos, definitely not like the face of a *cubano,* shaped long like *azúcar de caña. Somos nosotras las hijas de Coyolxauhqui,* full moon faces. *Y yo con una panza* to match. Big, round, beautiful full moon *panza* to match my *olmeca* head.

You see, well yeah I guess you see, I'm a big woman. That's why I spell *panza* with a "z" not an "s," cuz it takes up more space.

> Gestures the "z" in the air, Zorro style,
> showing exactly how much space it takes up.

And I'm a big woman goddammit.

Me dice el cubano, "Have you noticed that my people aren't fat? How many fat *cubanos* have you seen since you've arrived on the island?"

I want to ask, "You mean cept for Fidel right?" *Gusanos* abstain cuz I do believe in the Revolution but the Revolution has been better to some than others and Castro has put on a few pounds since the overthrow of Batista. There's no denyin, that man's *panza* is well fed. Anyway, cept for Fidel, it's true I've seen very few *cubanos* with *panzas.*

Infectious mambo music rises. She catches
the beat and begins to dance for a time.

Lights shift.
Mambo music underscores throughout the following.

Driving from the airport to Habana, I saw a woman get off the *guagua,*
a woman as big as me get off the *guagua*

She lifts her shirt, tucks it into her bra.

dressed in hot pink Spandex leotards and a T-shirt gathered and tied in
the back. Her *panza,* completely exposed.

She pulls her pants below her waist, now fully exposing her panza.

I don't know what it was—maybe she was just hot—but the woman
walked *panza* first, belly out with absolutely no shame. It looked like
she had more important things to worry about—places to go, people
to see. She probably had to wait two hours for that damn bus, probably had to stand jammed right up against someone else ridin the *cameo*
so when they let her loose on the streets she wuz walkin head up, back
straight, *panza* out. She made me turn around in my seat just to look
at her, pink leotard lady, in all her confidence.

You see, I talk a lot of *panza* power trash. Hell, I just talk a lot of trash in
general, call attention to myself—look at me! Flash you a little *panza.*

Truth is, I want you to look at it. I want you to know that I know it's
there. I want you to tell me to put it away so that I can say, "Hell no."
I'm proud of my *panza.* But this woman, she didn't need to say a word
cuz she was livin it, walkin the talk, in all her pink leotard glory, in
all her confidence. You know what? She looked good too.

Before I can tell the *cubano* about my *panza* positive image,

She snaps her pants back into place over her panza.

he begins to explain to me why *cubanos* aren't big people.

"Obesity," he explains "is an illness of capitalism. You," looking straight at me, *"comes mucho,* you eat too much, *demasiado.* We only eat what we need—beans, rice, yucca, *pollo frito.* We don't eat more than we need. You eat everything. You probably even eat when you're not even hungry. We only eat enuf to keep us fed. That's it. *Es todo.* It's all you need really, *un potiko.* You Americans are capitalists so you want to take more than what you need."

So, if obesity is a disease of capitalism, why is it that San Antonio is one of the largest cities in the nation

Exaggerated gesture to demonstrate the size of San Anto's panza.

and at the same time one of the poorest?

Music fades out. Lights dim.
She places chair center stage, sits with her back facing the audience.

EL VIENTRE

Music underscores throughout.
This monologue is performed in a highly stylized manner whereby Vicki makes
use of the chair in a variety of seated positions to enact the story.

dressed
in a bare-bottomed gown and socks.

sedated. alone.

my back cold. looking.
staring at ceiling lights. bright.
reminding me of moments
less than beautiful.

lying on my back.
legs open.

hands on my *panza.*
holding onto you.

hands on my *panza.*
holding onto you.

last night
i drew a bath of hot water.
held my breasts.
looked at my naked body.

life

i wanted to tell you
i was sorry.
that i Loved you
but instead i hit you.
hit my own *panza.*

fist clenched.

life

that ends inside of me.

i tried to kill you myself   with alcohol.
i drank and drank and drank and drank.
tried to make myself sick enuf   but you fought to be born.

life

from my broken body
broken Heart.

Life

hands holding onto you.
i'm opened from the outside in
from a stranger.
he reached inside.
took you from inside of me.
i felt you leave.

unborn

scar in my womb.
no fig tree planted in your memory.
still photograph of regret.

Music rises. Lights dim.

*She rises, places chair stage right. She moves to altar
and puts on a feather boa, sits in the chair.*

El Vientre by I. Mayorga © 2005. Courtesy of I. Mayorga. Virginia Grise in *The Panza Monologues*, presented by Cara Mía Theatre at the Latino Cultural Center, Dallas, Texas, March 2005.

POLITICAL PANZA

Music and lights rise. Vicki plays with a long, black feather boa.
She is now a flaca *(a skinny woman) persona.*

(petulantly) And what about us *flacas?* It's true, I *don't* have a *panza.*

"*Vas a perder tus nalgas* with all that exercising, and men want something they can grab, and then what?!" That's what my *panza* sisters say to me.

Women like me in this *panza*-city need our civil rights. I get harassed all the time by the *panza* majority who I *thought* were my *hermanas* in the struggle.

People just expect me to have a *panza.* I'm a fifty-year-old woman after all. *Sí,* it's true, I'm fifty.

Sometimes I think I was chosen not to have a *panza.* So that I would learn that there is a *panza* inside my *panza.* And inside those *panzas* you can't see—there are little boys who will one day grow up to be men. If we raise them by what we know to be true, they will love the *panzas* they came from, and they will bow down to the *panzas* they are now destroying for golf courses and petroleum wars.

You see, *this* is why I am in solidarity with my *panza* sisters, because the *panza* is political. If we asked how the *panza* was for all the citizens of a given society, we might not have hunger for our children or our elders. If we asked how the *panza* was for a woman with child, we might have quality prenatal care for all expectant mothers. If we asked, how is the *panza?* Is it fed, is it warm? Is it nourished? Was this *panza* living next to an electrical plant? A lead site? A cancer cluster? Will it get the medicine needed for a healthy *panza?*

Perhaps, if our government instituted *Panza Positive Policies* we might have world peace because we can see our humanity by the well-being of all our *panzas.* So don't be afraid of what we have to do because we are the *panza,* and to claim the *panza* is to be free, free, and it's mine and yours, and we are all *panzitas* in one big round *panza,* and she loves us very much.

The *panza is* political.

Music transition. Vicki rises.

PANZA BRUJERÍA

The introductory narrative to the monologue below changed for each show,
although its focus always concerned "talking" with the audience about con-
temporary issues that directly affected our collective panzas. At this moment
in the performance, some of the people and figures that we performed brujería
on and issues we addressed with our limpias included George W. Bush; former
Attorney General Alberto Gonzales; the Iraq War and war in general;
SB 1070, HR 4437, and other unjust immigration laws; and the presidential
candidates of both the 2004 and 2008 elections. Here we include the
narrative from our performance DVD.

I was living in Austin, Texas, when George W. Bush was governor,
and we all knew what to expect when he announced he was running
for president. And we watched as he stole the elections in Florida,
and I, like you, I'm sure, watched for hours and hours and hours into
the next day as he became our president for a second time.

Vicki grabs the stool and places it stage right.

Over half the nation had voted for a man who had lied, cheated,
and murdered.

She grabs a large bowl from the altar, places it on the stool. The contents
inside the bowl are hidden.

In the South, 60 percent of Latinos voted for him.

She takes out a small American flag on a stick from the bowl and unfurls it.

And we are going to feel the repercussions of that presidency in our
panzas for generations to come, and it's gonna take a lot more than the
promise of change to make it all better.

She turns the flag upside down and places it in the bowl.

I think what we really need is a collective healing, a national *limpia.*
Hay que curar el susto.

She takes a white rock, piedra alumbre, *from*
the bowl and raises it in the air.

We have to get rid of this fear, and this pain and this *coraje* that
we feel in our *panzas*.

> *She passes over her body with the rock, both arms,*
> *both thighs, both legs, her panza—giving herself a limpia.*
> *Then shakes the rock at the audience sitting on the left,*
> *in the center, and on the right, to "clean" them as well.*

We might have to do it more than once.

> *She takes out a lighter from the bowl and "lights"*
> *the rock, lets it catch fire for a brief time.*

In times like these, I think it's important that we look to the teachings
of our ancestors.

> *She puts the rock back in the bowl.*

And my grandmother taught me that as a people we have enough
power inside of us that we could curse somebody just by the way
we looked at them.

> *Points at someone in the audience, giving them the evil eye.*

So what I would like for us to do today is to put our collective energies
together to give George W. Bush and all other evil *políticos ojo*.

> *Finds someone new in the audience, cuts the person with her eyes.*

Can you imagine the power? I think he'd die.

That would be my . . . *Panza Brujería*.

You see, I feel heartache in my *panza*. Comes from the side like a
sucker punch, the kinds you throw when people ain't lookin. Causes
me to bend over. Grab my *panza*. Anger flush. Cheeks red. Heartbeat
fast. When the shit's bad I feel it here. Right here in my *panza*, not
my heart. I feel deep within me.

So when I send that shit back out into the universe. When I gots to do some of that old school *brujería*. You know, the shit our grandmothers use to do. I throw 'em *ojo* from the *panza*. That's why you gots to keep the belly button clean. You don't need no *mugre* up in there cloudin up your vision, half blind. Keep the third eye open, *mugrosa*, cuz sometimes you gots to give *ojo* to protect yourself.

When I give *ojo*, I reach my right hand over to my back. Fingers open. Palm touchin skin. I send the energy from the bottom of the spine through the body & out from the depths of my *panza*, full moon belly. The *ojo* of the *panza* shoots the energy through my left palm facing away, and I unleash from the depths of my *tripas* all the fury of my grandmother, María de Jesús Yee Cortez, *curandera* life healer with broken heart.

So don't fuck with us. Me and my ancestors. Me, my ancestors, my *ojo*, my *panza*. Don't fuck with us, a'ight.

> *Music swells, loud funky beat. She strikes stool and bowl and begins to move to the beat of the music. Lights rise.*

Panza Brujería by I. Mayorga © 2004. Courtesy of I. Mayorga. Virginia Grise in *The Panza Monologues*, presented by Cara Mía Theatre at the Latino Cultural Center, Dallas, Texas, March 2005.

PANZA GIRL MANIFESTO

*Music underscores throughout. Vicki dances during the manifesto in between
each item she lists. Music lowers each time she speaks and swells between the
manifesto's items.*

(shouts) Panza Girl Manifesto!

UNO:
Sin la tortilla y el frijol no hay revolución.

DOS:
Don't fuck with our *chicharrones,* the lard in our *tortillas de harina,* the
gravy of our *enchiladas,* the ooze inside our *barbacoa,* our red hot cheetos
dipped in sour cream, our *chamoy* flavored *raspas,* the *sal* in our Chinese
candies, the *cremita* on our *elote,* the *grasa* in our *masa,* and most of all,
don't mess with our processed yellow cheese!

THREE:
Don't trust skinny people, and don't eat at their houses.

CUATRO:
Don't let your *panocha* rule your life. It don't know shit! Let your *panza*
be your guide.

FIVE:
The only love you can ever trust, that will never betray you, lie, cheat,
steal, or break your heart is your love of food.

SEIS:
Give the *panza* what she wants. You gots to feed the *panza.*

SEVEN:
San Antonio is the *panza* capital of the world! Home of Chicana
heavyweights!

She climbs onto the first level of the altar and stands.

Panza *Girl Manifesto*, *The Panza Monologues* DVD still © 2012. Courtesy of the authors. Virginia Grise in *The Panza Monologues*, presented at Plaza de la Raza in Los Angeles for a special one-night performance on August 2, 2008.

OCHO:

You gots to love the *panza*.

> *She turns around, bends over the small cube on the altar, and shakes*
> *her booty for the audience. Then she turns to face them.*

NINE:

You gots to love yourself.

> *She sits on the top cube of the altar.*
> *Rolls up her shirt and lowers the waistband of her pants to expose her* panza.

DIEZ:

When all else fails, when you're feeling really low, just remember:

POWER TO THE *PANZA*!

She claps her hand against her bare panza *twice, raises her
right fist high into the air, and hugs her* panza *with her left arm.
Lights fade out.
Music fades out.*

El Fin

GLOSSARY

panza. (1) The core. (2) Center of the body. (3) Center of life.

Prologue

pachuco. Mexican Americans in the 1940s who donned zoot suits and a
  serious gangsta lean. Old skool cool.
son jarocho. A traditional style of music from the Sotavento region of southern Veracruz, Mexico.
"El Cascabel." "The Rattlesnake," a standard of the *son jarocho* repertoire.
  Utilized to revive the fandango and express the sheer power of *son jarocho.* This song began our show in Los Angeles.
objetos. Objects; *cositas; chucherías.*
chocha. Vagina, also commonly referred to as *panocha, concha, punani,* va-
  jajay, coochie, cookie, goody, kitty cat, honey pot, papaya, na na, lala . . .
  The list can go on and on and on. We'll stop here.
café con leche. Coffee with milk.
color de la tierra. Color of the earth.
tú sabes. You know.
panocha. Pussy. See *chocha.*
sí. Yes.
ándale. C'mon.

fideo. Vermicelli noodles. Often an end of the month staple for families who live month to month cuz you can buy three boxes of *fideo* for only 99 cents.

pan dulce. Mexican sweet bread. Paired with coffee it's the perfect breakfast or late-night snack.

menudo. Beef tripe soup. In an act of working-class ingenuity, campesinos in prerevolutionary Mexico used the parts of the meat discarded by the elite classes to make *menudo.* Also known (and personally tested) as an effective cure for hangovers. As Fred Sanford says in the 1970s television show *Sanford and Son,* "Life is like a bowl of warm *menudo.*"

tripas. Tripe (small intestines); beef or pork commonly eaten fried in a taco and often sold at booths at the local *pulga* (flea market). In 2004 the U.S. Department of Agriculture issued a ban on *tripas* because of a possible connection to mad cow disease. The ban lasted over a year. In San Antonio, we were convinced it was a racist conspiracy against Mexicans. *Tripas,* smuggled across the Mexican border like contraband, secretly made their way into markets, fiestas, and backyards all across South Texas despite the ban.

Sea Island. Six locations in San Antonio. Sea Island is a family-owned restaurant specializing in fresh but often deep-fried seafood.

El Camarón Pelado. Literally, "peeled shrimp." A seafood restaurant located on the south side of San Antonio that serves ice cold beers and where you can still find many items on the menu for under $10. On most nights, you can also find some of the best traveling taco shop musicians in the entire state of Texas.

China Sea Buffet. All-you-can-eat Chinese-style buffet; popular for quantity of food, not necessarily quality.

Luby's. Cafeteria-style restaurant. Luby's is a San Antonio institution. You get in line, use a tray, choose your food, and pay at the end. Waitresses refill your iced tea for free, from rolling carts in the dining room so that you don't even have to get up from your table once you sit down. That and the cloth napkins make it "*bien* classy" and a spot to take your children for special occasions and celebrations. At the Luby's on the west side of San Antonio, you can often find live musicians playing for lunchtime crowds, and the Luby's in Laredo off I-35 was the last restaurant on the U.S. side of the border that Virginia's family stopped at before crossing into Mexico to visit relatives.

lonja. Roll of fat. That little bit of fat that hangs over the jeans. Also commonly referred to as love handles or muffin-top.

mujeres. Women.

ritmo. Rhythm.

patas. Feet, used specifically to talk about the feet, paws, or claws of animals. Sometimes used by Chicana/os as a derogatory term for human feet, but anything spoken in the diminutive, such as *patitas,* has a softer feel to it and pairing *patas* with *pies* (the actual word for human feet) is just a fun use of alliteration, and Virginia's response to her mother yelling, "Don't call your feet *patas.* You are not an animal."

Historia

historia. History.

las diosas dijeron. The goddesses said . . .

esta parte tan importante de nuestro cuerpo. The *panza,* this very important part of our bodies.

allí va todo. Everything goes there.

los ovarios. The ovaries.

la matriz. The uterus.

el vientre. The womb.

velas. Candles.

cada factor. Each and every element.

cada molinito de su cuerpo. Each and every little piece or part of your body.

un mundo donde la gente no tendrá que sufrir hambres. A world where people don't have to suffer from hunger.

abuelita's remedios. Grandmother's remedies, often involving things she could find in kitchen cabinets, the refrigerator, or in plants from her backyard garden.

aceite de olivo calientito. Warm olive oil.

un tecito de canela o manzanilla. A cup of cinnamon or chamomile tea.

Curarás con tus propios manos. You will heal yourself with your own hands.

¡Que vivan las lonjas! Long live the love handles!

¡Que vivan! Literally, "May they live": a sort of call and response. We think of it more like "Hell Yeah!"

¡Que vivan las chichis! Long live the breasts.

panzoncitas. Big women; women with big *panzas,* not little *panzas.*

¡Que viva la panza! Long live the *panza.*

Aztlán. Aztlán gives name to a Chicana/o homeland. The site of what is now the U.S. Southwest where the Mexica (Aztec) Indians lived as a people before migrating south into what is now Mexico. Some say it's a mythical site; others have located it on maps, attempting to document the history of the Américas before the Conquest. It is all very confusing, as is the very complicated history of settler colonialism and what happens to a people when their land is taken away, and they are not completely wiped out in genocide. "Go back home, Mexican." Where is that exactly?

From Cha-Cha to Panza

gringo. A colloquial term meaning "white person," typically from the United States of America.

tacones. High heels.

piernas. Legs.

puta shoes. Higher than high heels; can be translated as "come fuck me heels."

Virgen. Our Lady of Guadalupe, patron saint of the Américas. Renderings of her image can be found painted on the hoods of lowriders, tattooed on the backs of *cholos,* and drawn on murals in barrios all across the United States.

Yolanda López. A Chicana visual artist, well known for her *Virgen of Guadalupe Triptych* (1978), depicting her grandmother, mother, and herself (working women) in the image of the Virgen of Guadalupe. As is the tradition of the Chicana postmodern pastiche, or more accurately Virginia's lack of historical, political, and/or cultural specificity (meaning she collapsed all them Chicana artists painting the Virgen into one person)— the piece of art referenced here is actually a mash-up of López's *Walking Guadalupe* (1978) and a silk screen by Ester Hernández titled *La virgen defending the rights of the Xicanos* (1976).

pues yo también. Well, me too.

raza. Often translated as "my race." More accurately defined as my people, my homies, my community, my crew. As Kid Frost says in his 1980s Chicano rap classic, "Some of you don't know what's happening, *qué pasa?* It's not for you anyway, cuz this is for the *Raza.*"

I throw punches for my *raza*. A riff on the title of an article by the Chicana scholar Angie Chabram-Dernersesian, "I Throw Punches for My Race but I Don't Want to Be a Man: Writing Us—Chica-Nos (Girl, Us)/Chicanas—into the Movement Script." See "Further Reading" in Chapter Five/ *Cinco*.

cholas. Chicanas skooled in the fine art of hair and make-up, with an advanced degree in street ethics. Their skills include mean control of a sharpie and the precision of lip liner application, a tuff attitude, and a razor-sharp wit.

cantina. A bar; in this case—a bar kinda on the shady side. You know, the kind without windows.

polka. German and Czech immigrants brought the polka with them when they first settled in Texas. Texas Mexicans made it their own, introducing elements of *ranchera* music into the sound. Marked by the fierce rhythm of the button accordion, polkas are danced in a circle, moving counter-clockwise, in *conjunto* dance halls all across South Texas.

Daddy O's. A bar next to the railroad tracks on the east side of Austin, Texas, where Marvin Gaye *and* Michael Miguel Salgado were played. The bar only served beer in bottles or wine from a box, but you were allowed to bring in your own bottles of liquor if you bought a setup at the bar. Daddy O's was known for the OGs (original gangstas) in suits who would play dominoes on the outside patio, the meanest pool hustlers in East Austin, and the fact that they didn't card most women under twenty-one. The bar wasn't actually torn down, but it was shut down after a very bad bar fight. Another bar by a different name was opened soon after, but the clientele was never quite the same.

vatos. Homeboys.

cholos. Like *cholas*, *cholos* are versed in the fine art of grooming, with an advanced degree in street ethics. Their skills include a smooth swagger, gangsta lean, and mean control and precision with the iron and a bottle of starch.

barrios. Neighborhoods; hoods; ghettos.

bloque. A boxy body type; block.

chanclas. Flip-flops, sandals; the opposite of *tacones*.

meternos un chingaso. Hit us real good.

gordis. A term of affection (or at least that's what they say) derived from *gorda*, "fat girl." *Dis* is short for *gordis*.

panzita. A little paunch.

lonjitas. Love handles; little rolls of fat.

tacón. The heel of a high-heeled shoe.

medias. Stockings, pantyhose.

A Hunger for Justice

mexicana. Mexican woman.

pan-son-cita. Someone with just a little *panza.*

pan-zona. Someone with a big ol' paunch.

yo siempre fui gruesa desde chiquita. I was always very thick, ever since I
    was little.

venimos de otros tejidos de herencia. We come from other fabrics of
    inheritance.

con facciones toscas. [Someone] with hard, tuff characteristics or traits.

yo nací en un pueblo en México, un pueblito que se llama Bustamante, Nuevo
    León. I was born in a town in Mexico, a little town named Bustamante,
    Neuvo León.

*en el rancho, en aquellos tiempos, la vida era muy diferente pero éramos felices;
    éramos bien felices.* On the ranch, during those times, life was very differ-
    ent, but we were happy; we were very happy.

me acuerdo que mi abuela se levantaba bien temprano. I remember that my
    grandmother got up very early.

*cocíamos el maíz, este, lo molíamos en el molino de mano, este. O si no, lo que-
    brajaba en el metate.* We would cook the corn. We would grind the corn
    by hand, or she would break it, grind it on the *metate.*

metate. A stone block used to grind corn for tortillas. Very old skool.

hacía las tortillas sobre leña. She made tortillas over a fire.

esto era divino. That was divine.

esta era nuestra cultura. That was our culture.

estos eran nuestros valores de saber valorar lo que teniamos y apreciarlo. Those
    were our values, our way of knowing what we had, valuing it, and
    appreciating it.

entonces, era una vida bien bonita, bien bonita porque teníamos lo básico. So,
    it was a very good life, very beautiful because we had what was basic.

mole. A sauce, usually paired with chicken or pork, made with chiles and in
    some cases chocolate. The word itself comes from Nahuatl, which indi-
    cates that our people have been making and eating *mole* for a very long
    time.

Levi's jeans factory. In 1990 the Levi Strauss factory on the south side of San Antonio closed its doors and relocated to Costa Rica, leaving more than one thousand seamstresses without work. Petra Mata was one of those workers and is currently the executive director of Fuerza Unida, an organization that continues to work for the rights of workers and women.

entonces. So.

pensábamos que íbamos a sufrir hambres. We thought that we were going to go hungry.

tiene un motorcito. It has a little motor.

flexibilidad. Flexibility.

My Sister's Panza

como. Like.

comidas. Foods.

tortillas de harina. Flour tortillas.

barbacoa. The head of a cow wrapped in *maguey*, banana leaves, or cloth cooked in a pit about three feet deep for many hours until it is fall off the bone tender. Often served only on weekends in restaurants and *carnicerías* [meat markets], *barbacoa* is bought by the pound and in San Antonio is often eaten in flour tortillas and paired with a three-liter bottle of Big Red. The Chicano blues man and San Anto legend Randy Garibay sings about *barbacoa* on his album *The Barbacoa Blues* (2000): "I went down Nogalitos looking for some *barbacoa* and Big Red. I could have had *menudo* but I got some *cabeza* instead." That's how good it is.

arroz con pollo. Chicken and rice. Cooked in one (usually big) pot.

capirotada. A sweet and savory bread pudding made with cinnamon tea and cheddar cheese, usually served during Lent. There are *capirotada* wars over who prepares the sweet treat the best. People take their *capirotada* very seriously.

bebita. Little baby girl.

Praying

cállate el hocico. Shut your mouth.

The International Panza

cuando yo metí la palabra. When I started talking; when I gave my two cents.

oiga, tú no eres de México. Hey, you're not from Mexico.

Mexican-American War. A war between Mexico and the U.S. between 1846 and 1848, which ended with Mexico ceding one-third of its land, including all or parts of present-day California, Nevada, Utah, Arizona, Colorado, and New Mexico. Or, as Virginia's mother says, "*Donde nos chingaron* [Where they fucked us]."

la migra. A derogatory term for the U.S. border patrol. Even saying the word *migra* naturally causes your right upper lip to lift, like you're scowling, and given the fact that the Obama administration has deported even more undocumented people than George Bush (because everyone hates Mexicans), the word *migra should* make you scowl, or better yet, make you angry and want to organize.

Treaty of Guadalupe. The contract that sealed the deal of the Mexican Cession. Or, as Virginia's mother says, "*Donde nos chingaron* real good."

mexicanas. In this context, *real* Mexican women (as in Mexican nationals), not Mexican Americans (not that we're not real).

cubano. A Cuban national.

gusanos. Literally, "worms." A derogatory term used for Cubans who fled the island after the Revolution.

paisanos. Countrymen.

chichimeca. A grouping of tribes of different ethnic and linguistic characteristics that lived mainly in what is now known as North Mexico and the U.S. Southwest.

rasquache. "Ghetto fabulous," meaning not just making do with the limited resources you have but turning them into something new, sometimes beautiful—like the grandmothers who make outdoor planters out of discarded tires from the neighborhood salvage yard. For a more detailed discussion of the term see Tomás Ybarra-Frausto's essay "Rasquachismo: A Chicano Sensibility."

güera. Light- or fair-skinned; the opposite of *prieta.*

alta. Tall.

gorda. Fat.

prieta. Dark-skinned; the opposite of *güera.*

baja. Short.

pocha. A Mexican American who does not have perfect Mexican Spanish or doesn't know Spanish at all, whose ways are a little more Americanized. Apparently *parkear, háblame pa tras, me trujo, lo chequiates, ansina,* and *barbacova* are not "real" words according to "real" Mexicans or Chicanas from Laredo who *think* they're "real" Mexicans.

tu gente sí era mexicana. Your people were in fact Mexican.

lo ves en tu cara. You see it in your face.

tierra of nuestros antepasados. Land of our ancestors.

es que la cara de México está más gorda, más redonda. It's just that the face of Mexico is fatter, more round.

compañeras. Homegirls, sistahs.

flacas. Thin, skinny.

luna. Moon.

pan. Bread.

Olmeca. An ancient Mexican indigenous tribe thought to predate the Maya, Inca, and Aztec civilizations. The original gangstas of the Américas. The Olmecas carved colossal round stone heads, which have been found in southern Veracruz and Tabasco, Mexico.

azúcar de caña. Sugarcane.

Coyolxauhqui. A Mexica goddess and the daughter of Coatlicue. According to mythology, Coyolxauhqui's brother Huitzilopochtli (who emerged full grown from their mother's womb) killed his sister, cut off her head, and tossed it into the sky where it became the moon. In 1978 while excavating for the subway in downtown Mexico City, an ancient—and now iconic—stone relief of Coyolxauhqui was unearthed. The pose that Virginia strikes at the end of the line, "*Somos nosotras las hijas de Coyolxauhqui*" [We are the daughters of Coyolxauhqui] is an *homenaje* [homage] to the image of Coyolxauhqui depicted on the stone disk.

y yo con una panza. And me with a *panza.*

me dice el cubano. The Cuban says to me.

Batista. Fulgencio Batista was the Cuban dictator overthrown in the 1959 Cuban Revolution.

guagua. The city bus, pronounced wa-wa. A small microbus or omnibus in Cuba. Sometimes you have to wait for hours for a *guagua,* and there is almost never a spare seat. You have to pack in tightly if you want the ride.

cameo. Literally, "camel." A "modern" type of Cuban bus, though not necessarily more comfortable, consisting of a huge truck pulling boxcars that are connected to each other in the center, creating a visible "hump." Yet another example of *rasquachismo*.

demasiado. Too much.

yucca. A starchy root that can be eaten boiled, baked, or fried.

pollo frito. Fried chicken, but not breaded and deep-fried like in the South. Chicken sautéed in olive oil and often fried together with black beans and rice (*moros y cristianos*). When Virginia was in Cuba, she would eat black beans and rice with *pollo frito* and a shot of *café cubano* every day in Havana's Chinatown.

es todo. That's all.

un potiko. Just a little.

Political Panza

vas a perder tus nalgas. You're going to lose your shapely bottom.

hermanas. Sistahs.

Panza Brujería

brujería. Old skool magic.

limpias. Spiritual cleansing or healing often involving freshly cut herbs, roses, smoke, eggs, melting rocks, holy water, and a whole lotta prayers.

hay que curar el susto. We have to cure the fear.

piedra de alumbre. A white rock that, when burned, will melt into the shape of your fear. Used in *limpias* to get rid of what you are scared of, and while we cannot reveal the specifics of this ritual, we can say it really does work.

coraje. Anger, rage.

ojo. Evil eye.

políticos. Politicians.

mugre. Dirt.

mugrosa. A dirty girl.

curandera. A healer versed in the traditional ways. In addition to knowing the medicinal uses of herbs, a *curandera* usually knows how to cure people of fear and sadness with things like roses, smoke, eggs, melting rocks, or holy water.

Panza Girl Manifesto

sin la tortilla y el frijol no hay revolución. Without tortillas and beans there is no revolution. At the end of the day, all our political rhetoric is bullshit if we can't sustain and feed our own people.

chicharrones. Pork rinds, often eaten deep-fried. You can buy them in large plastic bags in the chip aisle at almost every corner store in San Antonio, or you can buy them fresh from the *carnicería* and fry them yourself in huge vats in your backyard. Best eaten with *tapatío chile* sauce.

chamoy-flavored *raspas. Chamoy* is a sweet and savory paste made from the salty brine of dried fruit mixed with vinegar and chile. A *raspa* is a snow cone. A *chamoy*-flavored *raspa* is sweet, salty, spicy, and cold all at once— and a great cure for the summertime blues.

sal. Salt.

Chinese candies. A very salty dried plum, with a little flesh on the seed, that can be found at most corner stores in San Antonio in huge glass containers on the counter for ten cents each. There are many ways you can eat Chinese candies: (1) you can suck the flesh off the seed; (2) you can cut a lemon in two, put the candy inside, and eat the lemon and Chinese candy together; or (3) you can eat it with a pickle and powdered chile. This makes your cheeks pucker and your mouth water.

the *cremita* on our *elote.* The cream in our roasted corn; not sour cream but a thicker Mexican cream. It's kinda like food crack—once you hit it, you can't quit it.

the *grasa* in our *masa.* The lard in our dough; used to make tortillas, or tamales, or *gorditas.*

A CHRONOLOGICAL PRODUCTION HISTORY OF *THE PANZA MONOLOGUES*

Creating *The Panza Monologues* involved many different and unique kinds of presentations each of which was an important step toward the play's final manifestation. In the chronological production time line that follows, we broadly delineate key dates and also note the locations of each of our presenting opportunities or performance venues. Notably, the majority of these opportunities have been at people of color venues and queer organizations and through woman of color–led initiatives. Invitations to perform *The Panza Monologues* have always seemed to arrive in connection with word about the show spread by Chicana or Latina women.[1] We also include the names of the many talented people behind the scenes of each of our performances. We have continuously drawn on the resources within our immediate circle of friends or close allies for help with the finer details of putting together a performance. Allies have aided us with specialty tasks such as marketing, choreography, hanging lighting instruments, light and soundboard operation, moving and taking care of set pieces, cleaning and prepping venues, and front-of-house management.[2] Some supporters contributed their sophisticated theater training; more often, we helped to train volunteers for the tasks they performed. We were always working to mount the show while simultaneously in the midst of hands-on training with our crews.

Following the formal chronology, we have listed other types of development events. Often Virginia had the opportunity to try out materials from the play through invitations to perform in community settings, classrooms, or public readings. The audience response on these occasions made it possible for us to test the content of the performance and for Virginia to sharpen her performance techniques before a live audience. These presentations were also marketing opportunities, building excitement and anticipation for the play in progress in the communities and populations we desired to reach with a full production. We believe the community-based marketing strategy of these engagements truly enabled us to reach women, people of color, young people, and other potential audiences who might not otherwise have heard about a work of theater through more traditional marketing methods.

In the final list below, we document our different *Panza Pláticas* (see p. xxxi for a description of a *Panza Plática*). Equal parts presentation, demonstration, and *testimonio*, each *plática* allowed us to experiment with how to describe the story of making *The Panza Monologues*, to think through our Chicana theater production, or to articulate the sociopolitical dilemmas Latinas face that our play hopes to describe. These types of presentations became increasingly important to us because they put into practice our desire to think within a theoretical and creative dialectic.

— — — — —

The Panza Monologues was first presented as a staged reading at the Mujeres Activas en Letras y Cambio Social (MALCS) August 2003 Summer Institute: *"Reflexiones y Visiones:* MALCS Building the Future."[3] The institute's participants convened at the Esperanza Peace and Justice Center in San Antonio, Texas, for the staged reading.

Virginia Grise	Performer
Irma Mayorga	Director, Set Design
Marissa Ramirez	Sound and Lighting Design

Special thanks to MALCS 2003 Summer Institute
site chairs Dr. Norma Cantú and Dr. Gaye Okoh.

— — — — —

A second staged reading of *The Panza Monologues* was presented at the University of Texas, San Antonio (UTSA), in March 2004 as part of its Women's History Month, with funding provided by the UTSA Women's Studies

Institute (Dr. Sonia Saldívar-Hull, director) and the UTSA Campus Activities Board.

Virginia Grise	Performer
Irma Mayorga	Director, Set Design
Marissa Ramirez	Sound and Lighting Design
H. Esperanza Garza	Video Design
Rosie Torres	Choreographer
Jamila Reyes-Gutiérrez	Sound Technician

Special assistance provided by Carolyn Motley of the Women's Studies Institute and the staff of UTSA's Riklin Auditorium.

— — — — —

An abbreviated version of *The Panza Monologues* was presented at Northwest Vista College, San Antonio, Texas, on March 30, 2004, as part of their Women's History Month activities.

Virginia Grise	Performer
Irma Mayorga	Director, Set Design
Marissa Ramirez	Sound Design
Jamila Reyes-Gutiérrez	Sound Technician

Special thanks to Daniel Johnson, Asst. Coordinator, Leadership/Activities at Northwest Vista College.

— — — — —

A post–staged reading/pre–world premiere production of *The Panza Monologues* was presented at Theater in My Basement/SW Annex's *¡Teatro Caliente!* Festival in Phoenix, Arizona, on October 31, 2004.

Virginia Grise	Performer
Irma Mayorga	Director, Set Design
Marissa Ramirez	Sound Design
H. Esperanza Garza	Video Design

Special thanks to Dr. Ramón Rivera-Servera and Arizona State University.

— — — — —

The World Premiere of *The Panza Monologues* was presented by the Austin Latino/Latina Lesbian, Gay, Bisexual & Transgender Organization (ALLGO), Lorenzo Herrera y Lozano, Interim Executive Director, November 2004, at the Tillery Street Theater, Austin, Texas.

Virginia Grise	Performer
Irma Mayorga	Director, Set Design
Marissa Ramirez	Sound and Lighting Design
H. Esperanza Garza	Video Design
Rosie Torres	Choreographer
Sheree Ross	Production Manager
Tómas Salas	Lighting Design
Kristen Gerhard	Sound Technician
Chris Salinas	Media Assistant

Special thanks to Sharon Bridgforth, Artistic Director, ALLGO.

— — — — —

The Panza Monologues was presented by Cara Mía Theatre at the Latino Cultural Center, Dallas, Texas, and Rose Marine Theatre, Fort Worth, Texas, David Lozano, Artistic Director, March 2005.

Virginia Grise	Performer
Irma Mayorga	Director, Set Design
Marissa Ramirez	Sound Design
H. Esperanza Garza	Video Design
Rosie Torres	Choreographer
Christopher E. Edwards	Lighting Design
Jackie Elliot	Stage Manager
Cesar Hernández	Sound Board Operator
Sara Flores	Light Board Operator
Anacelia Alvarez	Media Assistant

Special thanks to Eliberto González, Cofounder and President of the Board of Directors, Cara Mía Theatre, and Artistic Director David Lozano.

— — — — —

The *Panza Monologues* was presented at the University of Colorado–Boulder for the "2005 Semana de la Xicana," organized by the *Raza* Womyn and Cultural Arts Board.

Virginia Grise	Performer
Irma Mayorga	Director, Set Design
Marissa Ramirez	Sound Design
H. Esperanza Garza	Video Design
Rosie Torres	Choreographer

Special thanks to Bernadette Garcia, Associate Director and Education/Public Outreach and Program Administration for the Colorado Space Grant Consortium.

— — — — —

The *Panza Monologues* was presented at *Las Hermanas* annual meeting at the Crowne Plaza Hotel in San Antonio, Texas, on October 7, 2005.

Virginia Grise	Performer
Irma Mayorga	Director, Set Design
Marissa Ramirez	Sound Design
H. Esperanza Garza	Video Design
Rosie Torres	Choreography

Special thanks to Sister Yolanda Torango, coordinator.

— — — — —

The *Panza Monologues* was presented at Plaza de la Raza in Los Angeles, California, for a special one-night performance on August 2, 2008, to record the performance for the creation of *The Panza Monologues* DVD. Filmed by Roberto Oregel. Live music by Los Flacasos.

Virginia Grise	Performer
Irma Mayorga	Producer, Director, Production Designer, and DVD Creative Director

LOS FLACASOS:
Alexandro Hernández Gutiérrez   Music Director and Musician
Eduardo Arenas   Musician
Laura Cambrón   Musician
Jacqueline Mungía   Musician

Additional creative assistance provided by:
Marissa Ramirez   Lighting and Scenic Technician
Abel Salas   Media Assistant

Special thanks to Karla Legaspy for community outreach and publicity, and Adelina Anthony, the evening's host.

— — — — —

The Panza Monologues was presented at California State University, Los Angeles, on February 27, 2009, by the Gender & Sexuality Resource Center as part of their "Love Your Body Week" activities. Live music by Los Flacasos.

Virginia Grise   Performer
Irma Mayorga   Director, Set and Lighting Design

LOS FLACASOS:
Alexandro Hernández Gutiérrez   Music Director and Musician
Eduardo Arenas   Musician
Laura Cambrón   Musician

Special thanks to Denise Carlos, Gender & Sexuality Resource Center Coordinator, and the staff of the University Student Union.

Other Selected Readings of *The Panza Monologues* Material

- When Fire and Rain Leave the Earth, Tillery Street Theater, Austin, Texas, 2004.
- *Lenguatazo:* Project of *Tongues Magazine*, Casa 0101 Theatre, Los Angeles, California, 2004.
- Amalgam, Resistencia Bookstore, Austin, Texas, 2004.

- Lee's Unleaded Blues Joint, Chicago, Illinois, 2005.
- Guadalupe Cultural Arts Center Inter-American Book Festival, San Antonio, Texas, 2005.
- Art and Social Criticism in the Americas, REDCAT, Los Angeles, California, 2007.
- Exquisite Acts and Everyday Rebellions: Cal Arts Feminist Art Project, Valencia, California, 2007.
- Prototypes Women's Center through the Center for California Cultural and Social Issues at Pitzer College, Claremont, 2007.
- Breath of Fire Latina Theater Ensemble, Santa Ana, California, 2010.

Panza Pláticas

- "Power to the *Panza:* Politics of the Body," Borderlands Conference, Arizona State University, Phoenix, 2004.
- "Performing the *Panza*," Pennsylvania State University, Dr. Susan Russell, University Park, 2008.
- "*Panza* Positive Strategies for Chicano Cultural Production," National Association for Chicano/a Studies, National Conference, Austin, Texas, 2008.
- "Art and Activism," California Institute of the Arts, Prof. Evelyn Serano, Valencia, 2009.
- "Reading/Writing Autobiography," Dr. Laura Harris, Pitzer College, Claremont, California, 2009.
- "*Panza* Performed," American Society for Theatre Research, Performance as Research Working Group, San Juan, Puerto Rico, 2009.
- "*Panza* Performed: A Case Study of Chicana Dramaturgy in Creating *The Panza Monologues*," Annual Meeting of the Association for Theatre in Higher Education (ATHE), Los Angeles, California, 2010.
- "*The Panza Monologues* Performance *Plática*," University of Texas at Austin, Gender and Sexuality Center, 2010.

THREE/*TRES*

TEJANA TOPOGRAPHIES

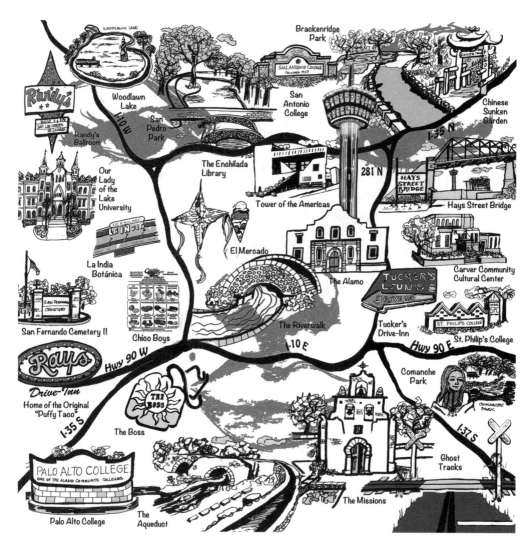

El Mapa de San Antonio by Debora Kuetzpal Vasquez © 2012. Courtesy of the artist. On this map, Debora Kuetzpal Vasquez has not only drawn in the most well-known San Antonio sites such as the Alamo, the Riverwalk, and the Tower of the Americas, but she has also placed sites and places deeply connected to Texas Mexican San Antonio such as Comanche Park on the south side, Ray's (home of the legendary San Antonio "Puffy Taco") and La India Botánica on the west side, a gay bar called the Boss, San Fernando Cemetery II—the "Mexican" Cemetery, Tucker's Drive-Inn, and the haunted Ghost Tracks—a place on the south side where if you park near the tracks, put your car in neutral, and wait a bit, the ghosts of dead children gently "push" your car over the tracks. It's true. Sometimes their handprints appear on the trunks of dusty cars. We—and dozens if not hundreds of San Antonio residents—have experienced the phenomenon.

INTRODUCTION

And I decide not to tell them that I was really born in Georgia because my father was in the military but I moved to Tejas when I was three, and I've never lived anywhere else and San Antonio is my home.
VIRGINIA GRISE, "The International *Panza*"

Mexican American . . . Chi-ca-na . . . Texas Mexican . . . Tejana. We both claim Texas as home, San Antonio as the town to which we belong. Yet as *The Panza Monologues* attests, we both recognize that San Antonio is a city of tensions and contradictions. It is the seventh largest city in the United States and yet can also feel like a much smaller city. It has fantastically wealthy residents and also boasts school districts where a school's entire population qualifies for free lunch programs. You can travel through neighborhoods where Spanish fills the air while *conjunto, cumbias,* or hip-hop pulse on the street, or find yourself in parts of town where you would never suspect that San Anto's a Mexican majority city. The city boasts several ultraconservative, nationally prominent megachurches and is also home to a 30 percent Roman Catholic population. It's a city with international aspirations but holds tight to its localized proclivities. As the Convention and Visitors Bureau's tagline for its recent tourism campaign offers, San Antonio resides "deep in the Heart." To this we can bear witness, but for entirely different reasons from those of the city.

As we note in our "Introducción," we often refer to *The Panza Monologues* as a "love letter" to San Antonio. We position the play in this manner because for us it has functioned as a response to the many insights about San Antonio that we gained as activists seeking to make palpable change, as residents with deep concern. As Tejana-Chicana artists, we've worked hard to locate our history, to discover the roots and origins of the material circumstances in our city and state. This has been difficult to achieve because our city so often tries to disguise the fullest dimensions of its story, especially events, people, and structures that have worked to subordinate its Mexican American people. Yet we believe understanding aspects of San Antonio's history helps to flesh out our Tejana-Chicana dimensions, to hear the things we ruminate about, and the things that haunt and impel us.

To better understand the socioeconomic and political dynamics that *The Panza Monologues* was created within, we present written topographies each of which in its own way attempts to map the history of our city, which in turn tells the story of people's relationship to economics, food, place, and other insidious forces of oppression. Each subsection of this chapter offers a historical account, including our own autogeographies, to contextualize the stories told in *The Panza Monologues*, highlighting the many dimensions of our city. Grappling with these historical forces, which continuously push through to our present, has deeply affected the theater each of us makes.

SAN ANTONIO PAINT(ED) BY NUMBERS

During the 1850s San Antonio transitioned from a small Spanish colonial outpost to a growing and bustling city. . . . San Antonio's physical structure changed such that by 1850 San Antonio was a city divided into four wards. The ward system resulted in a city structure where 80% of Tejanos and newly arrived mexicanos lived in two of the four wards. Early maps of San Antonio provide evidence of clustered Spanish surnames that are significantly segregated from non-Spanish surnames. These divisive forces were so strong that by 1877 San Antonio's physical structure was characterized by ethnic enclaves. Looking west of the downtown area, one found the Mexican community. . . . The Germans lived in the eastern and southern portions of the city. Anglo Saxons settled their homes in the northern and eastern parts, while the Irish lived northeast. In smaller numbers, the northwest part of the town became home for the Italians, and Blacks moved to the eastern edge of the city. . . . Chinese who came to San Antonio settled in the near west. . . . [T]he city was rife with ethnic divisions.

RAQUEL R. MÁRQUEZ, LOUIS MENDOZA, and STEVE BLANCHARD[1]

Instructions

Let's paint an image in our minds. Take a look at the map of San Antonio drawn by Debora Kuetzpal Vasquez that opens this chapter. Now imagine crosshairs covering the map and position the intersection of the crosshairs at the map's center, right about where, for example, you see the Alamo. Bull's-eye. These crosshairs have now divided the map into four quadrants—the "wards" mentioned in the epigraph above but not quite. The crosshairs I ask you to imagine most likely run north and south, like a plus sign; rotate them a bit to create an "X" over the city. There now. See how the crosshairs create wedges that radiate outward to enfold north and south, east and west? These are the shapes the numbers that follow will color in as we do a bit of imaginary statistical painting by numbers. In your mind, these wedges are fictional, but as the epigraph above notes, they have arrived from historical circumstances, and if you lived in San Antonio, you'd find they are all too real. And the racial contrasts within each of these wards, each with a distinct human hue—brown, black, white—color the conditions in our city.

Priming the Canvas

Present-day San Antonio painted in hard numbers requires some base coats—the primer of Texas's early formation. During the late nineteenth century Texas lands were increasingly parsed and divided, enclosed by barbed wire and under private ownership to accommodate the rapid commercialization of a booming cattle industry. Manufacturing rose as well. San Antonio became a hub for the cattle highway of the Chisholm Trail and a junction for cattle sent to New Orleans. Southern Pacific Railroad arrived in 1875, and Mexican Americans would find employment with both rail companies and stockyards in the city. Anglos established businesses and commerce around Main Plaza and the San Antonio River downtown. The U.S. Army used the Alamo as a quartermaster's depot, helping to secure the city's early military ties. Today San Antonio is also called "Military Town, U.S.A." All this expansion brought more pronounced Anglo influences into the city's cultural life as its racial demography shifted. The character of the delicate color play between Anglo and Mexican social and racial organization in the city changed as well.

The cattle industry's equally spectacular rise and collapse inspired the growth of commercial farming in twentieth-century Texas. Transformation from ranch to farm, cattle to cotton, created extreme conflict, yet, as the historian David Montejano explains, in this tumultuous transformation, Texas became "modern." Modern was Anglo, white; old was Mexican/Tejana/o. Eventually, Mexican cultural, social, economic, and political ways yielded to unbridled capitalism and commerce. The relentless quest for modernization helped to create a severe Jim Crow form of segregation that was wielded against Texas Mexicans in all "social arrangements" and would come to define them in ever-changing racialized terms: not black, yet distinctly *not white*. As the early twentieth century aged, newly resident *mexicanos* as well as Tejana/os, who had been established for generations on their once-Mexican, now Texan lands, were eventually viewed as "a racial menace, an unassimilable *alien* presence."[2] San Antonio's Texas Mexican peoples were pushed west of the city's center in the face of growth, west of the downtown area's San Pedro Creek, to establish San Antonio's "Mexican Corral" (so named, it was said, because Mexican families often made their homes in decrepit horse stalls), or the "Mexican Quarter," or "Little Laredito"—now known as the west side.

Yet Mexican nationals continued to stream into Texas in new waves of immigration that were of distinct benefit to Anglo interests: as renewable and cheap pools of labor for agribusiness. San Antonio's southern location, well-established Spanish-speaking community, and growing industry attracted a large number of these migrants. Also from this steady stream, San Antonio began to grow a small but distinct Mexican American middle class. Often monied and highly educated, these residents established important, politically active organizations and mutual aid societies as they attempted to forge ways in which to secure their civil rights and negotiate their highly fraught ties to "whiteness," often favoring Americanization and education as strategies to quell discrimination and racism raised against them.[3] Despite a growing middle class, the vast majority of San Antonio's Tejana/o residents lived in dire and reprehensible conditions throughout, roughly, over a little more than the first half of the twentieth century.

Fill in the Outline: Use Paint Colors #1 & #2, Race and Segregation

On this historical primer, San Antonio painted by numbers in our contemporary time exposes a city of widely divergent realities, which in turn reveal the material legacies of the city's history. According to the U.S. Census Bureau's "2008–2010 American Community Survey 3-Year Estimates," San Antonio had a 7.5 percent unemployment rate.[4] This would seem exceedingly good for one of the ten largest U.S. cities—especially in our era of economic recession. Yet other microdata sets collected by the Census Bureau help to fill in the full picture of the dynamics of social and economic forces in the city.

In *The Panza Monologues* we try to point out the city's various forms of poverty, but perhaps what is more accurate is not that people are deeply impoverished but rather that many are just getting by, and have been trying to do so for generations. San Antonio is the kind of place where you are born and then remain; 65.4 percent of the city's population was born in Texas.[5] Thus settlement patterns indicate lifelong residents' long-term choices in where and how to inhabit the city. For Anglo residents, the preferred site has become the north, the top wedge of the city we have mapped above; Texas Mexicans are overwhelmingly located in the city's southern reaches (the bottom wedge), with large concentrations on the west side (the wedge on the left). The images offered by the U.S. Census Bureau's data patterns for race exhibit this segregation dramatically. Above the north-south divide of Highway 90, which cleanly bifurcates the city, Census Bureau microdata show that white, non-Hispanics constitute from 24 percent to as high as 71 percent of the population. Below Highway 90, Anglos constitute less than 5.5 percent of the population.[6] As the census data evidence, the largest, densest, and wealthiest concentrations of Anglos are located in the far north central sections of the city, which slowly but surely reach toward Austin.

Another one of the most graphic ways to illustrate San Antonio's history of racial segregation in the past century is to examine the city's growth patterns over time. The political scientist Henry Flores has shown how the private sector's stake in San Antonio's decision-making processes has shaped residential growth. Thus private sector or business interests dominate public policy decisions as well as skew city planning to their best advantage. This has led to a tangible, systematic "bulking" of the city's north side, where white, upper-middle-class, and wealthy residents (along with a few super rich among the Tejana/o community) tend to reside—creating a deeper divide from impoverished and lower-middle-class Texas Mexican residents on the south or west side.[7]

As Flores's work documents, San Antonio city planning was in effect "captured" by the business and development community in the 1970s, whose interests favored the north side and neglected the city's west, south, and east sides.[8] This paved the way for explosive growth and development in the white-dominant north, with dramatic results. From 1980 through 1995, 88 percent of all new residential construction occurred on the north side. Census data of the same time period also show that the north side's population grew 80 percent, in contrast to the south side, which grew only 2.6 percent. Writing in 2003, Flores calculates that "fully 96% of San Antonio's population increases over the last 18–25 years has occurred in the northern portion of the city." By 1995, 69 percent of the city's population would be located on the north side, as compared to 31 percent on the city's Mexican American–majority south side.[9]

In turn, property values reflect the economic and cultural capital of the north side. In 2011 a single-family home in the north central part of the city sold for an average price of roughly $224,000, while on the south side, a residence sold on average for less than a third of this figure, $62,000.[10] The monetary value of individual business properties on the north side increased substantially from 1985 to 2000; on the south side, however, commercial properties were on average valued at less than half the value of those in the north. From a street-level perspective, this type of uneven, schematized growth may be best illustrated by the simple example of bookstores.

As late as 2005, on the city's south side, below the San Antonio "Mason-Dixon" line of Highway 90, there were no bookstores of any kind. A group of young south side residents formed Books in the Barrio, a collectively run community action group that lobbied major chain booksellers to set up an outlet in their part of town. These corporations responded to their petitions with claims that there was no market for books in that area of the city, citing that residents of the south side—poorer, with less educational attainment, and overwhelmingly Mexican American—weren't book buyers, nor would they form a book-buying market that could sustain a store.[11]

Fill in the Outline: Use Paint Color #3, Educational Discrimination

Access to education has always been a profoundly contentious battle for Mexican Americans in Texas. Racism, a legacy of cultural tensions, and racist assumptions about Tejana/os' intellectual abilities resulted in a strikingly uneven, segregated system of public education where for decades Tejana/o students were channeled into vocational or general education curricular tracks that limited their employment opportunities and choices. That is, if they made it through high school at all. In San Antonio, the groundbreaking case of *San Antonio ISD v. Rodríguez* exposed both the extent of educational disenfranchisement found in the city's public schools and the ferocious persistence on the part of Tejana/o students and their families. In 1968, at Edgewood High School, located on the west side, where more than 90 percent of the school's population was Mexican American and poor, students staged a walkout and demonstration to bring attention to the delapidated conditions in the Edgewood Independent School District (ISD). Among an array of inequities cited, the students also identified the urgent need for more qualified teachers. In San Antonio demands like this could be met only if school districts with a majority of lower income earning Mexican American residents received more funding from the state system. Edgewood ISD's poor conditions were a result of the superstructure of Texas's educational finance system, which relied in large part on local property taxes. Edgewood raised only $37 per student. In contrast, white majority school districts, populated with San Antonio's Anglo elite, such as the Alamo Heights ISD, raised around $413 per student.

The students' parents responded by forming the Edgewood District Concerned Parents Association. Demetrio Rodríguez and a group of parents filed a lawsuit against the state finance law on *federal* grounds on behalf of poor Texas schoolchildren. In 1971 a Federal District Court ruled that Texas had indeed violated the "equal protection" clause of the Fourteenth Amendment and that the entire state's school finance system had created an uneven distribution of tax monies and was therefore unconstitutional. The state appealed in *San Antonio ISD v. Rodríguez,* and the case went before the U.S. Supreme Court in 1973, which ruled against Rodríguez (and thus Edgewood and poor children throughout Texas). Justice Thurgood Marshall "called the decision 'a retreat from our historic commitment to equality of educational opportunity.'"[12] In the end, the uneven educational finance system persisted across the state until another historic decision, *Edgewood ISD v. Kirby.*

Taking up the cause of Edgewood parents, in 1984 the Mexican American Legal Defense and Educational Fund (MALDEF) filed suit against Texas Commissioner of Education William Kirby, "citing discrimination against students in poor school districts."[13] MALDEF argued that Texas's approach to education financing violated the state constitutional mandate to provide adequate, free education. In effect, MALDEF contended that adequate education could not be provided due to Texas's reliance on local property taxes for school funding. In 1987 a state district judge ruled in favor of Edgewood ISD, now finding that Texas's *entire* school finance system was unconstitutional under state law. However, in 1989 the Third Court of Appeals reversed this decision, declaring that education *was not a basic right* and Texas's system— unequal as it may be—*was* constitutional. The case went on to the Texas Supreme Court, and the justices ruled unanimously in favor of Edgewood ISD. In their sweeping decision, they "ordered the state legislature to implement an equitable system by the 1990–91 school year."[14] To meet this mandate, a new battle began in the Texas legislature.

The battle that ensued from *Edgewood ISD v. Kirby* was protracted and vicious. In the course of the fight, several possible plans were drawn up and rejected by both sides. Lawyers from the wealthier school districts fought aggressively against reform plans that would equalize school finance. Edgewood plaintiffs watched vigilantly as the process played out: they challenged the merits of several proposed plans, noting that the compromises offered still did not sufficiently resolve the uneven distribution. In one dramatic moment, the judge presiding over the Texas Supreme Court's mandated changes threatened to cut off *all* state funds to Texas schools if a just, feasible plan was not drawn up by the legislature. A plan was finally signed into law in 1993—twenty-two years after *San Antonio ISD v. Rodríguez*. Even so, many poorer school districts continued to contend that the new law left intact certain aspects of Texas's unequal school finance system.[15]

Unlike secondary education, for the majority of the twentieth century postsecondary education eluded the reach of the vast majority of Texas Mexicans. Therefore, providing a branch of the University of Texas system to San Antonio had the potential to open up many new possibilities. In 1969 the Texas legislature granted San Antonio a component of the University of Texas system—a hard-won achievement for the city—thus founding the University of Texas at San Antonio.[16] However, the campus was built on a donated "600-acre tract in the rolling foothills of San Antonio's northwest side," fifteen miles away from the city's downtown business district and what could be considered a world away from south or west side Mexican American residents.[17] The buildup around the campus in the next decades helped goad the city's urban sprawl. The University of Texas Health Science Center at San Antonio is also located in the wealthy suburban outreaches on the upper northwest side. To reach the main campus is an arduous journey if you are coming from the south or west side (especially without a car) but accomplished rather easily if you live in any of the ultra-exclusive communities within a few miles of the campus.[18] Today UTSA has grown into the third largest institution in the UT system overall, while it also, and ironically, has come to serve a roughly 42.9 percent Latina/o student population. Fully 94 percent of its students are Texas residents, and over half its population comes directly from San Antonio/Bexar County. Yet UTSA struggles with graduation rates for Mexican American students overall, acknowledged in recent initiatives to enhance its number of graduates.[19]

The results of the microdata thematic maps provided by the U.S. Census Bureau's American Community Survey for 2009 reveal that educational achievement follows the patterns of racial mircrodata as well. The "Percent of People 25 Years and Over Who Have Completed a Bachelor's Degree" dominates the city's north side, with a large number of areas gathering a density of 26 to 63 percent college graduates. In contrast, below Highway 90 most areas have only a 5 to 18 percent concentration of residents with college degrees. Despite this uneven balance, the city as a whole lags in college, much less high school, graduates. Overall, only 23.2 percent of the city's population has either a college or graduate/professional degree. About 10 percent of residents twenty-five and older have only a ninth-grade education or less, and 10 percent have had "some" ninth- through twelfth-grade education. Another way to consider the somber palette these numbers render is to compare San Antonio to neighboring Austin, roughly 75 miles north.[20]

With a population of 790,390, Austin—the "Silicon Valley" of Texas—is smaller than San Antonio, which has 1,327,407 residents.[21] Nevertheless, in the relationship between the two major metropolitan areas, Austin presents an important counterpoint to Mexican American dominant San Antonio. San Antonio continually competes with Austin in its bid to attract the burgeoning "creative class"—highly educated young professionals not native to the city, who are supposed to inspire gentrification, industry, and growth with their influx of "creative energy." Yet these usually young, mostly white, white-collar professionals tend to gravitate to Austin. As compared to San Antonio's 23.2 percent, Austin has a 43.9 percent college/professional degree population and an 8.1 percent population of residents with less than a ninth-grade education.[22] Granted, Austin may have the University of Texas's flagship campus, but you shouldn't forget that San Antonio boasts *five* separate colleges/universities as well as a large community college network.

Fill in the Outline: Use Paint Colors #4 & #5, Labor and Earnings

Given the low high school and college graduation rates for Mexican American majority San Antonio, the inclination of families to remain in the city, and a tourist-driven economy, a large number of residents find employment in nonprofessional jobs. Only 32.7 percent of residents find employment in white-collar jobs in management, business, science, and arts. Meanwhile, service occupations provide 20.4 percent of jobs, with 26.9 percent of people in sales and office occupations. Even during the economic downturn, 2010 data show that natural resources, construction, and maintenance occupations stood at 10.2 percent of employment occupations while production, transportation, and material moving occupations constituted 9.8 percent. In total, nonprofessional jobs make up roughly 57.5 percent of the city's employment.[23]

But the data that most surely bear witness to the city's tensions—despite its low unemployment rate—is that which describe wages earned. Income and benefits data show that 33.8 percent of households get by with an annual income of $35,000 to $74,999.[24] On the lower end, 40.2 percent of the city's households earn less than $34,999 annually.[25] On the upper end, 25.9 percent of households make more than $75,000 a year.[26] However, the vast majority of people in the city who live at or below the poverty level remain concentrated on the city's historically Tejana/o west side, with large areas awash in a 28 to 42 percent poverty rate. And while poverty should visit no person's family, in contrast, a vast swath of the outer northern reaches—notably the farthest geographic locations away from the Tejana/o majority south side—enjoy less than a 9.4 percent poverty rate. Ironically, the luxurious downtown core of San Antonio, where some residents still make their homes, is suffused with a 28 to 42 percent poverty rate as well.[27] Poverty in the city is nestled next to wealth, a fact that can be seen when driving around in downtown residential neighborhoods: one street might contain upscale homes while the next is lined with decaying shotgun houses. Moreover, women in the city suffer poverty in disproportionate numbers.

Fill in the Outline: Use Paint Color #6, Feminized Poverty

According to the U.S. Census Bureau's "2010 American Community Survey 1-Year Estimates," 15.4 percent of San Antonio's families grappled with poverty-level incomes.[28] However, 32.2 percent of families led by single women heads of households lived in poverty; this figure rises when there are young children in women's homes.[29] For example, single female heads of households with children under eighteen grows to 40.3 percent living in poverty, and if these women have children under five the number swells to fully 46.4 percent.[30] On the other end of the age spectrum, the elderly fare no better: a poverty income rate of 13.9 percent. But remember that the city enjoys a (seasonally adjusted) unemployment rate of 8.1 percent—a fact it proudly trumpets in response to the growing unemployment rate since 2008's game-changing shifts.[31] Given this low rate, it is unlikely that these women are overwhelmingly jobless. Rather, they work in jobs that do not allow them to earn a sustainable living wage, much less provide a promising future for "growth."

Place a Wash over the Entire Composition: Use Paint Color #7, Tourism

San Antonio has held the status of "tourist destination" since immediately after the Battle of the Alamo, when nineteenth-century sight-seers were drawn to the site of the Alamo's rubble. Tourism and hospitality now fuels San Antonio's economy—serving the vacations and conventions of nearly 26 million visitors a year and accumulating an economic impact of nearly $11 billion for the city. In official studies conducted by the city, tourism and the hospitality industry create more than 106,000 jobs, generating an annual payroll of about $1.99 billion. Hospitality also contributes more than $153.4 million in fees and taxes to the city.[32]

Therefore downtown San Antonio has been designed and groomed for the purchasing power of the city's millions of tourists and their billions of dollars. Downtown, you'll not only find the Alamo and gift shops, but you're also able to stroll along the immaculately manicured, winding banks of the city's famous Riverwalk, lined by hotels and restaurants far too expensive for lower-middle-class locals to stay in or eat at. On the river you'll see garish river barges carrying wide-eyed tourists, under the gaze of hundreds of restaurant workers hustling platters of food on the Riverwalk's signature outdoor patios, hoping for that big out-of-town tip to line their pockets, which these service industry workers will most likely spend on the south or west side. They'll have to—you can't find grocery stores downtown.

The growth of resorts and golf courses on the city's north side also provide important gauges for present-day struggles with tourism's machinations. Just to the north of the city lies the Edwards Aquifer, "one of the most prolific artesian aquifers in the world."[33] This pristine underground pool of millions of gallons of water is the city's only water supply. Yet in the early 2000s, private developers purchased land that sits atop the aquifer with the intention of placing large commercial properties (malls, resorts, business parks) and golf courses on the area of the aquifer known as its "recharge zone," a geologic formation where rain and moisture seep into the earth to help replenish its holdings. Placing anything hazardous in recharge seepage—such as chemicals and fertilizers from golf courses—would in effect compromise the water's pristine quality. Developers were willing to take that chance.

Over the course of several years, they fought tooth and nail to accomplish their plans, regardless of lawsuits and vehement community indignation. Not even city leaders stopped the developers; in fact, many San Antonio city council members strongly supported their efforts, all in the name of economic growth. The terms of the battle that raged between wealthy developers and concerned citizens were in effect waged deep in the trenches of racism and classism, which exposed how the city's wealth spreads, to whom, and why. If it was open land the developers wanted, there was plenty on the south side, which wouldn't have endangered the Edwards Aquifer even as world-class golf courses would have boosted the south side's industry, growth, and property values. A boon for the city overall, or so one would think. However, the developers wanted the north side, a preference shrouded in the sheep's clothing of "tourism." In the end, at the start of 2010 developers finally accomplished their goal and opened the 1,200-room JW Marriott San Antonio Hill Country Resort and Spa and the Tournament Players Club.[34] The resort boasts two tournament-level golf courses—so far. The future of the Edwards Aquifer's water quality remains to be seen.

Framed: Hang, Stand Back, and Admire Your "Masterpiece," Then Behave as if the Picture Doesn't Exist

These are the statistics rendered by a 400-year history that has seen San Antonio grow into Texas's second largest metropolitan area comprised of a nearly 60 percent Mexican American population. We believe the statistics tell the story of Texas Mexican people that continue to struggle for economic, environmental, social, and political justice. As *The Panza Monologues* attempts to show in some small measure, the conditions that manifest in our bodies come not only by way of personal choices but also by way of generations of struggle to negotiate racism and discrimination that have forced people to make choices that are driven by adaptations to survive. The high rates of obesity, diabetes, and physical maladies connected to diet that have afflicted Mexican American people must be assessed in the stead of underlying contributing factors such as these in order to be addressed in any meaningful manner. Justice begins at home. Only then can we render a self-made portrait of our city.

AUTOGEOGRAPHIES

Manuel Yee and Emma Lesi Yee Cortez, Monterrey, Mexico, 1948 by Anonymous © 2012.
Courtesy of V. Grise.

Margarita Patiño Gamez and San Juanita Gloria Mayorga (née Gamez), Houston St., San Antonio, Texas, c. 1941 by Anonymous © 2012. Courtesy of I. Mayorga.

VIRGINIA GRISE

My grandmother wrote poems on the back of old photographs, forgotten in shoeboxes, in dark closets, stored behind jars of brown Chinese alcohol, marijuana leaves, and holy water.

Se presenta para tus ojos y el recuerdo para tu corazón.

An intimate *conversación* I wasn't asked to join, I try to piece together the stories captured in a moment/still, simple, without color. *Para tus ojos. El recuerdo. Tu corazón.* Photograph. Monterrey, Mexico, 1948. My mother and her father on the corner of Padre Miel and Ubaldi. She stares directly into the camera. She is four. He tilts his head to look at her and smiles. He is holding her hand. My grandfather Manuel Yee was a Cantonese immigrant who traveled from China to Tampico to Monterrey, where he sold fruits and vegetables in the Mercado Colón, the old marketplace, the one they tore down in the 1950s. My mother walked with her father to work every morning before dawn. She spent hours at the market, even as a small child, took naps on stacks of old newspapers while her father ran the business. As a teenager my mother kept his books.

Why did he leave China, *amá*?
—For adventure.
Why did he go to Mexico?
—I don't know.

I never met my grandfather. He died before my sisters and I were born.

"Every morning my father gave red grapefruit offerings to Chiang Kai-shek, a picture mounted on the wall reminding us that he was not from here, that Cantón was not just a memory. He and your *tío abuelo* Andres Wah spoke Chinese across the kitchen table."

Andrés, who we called my *tío*, was family, but he was not related to us by blood. He traveled from China to Mexico with my grandfather and continued to live with my grandmother even after my grandfather died. Once when I was little I beat up a boy because he told me that Andrés wasn't my *real* uncle.

"He's older than your grandmother. *Ni es posible que sea tu tío.*"

I didn't understand. How could he not be my uncle? Andrés would cook dinner for my grandmother every night. He gave candy to the neighborhood children. Cooked me fish soup with chile. When I got sick he fed me warm rice and milk, and when I was little he made a special spot for me to eat on top of the roof all by myself.

"Pa que no te andan molestando."

So no one would bother me, he'd say. On top of a flat roof in México, I ate white rice with soy sauce.

Andrés lived until he was one hundred years old. I was twelve when he died. They held the wake at my grandmother's house. His dead body in a casket in the middle of the living room, bright light offerings, flowers and candles, a red pillow. I slept on the sofa, next to him. Coffin/open, satin and velvet, white calla lilies and carnations. His eyes/closed. When Andrés died, my family collected all of his belongings, his clothes, letters from his daughter in China, old photographs. They took them outside and burned them in a bonfire behind the house.

"It's a Mexican . . . Indian . . . Chinese . . . tradition."

Before the ceremony, my mother's brother took a stack of mud-covered records from the pile of Andrés's things, wrapped them in a plastic Soriana bag and saved them from the fire. My *tío* Andrés listened to those records over and over in his bedroom behind the kitchen, alone.

All those years so far from home.

— — — — —

I have a black-and-white photograph of my mother's *quinceñera en el salon Versailles*. The Lees, the Wahs, the Wongs, the Yees were all there. On the back of the photograph my mother wrote . . .

"Cuando cumpli quince años—mis papas y yo. Maria de Jesus Cortez, Emma Lesi Yee Cortez. Manuel Yee."

So that she wouldn't forget. *El recuerdo.* So that I might remember. *Tu corazón.*

As an adult, I went back to Mexico to try to find out more about the Chinese in the photographs. The Chinese who worked in the factories, the mines, the plantations, and the railroads. They worked for exploitative hacienda owners when Mexican campesinos went to fight in the Revolution *y tambien trabajaban en los mercados.* Green shoots and bean sprout merchants in the *mercado* in Monterrey, titles and deeds signed in the name of their wives half their age. The fruits and vegetables my grandfather and *tío abuelo* sold were from Tampico, and they would buy them from Angel, Carolina, and don Carlos Lee *en el* Mercado Asbastos. The *chinos* from the *lodgia masónica* wouldn't buy their produce from anywhere else. Rafael Lee owned a *yerbería* next to my grandfather's *puesto* and Luis Wong owned the Zapatería Justicia. Searching for my dead ancestors at the markets in Monterrey, the Chinese restaurants in Tampico, in the newspapers from Sonora, at the *henequen* plantations in the Yucatán, in forgotten photos from Arizona, lost cousins I knew I would recognize when I saw them. What did that migration across continents, oceans, languages, cultures mean to my grandfather and my uncle Andrés who *was* my family?

He was looking for adventure.
—But why Mexico?
I don't know.

At eighteen, my mother met my father. After marrying him she too would leave her family, crossing continents, oceans, languages, and cultures.

━ ━ ━ ━ ━

My father was a soldier who did three tours of duty in Vietnam. He enlisted in the military at the age of seventeen after running away from home. My two older sisters grew up on military bases with the enlisted man, the drill sergeant. I was born after the fallout of wars and posttraumatic stress, born to a deeply reflective and thoughtful man.

How did you end up in Mexico?
—What do you mean?
Why did you go there?
—Why not?

My father spoke very little Spanish, though he always understood more than he let on. My mother spoke English, an asset her father thought was important to running the business. My father would go to Mexico often even before he met my mother. He would spend hours on the city buses, discovering new neighborhoods, people, and places.

"Sometimes you don't know where the bus is going to take you, but eventually you'll get back to where you started except you'll have all these new experiences, these stories, you couldn't have imagined before you began, before you got on the bus."

The daughter of a working-class white father from Goshen, Indiana, my mother a Chinese Mexican immigrant, I was eleven years younger than my eldest sister, what they call a surprise. I was the child my parents hadn't planned or expected, the youngest of three girls, born in the South on a military base in Fort Gordon, Georgia. When my mother told my father she was pregnant, he went to the local library and calculated exactly how much it would cost to send me to college. He kept a 3" x 4" notebook with the figures in the breast pocket of his Dickies work shirt. I'm not sure what formula he used to figure it all out, but my sisters and I were the first to go to college on both sides of our family and all three of us graduated completely debt-free.

— — — — —

Standing behind a counter, surrounded by boxes and wooden pallets, a broom, a pencil sharpener in the corner, an old radio, and a scale—my mother holds a pencil in her hand. When I was four, my mother taught me how to write at her kitchen table. My hand over hers, the pencil never rested between two fingers. My middle, ring, and pointing fingers all touched each other as they held my mother's hand and followed the curves of the *letras* she wrote on the page. She knew I would have to read and write before I went to school. It was as if she had foreseen the challenges I would face in the Texas public school system. In kindergarten, my teacher would say I couldn't color inside the lines, didn't follow directions well, and that I held my pencil funny, not realizing that my right hand still remembered the presence of my mother's hand underneath mine even as I grasped the pencil all by myself.

"And she speaks funny too. You know, her English."

The teacher wanted to keep me back a year and put me in speech and English as a Second Language classes. My father was very confused.

"But English *is* her first language."

Even though I spent much of my childhood at my grandmother's house in Monterrey, at age five I still didn't speak Spanish. My parents didn't try to keep me from my mother's native tongue. I was just slow at learning languages. Even now, after having majored in Spanish as an undergraduate (I read *Don Quijote* dammit), I still speak like a *pocha*. I blame it on the fact that I grew up with so many variations of Spanish—what they call formal Spanish, Tejano Spanish, *norteño* Spanish, and members of my family who spoke Spanish broken, with a Chinese accent, because it was in fact their third language.

My father, who was a bus driver at the time, had to take several days off work to deal with my "language" issue and the possibility of me failing kindergarten. My mother, however, was ready to put me in ESL classes thinking maybe the teacher knew something they didn't. My father, again confused: "But she doesn't speak Spanish." I was given a standardized test to see if I was ready for the first grade, and when I passed the test (which was on a second-grade level) they accused me of cheating, all "Stand and Deliver" style. My father had exhausted his sick days in meetings with the school principal, so this time my mother had to go in to the principal's office alone. She was given clear instructions not to let them fail me. Who fails kindergarten anyway?! And if I was smart enough at age five to figure out how to cheat on an assessment test, then I was smart enough to go to the first grade. They eventually did pass me but not without a fight, and the following school year my parents sent me to Catholic school, not to learn the sacraments or the stations of the cross, but to keep me in class sizes that were capped at twelve, where I was recognized as the student that read the most books.

— — — — —

Like my mother, I was a Daddy's girl. She taught me how to write. He taught me how to read. My father read the paper every morning before going to work. Growing up, it was a given that we should think about the world around us critically and politically. My father believed that was everyone's responsibility regardless of one's education, race, class, or gender. He hated boredom and ignorance.

I remember when Ronald Reagan died my father bought a cake. He went to the grocery store, bought a huge chocolate cake, and threw a party. My mother was horrified, thought it was sacrilegious, screamed and yelled and begged for forgiveness, "*Ay dios mio*, please stop it." He struck a match to light the candles and said, "Ronald Reagan was an awful man, Emma. He was an awful, awful man," he kept saying it again and again, staring blankly at the wall in front of him. He lit all the candles of the birthday cake, blew them out, and then started to cry. It was one of the few times I remember my father crying.

I think I was way too young to *really* understand what Reaganomics did to this country, even though he did. As a kid, I spent most my time in garages choreographing dance routines to Michael Jackson's *Thriller*. I even had a silver sequined glove. Not a pair, just one. I'd wet my hair and put mousse in it pretending I had a Jheri curl. My mother tried to explain to me that Mexicans don't have Jheri curls.

But what about Menudo, ma?
—They're Puerto Rican.

Apparently I also didn't understand that not all brown people were Mexican or the fine art of hair grooming. You see, I just wanted to dance.

— — — — —

A first-generation Tejana with no roots or family in Texas, we moved to San Antonio when I was three, after my father retired from the military. In the highly militarized city of San Antonio my family could enjoy all the benefits of his early retirement. In addition to his pension, my family had access to free health care and to the commissary, an *almacen* located on the army base where we bought our groceries tax-free.

Like my father, I started running away when I was very young, imagining the worlds beyond my neighborhood. I rode my bike to the cemetery, the railroad tracks, the ditch down the street, the corner store, the dirt road behind our house, up and down hills, around sharp corners. I learned about scraped knees, stolen flowers, and things girls at five shouldn't know, no matter how grown they *think* they are. And I made up stories set in faraway places, like how I was born in a big blue house in California. As a kid, I had an imaginary friend named Karla. She was a fast girl and shit talker and taught me how to say motherfucker or at least that's what I told my mom when she asked me where I learned that word. My father read somewhere that creative, intelligent people have imaginary friends, so he encouraged my mother to set a plate for Karla at the dinner table one evening. My mother made it halfway through dinner before she threw the plate on the floor, breaking it, and then took me to the *curandera* (one of many childhood visits to the *curandera* that involved flowers, *huevos*, smoke, spitting, and/or holy water). She was trying to cure me of my badness, but it only made me think that being Mexican was magic.

As a teenager, I spent many nights on the roof of my parents' house, in the back of trucks, next to the river, in empty fields, on the hoods of cars, underneath the stars—dreaming. Like my mother, I wanted to be anywhere *other* than my mother's house. Like her father, my mother traveled many countries, before settling somewhere she actually had no connection to, no memory of, and called it home.

— — — — —

I grew up on the northeast side of San Antonio, surrounded by empty fields and railroad tracks, huge Texas skies. There was no public transportation near my house, and I could imagine how people *could* live their entire lives without ever leaving their neighborhood. San Antonio is encircled by several highways and a series of bridges that separate both communities and people, but my eldest sister had a car, and we traveled all parts of the city, crossing borders I didn't even know existed in her green Camaro, tape deck playing AC/DC and Judas Priest.

My sister had a boyfriend she was forbidden to date who would later become the father of her six children. He lived on the west side, the Mexican American side of town in a Mexican majority city, *en el mero wesaso*, over the bridge. She often took me with her for their secret rendezvous. I was her cover. At the Golden Star Café, next to the Commerce Street Bridge, I learned how to listen to things I wasn't suppose to hear, how to keep a good secret, and that I really liked bad Chinese food. I also learned all about Chinese candies, pickles, and the different flavors of *raspas* at the neighborhood corner stores.

When my sister was in college, she had her first child. I would go with her to the University of Texas at San Antonio, located on the city's far, far, far north side, *en el norte*, past Highway 1604. With my nephew in tow, I'd sit in the back of the room, listening in on astronomy lectures and discussions of Faust, hoping that he wouldn't wake up before the class ended because I didn't want to miss a word. I found it all so fascinating. I was twelve. When my sister graduated from school, she taught elementary school on the west side in the Edgewood Independent School District. As a teenager, I would go to the west side to watch independent movies at film festivals and to listen to poetry readings. At the Other America Film Festival and the Inter-American Book Fair I learned about Communist Cuba and Noam Chomsky. I watched my first lesbian film and listened to Sandra Cisneros read from *Loose Woman,* wearing a little black dress, cowboy boots, and red lipstick. I still remember.

— — — — —

In high school, I worked on a teen advisory board at the Brady Green Hospital in downtown San Antonio. Organized by the community activist Jefferey Hons, our group of young people met to discuss state policies regarding questions of sexuality education and reproductive health. I was trained to teach sexuality education classes at my high school and in community settings, spoke publicly about the need for comprehensive sexuality education for teenagers that included information about contraception and gay relationships/sex and organized a group of students to testify in front of the Texas State Board of Education, criticizing the adoption of health textbooks that focused only on abstinence-based education and ignored issues such as STDS and HIV/AIDS. Because Texas is the second largest state in the nation it is also the second largest purchaser of school textbooks, which means that books adopted in Texas and California are then marketed to the rest of the nation. I could see even as a teenager how the conservative climate in the Lone Star State could spread to the rest of the nation like wildfire—just look at what Bush Jr.'s presidency did to us. Through the teen advisory board I started mapping out the way in which power and politics played out on the local, state, and national levels and was introduced to traditional strategies for organizing so that we could have a participatory voice in institutions that make decisions about the well-being of our communities.

In between meetings I would spend hours at the Central Library at the corner of St. Mary's and Market Streets. Right on the river. The Aztec Theatre was within walking distance of the old main library. When my grandmother would come visit us from Mexico she used to go to the Aztec Theatre to watch films in Spanish. I have an old photograph of her where she's looking over her shoulder, hair pulled back. She looks like an old Mexican movie star. *Bien* made up, glass-colored earrings, *arreglada.* Buried under stacks of books sitting next to huge open windows that allowed a view of the green river that cut through the middle of town, I vowed to make it my personal mission to make sure that downtown was not just a place for tourists. As an adult, when I returned to the city, I always lived downtown because I wanted to live close to the San Antonio River.

— — — — —

From my apartment next to the Greyhound bus station, I started the Downtown Swimming Pool Liberation Party. We would put on our swimsuits and dark sunglasses and sneak into hotel swimming pools, where we would talk about ways to take back the city from corrupt politicians and how to fight capitalist expressions of cultural production, gentrification, and tourism. We often did so with a drink in our hands, celebrating the liberation of another gated pool, unlocked. I would also give tours of my city to people who came to visit, beginning downtown, going south on I-35 to the other side of Highway 90, to the city's south side, the Mexican side of town in a Mexican majority city, where I taught middle school in the Southside Independent School District. Southwest Military Drive cuts clear across the city, a military base on each end.

— — — — —

My father worked as an airplane mechanic, a civilian employee, at Kelly AFB on the city's southwest side until the base closed down in the nineties. Twelve thousand civilian employees lost their jobs when the base closed, including my father. He was forced to relocate to Macon, Georgia, when they refused to offer him early retirement. My mother stayed in San Antonio while my father tried to figure out how to financially make sure that I would graduate college, holding his 3" x 4" notebook where he kept his calculations close to his heart. My father lived in a tiny motel room right outside the military base in Macon. I remember going to visit him once, and the parking lot was filled with cars that had Texas license plates. He wasn't the only one who had to relocate.

— — — — —

Southwest Military Drive was also a favorite late-night cruising site, and on Sundays the street would line up with teenagers showing off cars and playing music from speakers they kept in the trunks. Tucked away in dark corners of the south side were sites like the donkey lady bridge and the haunted railroad tracks where as kids we would drink beers and have sex with both boys and girls under a blanket of a million stars.

On my homegrown tours I would take visitors to these places and to the part of the San Antonio River that didn't look like a mall, the part of the river where Mexicans still go to give offerings and pray. We would also go to cantinas, dance halls, juke joints, and gay bars like the Boss, the Zacatecana, the Wild Turkey, La Frontera, the Tenampa Bar, Salute, and Lerma's Dance Hall—where you could work off your *panza* on the dance floor to the best jukeboxes and live musicians in the city, and then build it back up again on beers 2 for $5. On Sundays at a juke joint on the east side called Santa's Place, you could also get generous helpings of fried catfish and collard greens. These bars were infinite sources of *chisme, guato,* and high, high real-life, for reals, drama.

I didn't grow up in the theater watching or reading plays, but I did grow up in a *cultura* that valued poetry, storytelling, ceremony, and the party. It is of course no secret that Mexicans tell the best stories, the perfect combination of *tragedia* mixed with humor, both *dulce* and bitter, fully enacted. It doesn't matter how many places I go—Tejas always feels like my *tierra*. Like many Tejanos whose families have lived there for generations even before the Alamo, I feel like that land is mine. It is from that point of beginning, the stories mapped on my people's bodies, from the poems written on the backs of photographs, the lessons learned at my mother's kitchen table, my father's expansive worldview, the places I went sitting next to my sister in her green Camaro, the stories mapped on my city's streets—this was a training I couldn't have learned in school, an education that was *puro* San Antonio. *Mi corazón.*

IRMA MAYORGA

She stands squarely facing the camera, a broad-shouldered woman, wearing what appear to be spectator pumps while holding her firstborn daughter in the crook of her left arm. It's the two-toned shoes and the wide-brimmed hat of the woman behind her that helps me place the black-and-white photograph in time: the early 1940s. On the back, the handwriting notes that she's standing on Houston St. in downtown San Antonio, Texas. On her way somewhere . . . errands? a Sunday stroll? She smiles the way I do—not a ready, toothy smile, but a slow, hesitant one. More a look than a smile. I like that we share this, that we have the same jaw-line and cheeks too. In her right hand she holds a slim purse and a small package. There's no bulky bag of diapers on her shoulder, no stroller packed with baby gear—just the baby tucked into a bonnet. She must be close to home, close enough not to worry about changing a diaper quickly, which means her home is somewhere near downtown—within walking distance. She looks incredibly proud as she stands in the center of San Antonio holding her daughter aloft against the strength of her torso.

At one time in the mid-twentieth century, commercial photographers haunted the main thoroughfare of Houston Street in downtown San Antonio. They captured passing people with the click of a shutter, collected their addresses, and offered to mail the photographs to their subjects' homes, all for a small fee. These entrepreneurs turned accidental ethnographers have left us remnants of San Antonio's past, usually passed down to our time through the treasure chests of family photo albums and personal archives stowed in shoeboxes. Images like these offer tender testimony to the day-to-day life of Mexican American people inhabiting the city, of the woman described above, my maternal grandmother, Margarita Gamez (née Patiño).

Born in San Antonio, Margarita Gamez raised her five children in the city. But she died before my birth. This brittle Houston Street photograph serves as one of the only documents I have of her existence, verification of my roots as a third-generation San Antonian and fourth-, perhaps fifth-generation Texas Mexican. My mother can remember back to her grand-mother, Isabel Patiño (née Morales), born in Waco, Texas, in the late 1800s. I especially like that one of the only physical remnants of Margarita records her actions in downtown; she plants my *historia* firmly in the center of the city. Now Margarita rests alongside my grandfather in the west side's San Fernando Cemetery II, the old "Mexican" cemetery where a statue of the Virgen de San Juan stands sentry over their shared headstone. Their shiny, black-and-white portraits adorn their headstone as well, pictures that both fascinated and frightened me as a child when we went to clean their grave and dress it with flowers held in a coffee can.

My *historia* and most of the things I tend to create are often preoccupied in some measure with these factors: my Tejana/o family's roots, my city and its activities, and seeing our present through the past. And yet I know so very little about my family history—lost as it has been in the skirmish of Spanish and English, the early passing of my older relatives, and the constant migrations of my youth. This is probably why I've always been continuously preoccupied by the search for it. This is most likely why the origins of family, of Texas hold such great importance to me.

— — — — —

Like many of San Antonio's Mexican American residents of the mid-twentieth century, my maternal grandparents lived on the near west side, where my mother was born in a house on Ruiz Street. That house is now gone, and in fact the entire neighborhood where it was located was razed in the 1950s for the construction of Interstates 35 and 10, which split the city—west from east, Mexican American from everyone else, as it sliced through the Mexican side of town. Because of the interstate's construction, my maternal grandparents relocated to W. Zavalla Street. They moved to a house my maternal great-grandmother Secundina Padrón helped her son secure, moving her kin onto the same street as her own in the northern section of what is known as the Union Stockyard District of the city, a crossroads where the railroads converged. Mexican Americans such as my grandfather Gilberto Gamez—born in the Rio Grande Valley town of Mercedes—found work in the railroad and cattle industries, which depended heavily on Mexican American labor. *La gente* considered proximity to the stockyards a good place to buy a home in the city. My grandfather could walk to his job at Swift Premium Meat Packing Company (once a major employer in the city) where for decades he cleaned out the cattle mess in railroad cars. There was once an alley behind their house where wranglers would run herds of cattle through the neighborhood to move them from Nogalitos Street straight into the stockyards. Gilberto surrounded the *very* tiny house for his family of seven with one of San Antonio's signature chain-link front yard fences—the kind with galvanized steel cocker spaniels that stood atop each gate. This house still stands on W. Zavalla, where it sits in the shadow of I-10 nearby, as does the fence and the huge Chinese plum tree in the front yard, but the bustling stockyards have gone. This home was eventually paid for in full with payments made from Gilberto's manual labor wages, but the family sold it at his death. He died when I was four years old; I only have vague memories of knowing him. He had a large frame and spoke to me in Spanish. My mother has always mourned the fact that the family sold *her* house on his death.

Margarita Patiño and Gilberto Gamez were poor people, barely working class. Margarita could neither read nor write and spoke only a smattering of English. My mother remembers her father regularly reading *La Prensa,* a Spanish-language newspaper, but he did not speak or write fluent English. San Juanita Gloria Gamez would be the first to acquire these abilities in my maternal generations of family, and she would also be the first to graduate from high school—Fox Technical, San Antonio's "vocational" high school, filled with Mexican American students who were taught work-ready skills and trades. In an era when so few Mexican American women completed high school because of segregation, marriage, poverty, or cultural attitudes about education, my mother has always been proud of earning her high school diploma. She wanted more education, but instead she put her training to use and began working as a secretary at Santa Rosa Hospital, also located downtown. She worked in order to contribute to her family's income, to help pay off her family's house on W. Zavalla.

Margarita Patiño Gamez died from blood cancer when my mother was twenty-two, but her terminal illness had begun years earlier. After Juanita nursed her through the illness, she took up the task of looking after her four younger sisters and brother. And she helped her family by turning over the entire sum of her income to help her father. It was an act she did without hesitation, without protestation. She turned over her salary because it's what eldest daughters did back then—out of duty, honor, and love.

As Juanita would be quick to tell you, her father was a gentle man who loved his children. From what I can gather, he was also a great storyteller, an extremely detail-oriented person, a very hard worker, and yet didn't mind cooling down on Friday nights with an iced beer out on his *porche.* He had wanted his only son to go to college. Gilberto Sr. knew his children *had* to complete high school—even if some of his daughters wandered off, and Gilberto Jr. joined the army instead. In those times, Juanita never questioned why it was that she shouldn't go to college too.

— — — — —

My father was a slight and delicate-boned man. Regrettably, I do not carry forward these particular features. Instead, I inherited his short stature and the insistent wave in his hair. In his late teens, Rojelio Mayorga signed up as a soldier down in his South Texas hometown of McAllen and was eventually stationed at Fort Sam Houston Army base. My father passed away in 2007, but when he was alive he too was an itinerant storyteller, a devotee of the Beatles, Freddie Fender, *conjunto*, Pink Floyd, the keeper of a huge inventory of jokes, and the first to laugh, be it at Johnny Carson's late-night antics or a Muppet's silly song on *Sesame Street*.

Rojelio Mayorga liked being a soldier. Not the military per se, but the fact of a dependable income, the patriotic fulfillment of service to country, and the superstructure of orderliness. This is how I remember him even now: as a soldier in uniform. A tight crewcut on his head. A crisp white T-shirt peeking out at the neckline from his standard issue olive green fatigues, an embroidered name patch—"MAYORGA"—sewn above the left shirt pocket. Pants cinched right above the long throat of his black army boots. Dressed in his hat, black army glasses, and fatigues, sometimes I couldn't tell him apart from the other soldiers at a distance.

My paternal grandparents lived down in the Valley, a six-hour drive and what seemed like a world away from San Anto . . . and our travels in the army. I only know slight sketches about Roy's youth and my extensive paternal family—mostly because he held great shame about his impoverished beginnings. He would rarely speak about his childhood, nor would he speak about his tour of duty in Vietnam, no matter how often I tried to draw him out. We didn't make regular visits to the Valley, and my paternal family didn't come up to the big city. They preferred the Valley; they were *sin papeles*. Besides, he was a son, a man; he had left.

Roy's mother and father were also poor. They were migrant farmworkers. Rojelio was the firstborn son and the first U.S. citizen in his family. Vicente and Clara Mayorga (née Vasquez) both died still retaining their Mexican citizenship. Yet they lived their entire adult lives in the United States, going back and forth, to and from McAllen. They would eventually settle there when they were older—less than ten miles from México. They both died *on this side* of the border. From my paternal line, I am more recently arrived, a second-generation Tejana, which often seems incredible to me because México has always felt so far away.

Clara and Vicente's eldest son joined the army as one of his only alternatives to escape a lifetime in migrant farm labor. He believed life would be better in the army. And, of course, it can be for certain young single men and women . . . especially if there isn't a U.S. war being waged. But entire families trying to live off an enlisted man's pay are destined for a unique sort of functional poverty in their army lives—one fueled by financial adversity but not necessarily outright destitution. For my family, paychecks were stretched to their outermost limit, down to pennies we counted around the 15th, 29th, 30th, and 31st each month, the end of each two-week pay cycle. But as long as my father stayed in the army, the checks would keep coming.

Juanita Gamez successfully passed the exam to join the U.S. Civil Service and left Santa Rosa Hospital, finding office work at Fort Sam. Little did she know that she had begun her lifelong relationship with the military. The story goes that my father spotted my mother at a cafeteria at Fort Sam where they both ate lunch sometimes, and he asked a cafeteria worker to introduce them. From this introduction eventually they married. My mother was twenty-four, late by the standards of that time, and my father was twenty-six. My mother married not only my father, an enlisted man who hadn't completed high school (he would later *proudly* earn his GED in the army) but also the army way of life. For the next twenty years, Janie Mayorga would rear her children in the military, survive moves every three years across the United States and through Europe on an enlisted man's pay, and eventually settle back in San Antonio when my father retired, where they would buy the first and only house they would ever own. Not on the west side, a side of town she refused to reinhabit because now she had choices. She chose to locate us farther out, on the far northeast side of town, the side of town that was near Fort Sam Houston Army Base and Randolph Air Force Base where she could have access to the free medical care the army had promised for her children and the military base exchanges that sold food and goods at cut-rate prices, compensating for the military's low pay. Juanita remains at this house today—now paid for in full with the working-class wages she and my father earned. Like her father and grandmother before her, she became a person of property in San Antonio. My father also died a man of property, a fact that was never lost on the migrant farmworker boy that he once was.

— — — — —

If it hadn't been for the army, I too would have been born in San Antonio. I am the firstborn, one of two daughters. My parents were married in the city exactly nine months before my birth; you can count the months. However, with my mother about five months pregnant, the army stationed my father at Heidelberg Army Base in what at the time was West Germany. They served a three-year tour of duty there, just enough time for my younger sister and I to be born with both West German and U.S. birth certificates. Just long enough for the two of us to have to forever explain that *we are* from San Antonio . . . but no, we weren't born there. When we returned from Heidelberg, my mother, sister, and I resided with my grandfather at the house on W. Zavalla Street while the army sent Rojelio to serve in Vietnam. This became a cycle for our family: stationed in a new city, return to San Antonio. Back and forth. Constant movement. We became a typical military family: it wasn't just the father who served the time—*we all served.*

I believe that this type of far-flung travel, imposed as it was through military service, created a very specific way in which I came to embrace the world. As a very young child I quickly learned not to fear new places, not to grow attached to houses or cities, and to face impending change with a sense of welcome. For my family, constant travel was both a gift and a hardship, financially and psychically.

Until the age of sixteen, I only attended army schools on military bases. Built of scores of enlisted men of color and their families, the army provided an environment of extreme diversity, a world always filled with poor people from many different backgrounds, geographic locations, and races. My sister and I were never the *only* Mexican American children: there were many Mexican American children among our friends, even then, a testament to the army's recruiting strategies. Army schools and bases provided a systematic admixture of races, a startling array of peoples.

The majority of the children at army schools were not rich. The majority were young enlisted men's kids.[1] We all shopped at the same post exchanges for our clothes or household goods.[2] We all often showed up at school wearing the exact same shirts—the exchange's inventory was very limited, especially in Germany. My classmates and I usually lived in identically constructed housing units on the bases. Only the officers were treated differently. Officers were usually white (you have to hold a college degree to be an officer) and always had the better homes assigned to them—larger homes. The class segregation the army cultivated was clear-cut, with no façade to disguise the fact that higher rank meant better resources, better pay, and better living. As a young girl, I remember asking my father, "Why?"

"Because they're officers, *mi'ja.*"

I believe the army's rigid, yet transparent hierarchy stoked some of my earliest sense of indignation about social inequality and my strong personal resistance to ranking, ranks, and hierarchical structures of power.

Yet at the same time, ironically, the army opened up the world to my family. This played into my mother's adventurous spirit. Janie Mayorga wanted to explore the world, and she cleverly used the opportunity of our reassignments to find the means to do so. This was an important precedent for my sister and I because although Juanita detested the constant moving, her sheer optimism and sense of wonder about what we could see and do (because we really couldn't do anything about the moving) surpassed any sense of frustration.

In Germany, when my sister and I were toddlers, she made my father drive our family into Italy, just to look around. She knew something was there to see, and she wanted to experience it, show it to "her girls." On our second tour of duty to Germany, when I was a preteen, she trekked our family to Paris, Luxembourg, Oktoberfest, Berchtesgaden, Oberammergau, medieval castles, geographic marvels like mountains and waterfalls, Volksmarches, and World War II memorial sites such as the Maginot Line and Dachau, a profound experience that remains with me even now. The funds for these trips were painstakingly carved out of my father's enlisted man's pay. We almost always camped to offset costs—even in Europe—with my mother hauling around an old Coleman stove to cook meals on in order to save money. In Paris we lived off baguettes bought at bakeries and slices of ham purchased at butcher shops for almost every meal of the trip. We used the money saved to buy tickets to ride up the Eiffel Tower and walk around the gilded rooms and painted ceilings of Versailles.

In the United States, every reassignment was preceded by scouring a map to inspect the path we had to drive along the interstate in order to discover the places we could see along the way. These sites included national parks, zoos, aquariums, gardens, amusement parks, historical landmarks of every kind, and museums—especially museums, art or otherwise. The Smithsonian was a particular favorite of Juanita's; she was so impressed she maintained an annual membership to it for over twenty years.

Juanita Mayorga was also a pathbreaker in more prescient senses. In raising her daughters, she worked against almost all the gender constraints she had faced as a Mexican American girl and woman. Although Rojelio could be given to displays of *machismo*, he reluctantly acquiesced to his wife's decisively progressive decisions regarding rearing "the girls." He had no choice:

Juanita's feminist ethos only grew more articulate as the years passed. When I was about eight, my mother declared to my father that she was *done!* making flour tortillas every night for dinner by hand. He'd have to do with store bought. And he did.

Born in San Antonio in 1940, my mother has only disclosed a small fraction of the prejudice and hardships her family endured. She remembers severe punishments in school for speaking Spanish, which is why she refused to teach the language to her girls. Yet she used enough of it in our home to plant its cadences in our consciousness, to discipline us when need be with Spanish commands (that's how we knew we were in BIG trouble), to shower us with its terms of affection, or to speak privately with my father, usually about money. She remembers her frustration at the fact that she had to speak only English at school and only Spanish at home—at mastering neither and living between them as best she could. At quiet moments when plied, she can vividly recount the apartheid-like San Antonio of her youth. Her experiences with the special brand of South Texas racism and discrimination only shored up her decision to refrain from using Spanish. My father concurred. I can still hear him telling me:

"English is the money language, *mi'ja.*"

In the fleeting glimpses Janie has let slip over the decades, I have come to know that surviving San Antonio from the 1940s to the 1980s as a Tejana was a constant fight for justice, dignity, and survival. Both of my parents have always wanted the future, not the past. I'm the digger, the one who has kept asking them to reach back.

Most of all, Juanita was bound and determined to redress the educational limitations she had faced. She was determined to have her daughters go to college. This decisiveness steered many of her decisions—even if she couldn't explain *exactly what* college was to my sister and me. But she made it sound like the most important, fascinating place on earth. To prepare us, she also empowered us mentally: she never, never implied that we had shortcomings of any kind simply because we were female. She steered us away from activities that ingrained traditional gender roles in our thinking: my sister and I were not permitted to cook or clean or serve. She also filled our house with a constant flow of books, including the most treasured books of all: a complete set of *World Book Encyclopedia,* each lettered volume bought month by month. She never insisted we had to marry to become our fullest selves or have children to make her a happy *abuela*. If anything, she begged my sister and me to pursue our dreams in every way we could.

Instead, we were encouraged toward creative activities of any kind; we made things. The financial lack we faced as children was never our stopping point; we launched creative adventures from its inescapable fact. If a Barbie doll needed a pink car like the one on TV, we would build it from a shoebox. We learned to maneuver my mother's Singer sewing machine and sewed outfits for raggedy stuffed animals from fabric scraps. We made sleds from cardboard cartons, complete with racing stripes painted on the side (those didn't work too well), and learned to crochet, paint, knit, macramé, weave, embroider, make pottery, and bead. These are only some of the things I re-member—there were more. The army offered low-fee classes for these types of things at their DYA (Dependent Youth Activity) Centers on each base— and my sister and I indulged in everything from crafts to dance. My sis-ter was the one who baked, starting off with her much prized Easy Bake Oven—bought through layaway—and moving on to ambitious culinary ex-periments that widened our Tex-Mex staples of *arroz con pollo,* weenies and eggs, and tortillas and beans. Creative activity has been a part of my life for as long as I can remember.

In her own organic way, Juanita Mayorga practiced what I tend to think of as a self-hewn, radically interventionist form of Chicana feminism. She jetti-soned from my childhood cultural constraints that could impede the future woman I would become. She has never identified herself as a feminist and has only recently actually used the term "Chicana" in a positive vein—only after having me claim it for so many years (before that, her unease with the term was extreme: *¡Ay, cochina!*). Yet functioning in all measures as a Chi-cana, she broke down barriers for her daughters in ways that clearly mani-fested her self-made feminism. Instead of our participation in the kitchen, she would chase us out, insisting, "You could be reading a book! You could be coloring a picture! This is not what I want you to do with your time, with your life!" She never said it outright, but you could hear the unspoken "like me!" that hung at the end of her scolding.

– – – – –

My family moved back to San Antonio at the end of my sophomore year in high school as my father prepared to retire from the army. After consider-ing her choices, Janie made a crucial decision not to settle near her sisters, who, along with a growing number of Mexican Americans, had made their homes on the city's far west side. She did this for one sole reason: to be in a better school district. She shot for the northeast side of the city where the schools were more highly funded by the property taxes they drew on. As she knew all too well, education was the vital linchpin that could help her daughters get into college—Janie's biggest, most audacious dream.

In the early 1980s, the eastern side of the Northeast Independent School District sat amid upper-middle-class and higher-end homes.[3] In our own limited fashion, my sister and I knew a different world, a wider world, and we wanted to go back to that world—not to the halls of MacArthur High School, a Class 5A school that boasted thousands of students. The student population at MacArthur reflected this side of the district's higher property values. The wealth on display was outlandish and conspicuous; it was the early 1980s after all. Kids drove BMWs to school, dressed in designer labels, and spoke with brawny Texan drawls. There were also wealthy, upper-middle-class Mexican American students, and they firmly attached their allegiance to packs of wealthy white kids. And, of course, there were poor Mexican American students, but unlike west side schools, this was not a *majority* Mexican American school. In the midst of this mix, my sister and I had a very rough transition. We were not only poor, but worse, we were persistently and visibly "artsy" in a place with a rabid sports culture where football was (and still is) king. We could have cared less about wins, losses, or the glory of state championships. Instead, I buried myself in MacArthur's theater classes and play productions. My sister made her home in German Club and with her fine arts teachers and classes. We both counted the minutes until high school would be over.

Despite Juanita's best, most heartfelt efforts, it seemed simply that the discrimination battles of race and ethnic identity had been exchanged, unwittingly, for those of class.

— — — — —

When I considered the possibility of going to college it was always with a drive to leave Texas. I did my scheming without informed guidance, models, or good suggestions. I didn't know what I was supposed to look for other than the fact that I wanted a place far, far away. Juanita Mayorga plotted with me. She didn't know what we should be looking for either, except that I *was going*, and I needed scholarships. Juanita never begged me to stay close to home. A public university would have been more affordable for our family, but I think the travels of our army life prepared us both for a place far away.

She let me go, and so I did—the first in our generations of family to attend college.

I had a small scholarship, student loans, a parent loan, a Pell Grant, a work-study job, and $300 to my name when I stepped off the plane in the Twin Cities with two suitcases. Juanita thought this *huge* amount of cash would last until Christmas. After buying books, a coat, and laying out money for countless incidental fees, the $300 was gone by mid-October. She sent more through the mail; from which bill payment she leached it, I have never known. Juanita had begun an ever faithful postal relationship between us that lasts to this day.

— — — — —

When I started college, my mother began to send newspaper clippings of every major action or change approaching San Antonio, especially for Mexican Americans. I learned of new developments concerning San Anto *gente* of note: politicians, bigwigs, luminaries—often with her carefully placed annotated commentary on Post-it notes stuck to the clippings, usually with arrows pointing at what I should pay particular attention to in a certain paragraph (it was all usually analysis—she's the organic intellectual in the family). She liked the epic stories about the city best: the contentious elections of new mayors and city council members, the changes to her bus routes (she rode the city bus to work and all over town for over fifteen years), the messes created by major road construction, the budgetary fights in City Hall, and the gentrification of neighborhoods. Juanita monitored the press with intense interest during the entire saga of the Chicana author Sandra Cisneros's 1990s "purple house" controversy in the King Williams neighborhood.[4] Every news column, op-ed, or magazine feature about the purple house was clipped and sent to help me follow the stakes at hand.

"It's *real* pretty Irma. Why would people complain?"

This is how she moored me to our city, even as I was far away.

— — — — —

I entered the College of St. Benedict knowing full well that I would pursue theater. It honestly never occurred to me to major in anything else.

My school of choice was a Catholic women's college.[5] This, no doubt, contributed heavily to the factors that eased my mother's fears about allowing me to go out of state. Female students were always referred to as "women," never "girls," and we were empowered to think of ourselves as *the* primary figures of our school as well as our own lives. It was a powerful thing to participate in a place where every club president, student government position, or leadership role in an institution that a student can have is led by a woman. Here, women in leadership roles became naturalized in me.

The college had a small but thriving theater department and a holistic approach to a liberal arts education for theater students. We were encouraged not to specialize but rather to generalize—to learn about every aspect of theater and the world that we could. I took every acting, design, and theater literature or history course available to me. In fact, the only particularities that I did not "try on" in those years were directing and playwriting, an irony not lost on me today. I tried to participate in learning about or making theater in every way that the department offered—in classes, in productions, and with guest artists. I had a work-study job in the Costume Shop and spent much of my college career in my campus's Fine Arts building, making things.

I also traveled to the Twin Cities of Minneapolis and St. Paul, seventy miles south—cities rich with theater making as well as literary and visual arts. I was able to see groundbreaking work by Theatre de la Jeune Lune, a company whose startling aesthetics remain one of my deepest influences. I also took in shows by the renowned African American Penumbra Theater Company. At Penumbra, I observed that theater made by nonwhite people looked and felt fundamentally different. This resonated with my cultural sense of self (something I often left at the door for Euro-American productions). I also attended numerous performances at legendary Minneapolis theaters such as Mixed Blood and the Guthrie.

As I have observed, almost everyone who aspires to work in theater starts with some type of relationship to acting, but as my time in college progressed my ideas about how I wanted to participate as a professional in theater changed. I discovered that the skills I had accumulated as a child to endure a working-class life in the army were almost always essential skills for creating work and in fact were needed and valued in order to make theater. The sewing, the crafts projects, the conscientiousness about budgets and price, the creative solutions for making something from nothing, learning to navigate an ever-shifting world, thoughtful experimentation, thinking about structures and groups, and suspecting the rules of the crowd—these were all skills called on in theater making. I also quickly came to realize the realities of the racial politics surrounding casting: I was a Latina with very *china* facial features.[6] In my last two years, I moved away from acting. I set up new goals and focused on design. Supportive and prescient professors helped me to gain admittance and a fellowship to an MFA program in theater design. I obtained my MFA in 1992 from the University of Wisconsin, Madison.

— — — — —

I worked as a theater designer in the Twin Cities area for a number of years before receiving an invitation to return to my undergraduate institution to teach. I taught for two years as a visiting assistant professor of costume and set design. During this time, I realized that although working in theater elated me, working as a designer often did not. At the time, I couldn't quite put my finger on what was missing. While teaching, I also realized I missed the academy and its environment of learning and thinking and the vast resources available to do so. I also longed for academic camaraderie—an assembly of learners. Now my colleague, my former literature and history professor instilled a new idea in me: obtaining a Ph.D. in theater studies. More important, she said she would help me with all the minutiae of applying, and she did just that. From working in mainstream theater, I knew that my investments had changed: I was driven more steadily toward work that addressed social issues and ideas of social change. Yet I never imagined, as I slipped my application into the mail, that I would gain a reply, much less an acceptance letter, much less a doctoral degree.

I sold almost every household item that I owned, plotted out my map, and drove from Minnesota to Palo Alto, California, in the fall of 1996. On the move, again.

— — — — —

A place such as Stanford University afforded me the opportunity to deepen my theoretical interests, work I had been introduced to at the University of Wisconsin during my MFA studies. In the Stanford drama department as a doctoral student, I had the opportunity to direct and design shows, write, read widely, and attend lectures to hear ideas from a star-studded line-up of thinkers. I also had the opportunity to take classes with powerfully intelligent scholar/artist/teachers who would sharpen my critical acumen.[7] And at Stanford, I met the Chicana poet/philosopher/playwright Cherríe Moraga, the drama department's artist-in-residence.

———

To be a student in Cherríe Moraga's classes is life changing. When someone such as Cherríe insists that you are a writer, that you must write, that you *can* write—it is a summons difficult to ignore.

Cherríe asked me to bring to bear the breadth of my theater training and career to the task of writing plays. From her mostly brown, working-class-student classes in an elite institution such as Stanford, she insisted that we were the scribes, the ones who must write our families, histories, legacies, subjugations, and dreams *as people of color.* And she insisted we do it with craft and care. Trained as I was by years of predominantly white and Western/American theater practices, her edict served as a form of permission—permission I needed to put *my* words to paper, to speak as a woman, a Texas Mexican, a daughter of working-class and military migrant parents, as a theater artist. I began my first playwriting class with her at the age of thirty; I had spent my entire adult life as a theater professional, but it had never occurred to me to think of playwriting as a pursuit. Under her tutelage, which included a thick mix of Chicana feminist theory, study of radical and revolutionary people of color literature and politics, thinking on sexuality, gender, and indigeneity, exploring postcolonialism, inspecting Chicano Nationalism and culture, interrogating mainstream theater, and attending to the voice and shape of our writing and its possibilities, I constructed my first play.

What my education with Cherríe did was to help me intellectually organize and formally articulate my *concientización* (political awakening) as a woman of color artist and more specifically as a Tejana. But I also knew that this type of work was building on political ideas and radical ways of thinking that had already been planted in me, learned through my mother's own counterhegemonic, and really, commonsense actions in terms of gender's shaping forces, her deep regard for education, and her racially and class-based searches for *dignidad* in San Antonio. I learned from Cherríe to name my mother's thinking: it was theory of the flesh activated. I consider myself extremely lucky and privileged to have built on my mother's theory turned practice in Cherríe's decolonized classroom.

———

It would be another four years before I returned to San Antonio as a more permanent resident. I had to fulfill the obligations of a dissertation fellowship, and I had begun work at a theater company in Massachusetts as a director and dramaturg for solo performances the company was developing at the time. In particular, this primed me for work toward what would become *The Panza Monologues.*

When I did finally move to San Antonio, I was thirty-five. I had completed college and two graduate programs specifically concerning theater. I had lived and/or worked in five separate states. I had a dissertation to finish. I had seen so much, learned from many people, worked very hard, and now I had chosen to return home, to the place I came from, to the place I seemed to need then. I was both a native daughter and a newcomer. My relationship to theater was set to change yet again as I took up the task of finding the place that existed between direct action, political activism, community-based art making, playwriting and directing, and scholarship in a cultural organization that was neither a theater company nor the academy.

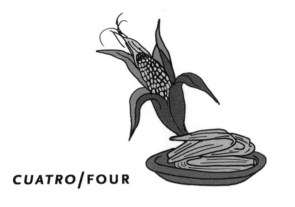

CUATRO/FOUR

A DIY PRODUCTION MANUAL

INTRODUCTION

While the previous chapters of our book have served as introduction, documentation, archive, and history, this chapter thinks on the future, moves your thoughts forward, and urges possibilities. It has always been our intention to publish a second edition of *The Panza Monologues* that offered helpful materials in addition to a copy of the script. This chapter responds to that intention.

We continue to receive requests from groups to stage independently produced performances of *The Panza Monologues*. We have also learned about public productions after the fact. Most often these inquiries have arrived from groups or individuals seeking to produce a piece of theater for the very first time. Requests also come for any advice we can offer as groups embark on their productions. Over the years, we eventually organized an informal "guidelines" letter as a response that helps organizers think about details to consider when mounting a production of theater as well as pitfalls to avoid. We include the compilation of that advice here, plus more. We have also put down some thoughts about the event surrounding your performance. Planning is always key when working on a theater production, so we have also compiled a "production checklist," organized by the timing of tasks (both large and small) that need your attention in order to put up a production. The checklist is not exhaustive, but it does help you to index and pace ideas and actions you should coordinate to make your endeavor organized and strategic. Believe us when we say, through our own journey of creating and

Inside the Panza, *The Panza Monologues* DVD still © 2012. Courtesy of the authors. Virginia Grise in *The Panza Monologues*, presented at Plaza de la Raza in Los Angeles for a special one-night performance on August 2, 2008.

producing *The Panza Monologues,* we know the many types of obstacles you will face in the throes of trying to produce a piece of theater. Don't get discouraged; making theater is always hard work.

But there is also the matter of seeking permission from a play's copyright holder to produce the work for a public event, especially if you intend to charge for tickets. As a professional courtesy, interested producers should seek a copyright holder's permission before they proceed with any stage of production. Copyright laws are clear for plays: the legal rights to produce a published script must be secured from the author. (A tip to ward off your trepidations about asking for permission: we almost always say yes.) The point of seeking permission is to think about the need to pay royalties to the artist(s) for creative work; this can be done in a variety of ways.

The availability of *The Panza Monologues* DVD (which can be purchased on our website) provides you with an opportunity to think about hosting a *Panza* Party with friends, family, or organizations. Now you can watch *teatro* in the comfort of your living room. A *Panza* Party takes some measure of planning for its success. Our suggestions here provide both organizational details for a screening party and recount creative measures that different groups or individuals have implemented to personalize their parties. We admire the thought that has gone into some of the more fabulous *Panza* Parties. Perhaps these examples will inspire you to host one of your own.

Finally, we give you our contact information: website, email, Facebook, and Twitter. We are always happy to hear what *actions* and futures *you* are helping to envision and materialize with *The Panza Monologues*.

GUIDELINES, ADVICE, AND GOOD WISHES FOR STAGING A PRODUCTION OF *THE PANZA MONOLOGUES*

First and foremost, if you are interested in staging a reading or producing your own performance of *The Panza Monologues*, we are honored. We're already excited for you. And we have some advice to offer to help make your production/event successful, as well as a few requests about the particulars of permissions and royalties connected to the public performance of copyrighted materials.

We receive many inquiries from groups who wish to produce some version of the play: staged readings, full-out production, or classroom performances. Typically, these groups plan to stage a production for organizations or activities connected to their gender and sexuality centers on campus, student organizations, and/or Chicano/a and Latina/o student-led events such as Semana de la Raza, Women's History Month, "Hispanic" Heritage Month, or Love Your Body Week. But some women and groups have launched into the journey of staging self-produced productions without institutional or organizational support because—as we've heard—(1) their campus or community does not offer the space or resources for *teatro* by Chicana/os, Latina/os, or other people of color; or (2) because their campus does not have a theater department; or (3) because their school's theater department doesn't regularly produce plays for or about Latina/o people or have roles for Latina/o actors; or (4) their Spanish department only produces plays from, say, Spain's "Golden Age." We also have learned about public productions or readings of the play connected to many sorts of goals and activities after the fact—very flattering but also quite unexpected. However, public performances of copyrighted materials should be done with permission from the copyright holders in hand—that's us. This is a simple process, especially with the guidelines we offer here.

We encourage your ambitions to make live theater in all regards, so we offer this advice to help all levels of producers understand some of the particulars about theater making, published works and playwrights, and ideas about creating your event.

PERMISSION TO STAGE THE PLAY

We would very much like to learn about *all* public productions or readings of *The Panza Monologues*. This includes classroom-based or college/university performances of all kinds, as well as plans to produce the play in other community settings or in support of community events. It's always a joy for us to discover and chart how the play circulates, and we like to keep track of its travels and manifestations. Therefore, if you are interested in producing a staged reading or other type of public performance event, *please let us know* so that we can provide you with a notification of permission to publicly present the play. (See the end of this chapter for our contact information.) Even if you are not charging admission to your staged reading or production, producers/organizers should obtain permission for their public performance. Ideally, you should contact us *well before* you stage a performance of the play in order to obtain permission:

- 3 months ahead of time would be very good
- 6 months before the date you are planning would be even better

This type of notification is not only a courtesy but also part of the normal process of gaining permissions and rights for public performance. All notification on your part initiates a conversation with us through a simple letter that states your intentions and asks permission to perform either (1) a public staged reading or (2) a fully staged production.

How are a "public staged reading" and "fully produced production" different? Generally, a staged reading involves some manner of reading the script aloud, with actors standing still (to a certain extent) or sitting. A fully produced production generally includes full memorization on the part of the actors, rehearsed movement on the stage (exits, entrances, transitions, blocking), and usually design elements as well (lights, set, sound). Staged readings are usually smaller, more intimate affairs—small audience, small venue. Full productions are usually much larger, formal public presentations—larger venue, larger audience. In your letter you should let us know:

- your name
- the name of the organization that will be producing/staging the event (if applicable)

- the proposed dates of the performance
- your contact information

To help guide you, we have also provided a sample letter that can serve as template for your request. Finally, when you send your letter/request, we'd also like to know:

- What is the occasion for your planned performance?
- Why did you choose to stage the piece?
- Do you plan on charging your audience members for tickets?

ROYALTIES FOR STAGING THE PLAY

The script of *The Panza Monologues* contained in this book is copyrighted material. Usually all published plays are copyrighted and are subject to royalties and permissions from the author(s) for *all* public presentations, especially if you charge your audience an entrance fee to the show. Public production means that

1. you plan on rehearsing the show;

2. you advertise its performance to the public to gain an audience; and

3. you present your rehearsed production to a public audience that responds to your advertising efforts.

A royalty fee helps to pay working artists for the use and presentation of their creative labor. When people or groups contact us about presenting the play, we ask if they will be charging audience members for tickets (some don't, for example, if it's for a class, fund-raising, consciousness raising, or private groups). We work with individuals/organizations on a case-by-case basis to determine the best form of royalty fee to solicit.

We ask for a royalty because we believe that artists should be paid for their creative work, whether it be monetary, fair exchange, or a symbolic donation. Creative labor is how artists earn their livelihoods; it's our life's work, and therefore it has a value. But, as Chicanas, we also believe in supporting our many communities, so don't be scared by the word *royalty* because we are not *princesas* and have been known to give Raza discounts![1] We realize the many obstacles Raza, women, and people of color face when we attempt to make *teatro*. Especially when *mujeres* try to make *teatro*. *We don't want to create more obstacles for you*, but we do want *gente* to understand that our hard labor—bodily as well as creatively (and especially women's labor)—should never be taken for granted, asked to be donated under duress of essentialist notions about gendered divisions of labor, or expected to be given away for free because we are female.[2]

PROMOTIONAL MATERIALS FOR/FROM YOUR PRODUCTION

We'd be extremely grateful to receive (via email or snail mail) copies of any documents you produce or press generated about your production: leaflets, posters, email flyers/images, local or campus newspaper stories, web features, or ads of any kind that you create to get the word out. We collect these often beautiful materials to add to our production archive. For example, the top image on page 169 features a poster drawn and created by Julio Salgado and commissioned by the Chicana feminist collective Conciencia Femenil for a production of *The Panza Monologues* they produced and performed at California State University, Long Beach, in 2009.[3] On the other hand, the bottom image is an example of a poster that we created to advertise the play in Los Angeles (used in emails, flyers, and handbills). Like the cover of this book, we typically feature Virginia (and her *panza*) in our print/image advertising. Both of these examples focus on the Chicana body—a great starting point for imagery to advertise the play.

We're trying to track how *The Panza Monologues* lives in the world and the marvelous aesthetic activity it inspires. Also, putting us on your contact lists created for email advertising would be very helpful. That reminds us: use email "blasts" to advertise your show and circulate your posters/PDFs/images—easy, cheap, and quick.

(facing page, top)
The Panza Monologues Promotional Poster by Julio Salgado © 2009. Courtesy of the artist. Poster commissioned from Julio Salgado for Conciencia Femenil's production of *The Panza Monologues*, California State University, Long Beach, December 4 and 5, 2009.

(facing page, bottom)
The Panza Monologues Promotional Poster by I. Mayorga © 2008. Courtesy of the authors. Advertising poster created for *The Panza Monologues'* live taping at Plaza de la Raza, Los Angeles, August 2, 2008.

CONCIENCIA FEMENIL PRESENTS:

"THE PANZA MONOLOGUES"

DECEMBER 4TH AND 5TH
LOCATION:
BEACH
AUDITORIUM

DOORS OPEN AT 6 P.M.
SHOW STARTS AT 7 P.M.

PRE-SALE TICKES ARE $7 AND $10 AT THE DOOR.

FOR MORE INFORMATION CONTACT NADIA AT
NADIAZ88@HOTMAIL.COM

Backyard Productions presents

The Panza Monologues

a play by Virginia Grise & Irma Mayorga

Special Appearance. One Night Only.

Plaza de la Raza
3540 North Mission Rd.
Los Angeles, CA

August 2, 2008 @ 7pm

Free Admission! * Power to the Panza!
For info see facebook website:

www.facebook.com/pages/San-Antonio-TX/THE-PANZA-MONOLOGUES/13733612511

NOTES FOR STAGING YOUR PRODUCTION

You've decided to undertake a production of *The Panza Monologues*. *Bravísima!* You've asked for permissions (and we've replied in turn), you've arranged plans for the royalty fee, and now you are ready to move into rehearsal even as you're working on advertising the event overall. You are busy. But what else should you know about making live theater?

Well, we can't tell you everything. Some things you have to learn by doing. But because many of the groups who contact us about their upcoming productions are setting off on their very first journey in making theater, we've developed a few *notitas* about staging the play that should help to make your production better all around. Some of this advice is basic to all kinds of live theater, while other reflections are particular to *The Panza Monologues* in live performance. You will still have a great number of creative choices as you proceed. You can also view our performance DVD, which offers guidance. Below is the most important advice we can offer in terms of staging.

Stabilize All Actors Onstage (This Is Called "Grounding")

Avoid what Irma calls "the wander walk"—where an actor seems to pace aimlessly throughout her monologue, usually in a slow, meandering way as she speaks. This is deadly to creating intensity or interest. Instead, we suggest that you have preset chairs, stools, blocks, or benches—"anchors"—at different places on the stage that your actors can use as focus areas for their performance. Virginia makes use of her chair or stool during each monologue (our performance DVD contains a good record of her blocking). When she moves away from an "anchor," it is with intention and purpose. And because she only moves away at particular moments (as when she launches into her dance during "From Cha-Cha to *Panza*"), these become more meaningful and powerful. Also, she returns to her chair (her anchor) after dancing. We recommend that any set pieces you designate as anchors *remain onstage throughout the performance*. We use one stool and one folding chair in our production. This cuts down on unnecessary traffic or moving stage pieces or carrying pieces on- and offstage—which we *strongly discourage* because it slows down the performance's pacing!

Don't Use Blackouts between Scenes/Monologues of the Play!

We've noticed that many producers of the play use a multiple-person cast in order to create wider participation opportunities—so you're going to have to figure out how to move from one person's monologue to the next. If you are performing the show indoors, the one thing that immediately kills the play's energy and pacing is inserting the deadly "blackout" between each and every monologue. We *never, never do this.* Instead, move things along! When one monologue ends have the next performer ready to come onstage (be creative in all regards at these transition moments). Use music during transitions— short "cuts" from songs that you feel are appropriate to the material—then (perhaps) dim or shift the lights onstage (but never insert a blackout). We also help our transitions through the use of projections, which state the title of each monologue. Or use specially chosen transition lighting to designate a shift between monologues. Pacing is everything! When we perform the show it runs only sixty to seventy minutes! Be quick, and don't bog down the energy.

Think of Ways to Make the Show a Reflection of Your Local Complexities

Collect facts about obesity or diabetes or access to healthy food or health care in your own community, neighborhood, city, region, or state to use in the section of the play called *"Noticias."* In our script we include obesity/food facts that are specific to San Anto, but here is the opportunity to tell your community/city/state's story. Make your production speak to your local concerns! We use projections to introduce these facts. If you don't have access to projection equipment, use a good old-fashioned easel and placards . . . or hand out leaflets to the audience . . . or unfurl banners . . . or have each cast member wear a T-shirt that states a fact . . . or speak the facts aloud. There are all sorts of things you can do to foreground and animate the issues affecting your community. Creativity is key.

None of the Monologues Should Be Overplayed, Overacted, or Overtly Melodramatic

The play's monologues are based on real people who shared their stories with us and on our own life stories—so keep it true to a person telling a good story (you know, like how Tía Chencha always has the *good* gossip). Don't overdramatize or hold on to anything like it's precious. Be careful about being melodramatic; it detracts from a story's power. The subject matter of many of the monologues is very tough and therefore moving or hilarious in its own right. The more honestly you play it, the more powerful it becomes, and the more resonance it holds.

Build an Altar Onstage

We have always built a large altar onstage dedicated to our loved ones (see script for description of the objects we use). A huge, fantastic altar can function as your primary set piece. We use a low platform or sometimes a table. Basically, we include objects that have given us strength, inspired us to act with love, or reminded us why we need to work harder. We also include mementos of the people who love us and symbols/objects connected to Texas and San Antonio. And, always, fresh flowers and foods. Also, be sure to ask your creative team to bring items to place on the altar too.

BEYOND THE PLAY: YOUR EVENT

Productions of *The Panza Monologues* staged by groups have been expanded on in an array of creative ways that have made *the event* of attending *teatro* rich and memorable. We only wish that we had thought of some of their ideas first! These ideas not only speak to the themes of the play but also invite an audience's active participation in generating connections about themes back to their own lives. We are pleased to pass forward three activities that you might consider for your own event.

Create a Symbolic Food Item to Give to Audience Members before or after the Show

At Cal State, L.A., one group sold lollipops molded into the shape of a naked female torso, wrapped the lollipop in cellophane, and attached a tag to the stick that stated the name of the show, their group's name, the date, and Love Your Body Week. If you can't get "female body" lollipop molds (where did they get those?), you could pick another food item and transpose this idea to that item or come up with other *panza* mementos for your audience. A couple of times, Irma made "Power to the *Panza*" stickers with her home printer and self-adhesive paper. We gave them away at readings and performances in San Antonio and Austin. Ten years later, people still ask for them.

Panza Photo Booth Project: What Does Your *Panza* Want to Say?

At the University of California, Davis, in February 2011, for a collective production of *The Panza Monologues* staged for Semana de la Xicana (Week of the Xicana), organizers set up what they called a *Panza* Photo Booth in their theater lobby in order to create an opportunity for their audience's participation. The organizers encouraged audience members to answer the question, "What does your *panza* want to say?" and handed them a small chalkboard and chalk to record their thoughts. The photo booth—actually a computer station—was used to photograph the audience members with their written thought. Then the photos were posted on the organizers' blog. This record of photographs is hilarious and ingenious. We encourage the idea of enabling audience members to insert their voices—and creativity—into your event's conversation. For a look at the photographs, visit our website.

Panza Placazo Wall Project: What Does Your *Panza* Want to Say?

In Riverside, California, organizers of a *Panza* Party did something very similar to the *Panza* Photo Booth Project but with butcher paper and Sharpies. They taped a large sheet of butcher paper on the wall and asked the audience to write down anything they wanted to share about their *panzas*. People drew pictures and wrote down their own *panza* positive messages. This group took their collective thinking with them to their next event and asked people to continue adding their *panza* thoughts to what was already created—kinda like a traveling mural. We loved this idea because, like our DVD, it's a compact and mobile way to share information. You can take it with you anywhere. *Mira que* smart!

PARA QUE NUNCA MÁS NOS VUELVAN A BORRAR: CONCIENCIA FEMENIL, A CLOSER LOOK AT *PANZA* POSITIVE ACTIVISM

All of our suggestions about staging *The Panza Monologues* are just that, suggestions. However, we believe Conciencia Femenil's production and organizing efforts offer an exemplary case study for thinking about all the facets at hand and in motion—pragmatic and ideological—in organizing a production of *The Panza Monologues* in an academic setting. Here we offer the story of their process as a means to highlight feminist action and collectivity in practice through theater production.

In 2009 we were contacted via email with an inquiry about staging *The Panza Monologues* by the women of Conciencia Femenil (Women's Consciousness), a recently formed Chicana student feminist *colectiva* at California State University, Long Beach. What we didn't know was the larger-scale struggle in which the women were engaged. As the women explained on their Facebook page, the *colectiva* had modeled their activism in honor of a historically important Chicana feminist organization, also started at CSLB:

> Conciencia Femenil is a Chicana feminist organization formed in 2009 to address the cycle of zero, or chronic erasure, of Chicanas on the California State University, Long Beach, campus. Conciencia Femenil follows in the footsteps of their foremothers Las Hijas de Cuauhtémoc who in the early 1970s established Chicana feminist written thought, standing up valiantly for the rights of mujeres in a Chicano Movement that though inspiring, was strongly machista and exclusionary.
>
> Conciencia Femenil is currently undertaking the task of cementing history and establishing the present. It is our goal that future generations of Chicanas and their allies will no longer have to ask the basic questions about Chicana history that in a validating environment would be long answered. We hope to aid ourselves and our compañeras in the acquisition of an informed and empowered identity, para que nunca más nos vuelvan a borrar.

While the formation of Las Hijas de Cuauhtémoc stands as a landmark moment in Chicana feminist history, we were not aware of some of the more unfathomable facets of Chicana/o history "staged" at cslb,[4] as Conciencia Femenil's Facebook page recounts:

> In 1971, M.E.Ch.A.[5] held a mock funeral procession that was a ritualized attempt to kill Las Hijas [de Cuauhtémoc]. They carried caskets and walked with candles to a makeshift graveyard with gravestones for Hijas leaders and a lynched effigy of Anna Nieto Gomez[6] (with her name inscribed). [Las Hijas] faced this for trying to transform the sexist oppression within M.E.Ch.A. This history has never been written nor confronted which is why we feel it has repeated itself.[7]

At Cal State Long Beach, with Las Hijas de Cuauhtémoc serving as their reference point, Conciencia Femenil had come together as an act of resistance to present-day misogyny—forged from a cycle of aggression against Chicanas on their campus that has spanned decades and today has newly ignited to attack the out presence and actions of queer Chicanit@s. A new intracultural battle had erupted in the theater of an old war.

Conciencia Femenil had requested a script for a production. But it wasn't just a performance of the play for them, as we would come to learn through communication; it was a production organized to help raise funds to support their Chicana Feminisms conference. Moreover, they wanted to use their performance of *The Panza Monologues* to create collective feminist action on their campus that culminated in a visceral marking of their presence even as it gave voice to their feminism through creativity, through *teatro*. They were cultural warriors in action. And we remain their admirers.

With that hope, after contacting us via email for permission to use the play, Conciencia Femenil did the following:

> 1. They started researching grants and campus monies—looking to their Student Government at Cal State for funds. Often, campus monies for student-led initiatives go unused. The women received a grant from the President's Commission on the Status of Women at Cal State Long Beach (which many campuses have in reserve, so we encourage you to ask around your institution).[8] They used this money for the facility they rented to stage their production. (Yes, even though you pay tuition and student activity fees, sometimes you still gotta pay to use the spaces in your own school).

2. They made a flyer announcing an "Open Call for Volunteers" to advertise their production plans and gather allies.

3. They decided not to hold traditional auditions. At their open call, *mujeres* read the script and chose which monologue/s they wanted to perform. They were very inclusive: they wanted to work with everyone who wanted to work with them. Most people had never acted before, yet the play spoke to them and their community. Women were encouraged to choose monologues they could relate to. Each woman performed a monologue. In some cases, when more than one woman wanted to do a certain monologue, they would split their performances: one woman would do it one night, and the next night another actor would perform it.

4. After assigning the monologues, they watched the performance DVD together. They studied the directing, staging, and performance, but then they put their own interpretation into their individual monologues and production. They did not want their monologue performance to replicate Virginia's.

5. They held about six to ten rehearsals in total. To begin, they read the script aloud together. This allowed them to get comfortable and become acquainted with each other and the words. Then they started working on their feet and giving each other feedback, thinking through what they thought was funny, what needed to be emphasized. This was done collectively. *No one woman served as the director.* They did, however, ask one of their professors to watch a run-through to get help from an "outside eye." Rehearsals often turned into conversations, women talking, *comadriando,* and the cast sharing stories. This was in part inspired by the language and cultural references of the piece. They talked about everything from how they felt about their *panzas* to the different ways they eat our hot Cheetos. (The cycle continues! See *"Introducción"* and our essay *"The Panza Monologues:* From *Cuentos* to DVD" for how *The Panza Monologues* originated through activities just like these.)

6. They looked to people they hung out with to help—like the artist Julio Salgado. They asked him to develop a "cool flyer." This request inspired what is now Julio's highly praised "Chubby Girl Art Series." On the evening of their performances, they provided a space for him to sell his artwork. In effect, the two purposes inspired each other's creative work.

7. On the night of their performance, everyone agreed to wear black, but they also agreed to bring their own *estilo* to their *trajes*. Some wore short skirts and shorts, others ties and pants.

8. Instead of using projections between monologues (as we do in our show), they had an emcee introduce each monologue.

9. All the people involved helped to build an altar for their performance. They brought a *molcajate* (mortar and pestle made from lava rock), food, *calaveras* (decorated skulls made from molded sugar)[9]— things that had meaning for them—creating a community-based representation of everyone involved.

10. For their production, they always tried to work collectively. Each person took on different roles: publicity organizers, logistics coordinators, rehearsal coordinators, stage mothers, front of house staff, or ushers. They learned that organizing as a collective is hard, and they felt they had few models to follow. But as they found out, you took on multiple roles to make the performance. No one did only one thing (ouch, traditional theater models). As one of the women put it, "It's like home, everyone pitches in." *Hijole*, what an analogy!

11. The women sold tickets at the door, but they also implemented a "pay what you can" option, because in addition to their fund-raising efforts, one of the goals of the organization was to have *gente* come see theater. They successfully met their fund-raising goals.

With great enthusiasm *colectiva* members Lizeth Zepeda, Nadia Zepeda, and Audrey Silvestre reported all of this activity back to us when we badgered them for materials from their event. The women were also careful to articulate what their performance instantiated: all of the people involved, audiences and performers alike, related immediately to the play's ideas and themes. Or as they put it, "You made me fall in love with my *panza*!" As they went on to report, the women who joined together for this production were all undergraduates, mostly Chicanas but also Latinas and even a Palestinian ally. The women were self-identified butches, queer, straight, or bi women, and they performed to packed houses: "As Latinos we can pack a house with our families alone!" Conciencia Femenil advertised their production through their Women's Studies program and other departments.

They asked individual, supportive professors to invite their students. They also advertised their show in their community. We have never intended to pit our play against other women's work, which is unhelpful, yet Lizeth's observations are quite striking and worth recounting in order to articulate a point of origin that inspired our own journey in creating *The Panza Monologues*. When she performed in *The Vagina Monologues* her mother could not bring herself to attend the production, but when she participated in *The Panza Monologues* her mother went to the performance. This was deeply affirming to Lizeth.

Even in the woman-affirming throes of their production, the women of Conciencia Femenil still faced the challenge of their conference. Their 2010 annual Chicana Feminisms conference intended to invite the renowned queer Chicana feminists Cherríe Moraga and Alma López, but it was met with a homophobic response from the student body:

> Conciencia Femenil was hit with the firsthand experience of history repeating itself. By bringing attention to hetero-patriarchy at Cal State Long Beach, within the departments, student organizations, and our Chican@ communities we too were attacked with misogynist and homophobic violence. In response to an article announcing the conference, hateful homophobic and sexist attacks against the organizers and conference speakers Cherríe Moraga and Alma López were displayed on our school newspaper's website ("the daily 49er"). The homophobic slandering attacks intensified and eventually escalated into remarks that referenced an appropriation of an Aztec calling for the murder of gays and lesbians with explicit instructions as to how to administer the killings.[10]

When we recount the shape of aggression and violence that women and queer folk face, as we often do at our talkbacks, Performance *Pláticas*, and other public opportunities, such as this book,[11] in our adamancy and earnestness, we do not exaggerate for dramatic effect or histrionics: this is the climate feminist women face, even within our own Chicana/o communities. The resistance and affirmation that describes Conciencia Femenil's production of *The Panza Monologues* truly astounds and humbles us. We offer their example as one of the reasons why we endeavor to work harder. We hope their example inspires readers as well.

– – – – –

Finally, we wish you the very best for your production.

Creating and mounting any type of theatrical event that calls upon a group of people to collaborate is always a remarkable and extremely rewarding journey.

– – – – –

As one saying goes, *break a leg*—or as we always say,

Power to the Panza!

PERMISSIONS AND ROYALTY REQUEST SAMPLE LETTER FOR *THE PANZA MONOLOGUES*

We recommend that you adapt this letter as necessary and send it on your own letterhead or stationery as a PDF via email. You can also find document templates for writing a request letter at www.panzamonologues.com to help you generate an inquiry.

— — — — —

[Date]

Irma Mayorga & Virginia Grise
Playwrights
The Panza Monologues
panzapower@gmail.com

Dear Irma and Virginia:

We are interested in producing a *[insert the appropriate choice here from the following list]*

- staged reading of *The Panza Monologues*
- fully staged production of *The Panza Monologues*
- classroom-based production or reading of *The Panza Monologues*
- community-based production or reading of *The Panza Monologues*

with/for/on behalf of *[insert the name of your organization here—if applicable]* at *[insert name of venue/institution here]*. We would like to perform the play on the following dates: *[insert dates of proposed performances here]*.

We would like to obtain your written permission to present the play, and we also write to inquire about royalties. We are interested in *[choose the most appropriate here: (1) staging, (2) reading, (3) presenting]* your play because we would like to *[insert an explanation of your overall project here]*.

We also understand that any public presentation of *The Panza Monologues* requires a royalty fee, and we seek further communication with you for our next steps towards discussing fees.

In exchange for permissions, we also understand that you would appreciate receiving copies of any documents we produce or press generated connected to our production such as handbills, posters, email flyers, local paper news stories, or ads. We will be sure to put you on our email lists and forward these materials as they are created.

[Let us know of any other pertinent information about your plans here before you close!]

[Closing],

[Your name]
[Your organization]
[Your mailing address]
[Your phone number]
[Your email address]

PANZA CHECKLIST: PLANNING YOUR PRODUCTION

Beginning

☐ Determine the dates of your production.

☐ Determine if you are going to produce the show as a solo performance or as a group production.

☐ Determine if there will be a singular director or a group effort of some kind.

☐ Set up a budget for your production. Be sure to think about costs for royalties, renting your venue, costumes, sets, lights, props, altar, and any special event activities beyond the play itself. Think about free resources (on your campus, for example) you could draw on for aid.

☐ Create cross-campus or intracommunity cosponsorships to help *fund* and participate in your production. Perhaps you would also like to coordinate with others for postperformance discussions or other types of intersections.

☐ Locate a venue for your production, check its availability for your planned dates, determine if you need to pay a fee to use the venue, and be sure to see if the venue is also available for rehearsals—especially in the three to four days before your production dates. If so, reserve the venue with its facilitators.

☐ Determine a venue for your rehearsals.

☐ Determine if you are going to charge admission for your production. Determine the price of your tickets.

☐ Send a letter to the playwrights of *The Panza Monologues* to notify them of your desire to produce the show for a staged reading or full production and to arrange royalties. On page 181, we include a sample letter of notification as a guide.

Early Planning/Work before Rehearsals

☐ If necessary, determine how you will sell tickets—person to person? or through some other outlet? Decide on which date to begin selling tickets prior to the date of your show. Determine if you need to create paper tickets/receipts for purchasers to present at the door on the night/day of your performances.

☐ Gather other collaborators who will *not be* performing. Sharing work makes the load lighter but coordination and commitment is key. It is helpful to find separate people from the actors to: create your set, help with lighting, help with managing the audience on the days of your performances and any activities in the lobby, help with creating programs, help with advertising/publicity, and help run the show from backstage. Now is the time to widen your circle.

☐ Think about any type of postshow discussion you might want to coordinate for your audience. Contact and invite guest facilitators if desired—they will need to save the date for their calendars.

☐ Begin creating your advertising materials.

☐ Schedule auditions and find a venue for auditions.

☐ Advertise auditions. This is a breaking moment when even your advertising can generate excitement and anticipation for your production. So we suggest creating visually compelling materials/announcements!

☐ Create an "audition form" that requests the following information from each person who auditions: name, contact information, unmovable commitments they may have (e.g., child care, classes, jobs). Also request their rough weekly schedules for the next two months or so.

☐ Plan a schematic for an ideal rehearsal schedule. Start backwards from the date of your opening to determine the time you will need to coordinate your cast members' multiple schedules—leave ample room in your schedule for unexpected events.

☐ After an advertising campaign of at least two weeks, hold auditions, recruit friends, and find your cast. When auditioning people be sure to emphasize about the time needed for participating in rehearsals.

☐ Based on auditions and casting, determine who will perform what part of the script. Mapping it out before rehearsals makes for a clearer path.

Rehearsal/During Rehearsal

☐ After casting your production, revise your rehearsal schedule with regard to your cast's potential schedule conflicts.

☐ If you are planning a full production, we suggest a four- to six-week rehearsal period before you reach the final week before a performance. The final week of your rehearsal period is usually composed of technical rehearsals to put all your elements together, thus its name: "tech week."

☐ Finalize your advertising materials. Distribute these materials via the Internet and through public posting at key community sites.

☐ Contact press outlets in your area to notify them about the upcoming production: think newspapers, online mags or notices, bloggers, Internet information outlets such as campuswide or community-wide calendars, public and private group email lists, and radio.

☐ Create an online presence for your production, and invite all collaborators/cast members' friends to the page. Post regularly to this page with updates about your process, rehearsal achievements, and forthcoming show information in general.

☐ Keep working on coordinating activities that you are planning for the day of the show/lobby. Try to finalize details *before* you hit the week immediately proceeding your production dates ("tech week")!

☐ Begin selling tickets to the show.

☐ Be sure to keep checking in with any sponsoring organizations you have secured if you need their help or to check on their efforts to spread the word about your upcoming show.

☐ Create your programs.

Before You Present Your Performance

☐ Intensify your advertising efforts about one week before your opening date.

☐ Finalize all lighting, set, costume, music, and prop needs at least one week before your opening date.

☐ Be sure to schedule, *at the very least,* one full-out, all-elements-in-place, nonstop run-through of the play in motion so your actors can feel and experience the totality of the show. Two to three of these full-out dress rehearsals are better!

☐ Coordinate how and when you will move your audience into the performance space on the days of your performance. Determine who will sell tickets and who will take tickets at the door, and monitor and facilitate all lobby activities.

☐ Think about how you will document the show and your effort. Try to take pictures during one of your full-out dress rehearsals as opposed to the nights of performance. Remember to take pictures to document your "off-stage" collaborators in motion as well!

Opening and Performance

☐ Breathe.

☐ Leave plenty of time on the day of the performance for last-minute details, emergencies, and calamities. They happen. Encourage your cast and collaborators to do the same.

☐ Arrive early at the performance space.

☐ Set up your lobby for the audience well in advance of their arrival, at least one hour before the play begins. Audience members appreciate your readiness and attention to details about their participation.

☐ You're tense and excited. Treat everyone and yourself with kindness, *pues* at the end of the day, it's only a play.

☐ Tell all your collaborators thank you again and again.

☐ Enjoy the performance. Watch your audience's reactions. Take it in.

Postperformance

☐ Return anything borrowed.

☐ Return your venue to its facilitators in pristine condition. Don't make more work for the people who work there, especially custodians.

☐ Thank sponsoring organizations with a personal gesture.

☐ Thank all collaborators with a personal gesture.

☐ Thank your online community with some thoughts about the experience immediately after the show.

☐ If necessary, coordinate and calculate your ticket sale monies.

☐ Determine who will send advertising materials like posters, leaflets, interviews, press notices, or images of the show to the playwrights.

☐ Share your photographic documentation online or in print or on a blog or in a newsletter.

☐ Celebrate yourself. You did it!

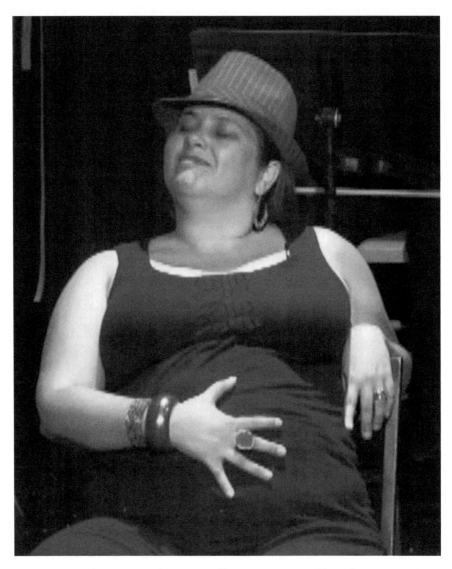

Panza to Panza, The Panza Monologues DVD still © 2012. Courtesy of the authors. Virginia Grise in *The Panza Monologues*, presented at Plaza de la Raza in Los Angeles for a special one-night performance on August 2, 2008.

TUPPERWARE MEETS TELENOVELA: HOW TO ORGANIZE A *PANZA* PARTY

The idea of the *Panza* Party was born in the kitchen of Dolores Zapata Murff's home in San Antonio. After the first round of *The Panza Monologues* DVD's editing process, our editor, Mirasol Riojas, expressed a desire to view the DVD with an audience before she made the final edits to the video. Dolores was gracious enough to open her home to our *panza* project and a group of ten *mujeres*, *comadres*, and girlfriends—along with Virginia in attendance—gathered in her living room on a Saturday night to screen a rough cut of the DVD in its entirety. Using the glow of the television as her only light, Mirasol sat next to a coffee table where she quietly took notes. Similar to the experience of watching live theater, everyone cried and laughed out loud together, but they did so in the comfort of someone's living room with plenty of cocktails, wine, and homemade food, including finger sandwiches and chips. In the kitchen, over the sandwiches, everyone joked about how this could be the artists' version of a Tupperware party.

The humble Tupperware party, those woman-driven gatherings that featured a household product and entrepreneurial chutzpah, provided a provocative idea for circulating our DVD, but we were also bringing the drama: Tupperware meets *telenovela*. As we saw it, it was somewhat easier to market the DVD to established institutions; we were glad to see the DVD purchased by community centers and university libraries—important points of access for a certain segment of our *gente*. But we also desired to put our portable *teatro* in the hands of people who don't normally have access to these places.

The Tupperware meets *telenovela* joke quickly turned from an idea into a plan—a "party approach to marketing" to help distribute and sell our DVD: the *Panza* Party.

What's a *Panza* Party?

Panza Parties are viewing parties, sponsored by a "fan," ardent supporter, or ally who gathers together a group of people in their homes to view our DVD collectively and, thus, in community—much like the event of theatergoing. Every *Panza* Party is a unique event dependent on the creative ingenuity of its host/s. The first official *Panza* Party was held in Claremont, California, at the home of Lydia de los Rios. Lydia, now a retired school teacher, had returned to California after receiving her master's in education with an emphasis on reading development and second language acquisition at Harvard University and spent her career teaching at Pomona High School (in a working-class suburb thirty minutes south of Los Angeles). Lydia invited colleagues from her school and a few close friends to her party. The guest list included teachers, principals, guidance counselors, graduate students, and her daughter Cati de los Rios, a *panza* ally and serious *chingona panza* power educator in her own right (who, by the way, also went to Harvard *and* was teaching at Pomona High at the time).

The group watched selections from the DVD in Lydia's family room, with Virginia introducing each monologue and offering personal anecdotes and stories. *Panza* Parties are excellent opportunities to initiate discussion about your community's health, power relations, historical circumstances, and your body. After Lydia's screening, the educators began a conversation that focused on the issue of obesity in Latina/o communities, specifically raising questions concerning free lunch programs and health and nutrition in the schools. The women present also shared stories about their relationship to their *panzas,* including thoughts from a pregnant graduate student in attendance. Some of the young male teachers bought copies of the DVD insisting that their mothers, *tías,* or *primas* had to see the show. Others said they were going to take the DVD back to their schools to use as a pedagogical tool in their classroom.

A *veterana pansonsita,* Lydia threw a huge *panza pachanga.* She and her husband, Miguel de los Rios, worked all day in their kitchen cooking plates full of delectable food and homemade *taquitos.* She is known for her chicken *taquitos,* while Miguel is an expert at *carne asada taquitos* (a distinction Lydia finds important to articulate—*pa que sepas*).

The *panza*-perfect evening ended with a *panza*-satisfying tequila toast before everyone said their goodbyes. A celebration with community *and* food has come to be a central feature of a *Panza* Party (food encourages rich discussions).

Other *Panza* Parties have been very intimate dinner or cocktail parties such as the one thrown by Sibyl O'Malley in her one-bedroom apartment in Eagle Rock, California. She cooked a vegetarian stir fry with lemongrass for some fellow writers, proving us wrong: maybe we can trust skinny people *and* eat at their houses.

Also a *flaca* like Sibyl and one of our biggest *panza* allies, Marissa Ramirez, threw a *Panza* Party in her house on the south side of San Antonio for Valentine's Day and called it the "Love Your Body *Panza* Party."[1] She decorated her home with paper hearts and red garland that she purchased at a local flea market. The south side after all is famous for its *pulgas*. You didn't know? Again, guests gathered in the living room of her *casita* around her gigantic flat screen TV to view the DVD. That evening Virginia performed "The International *Panza*" live. Those invited included college students, mothers and their babies, self-identified butch dykes, and even some *Panza* Party crashers who heard about the party from friends. Marissa let them in! "I thought you knew them," she later told Virginia. After the screening, everyone pushed back the furniture and danced to *conjunto* music, ate barbecued brisket hot off the grill, *frijoles a la charra,* and potato salad. It was *panzalicious* and so very Tejana/o.

Most recently, theaters and activist organizations have been throwing *Panza* Parties as fund-raising events. The Breath of Fire Latina Ensemble Theater in Santa Ana, California, organized a *Panza* Party that included screening clips from the DVD, a live performance of select monologues by Virginia (including "From Cha-Cha to *Panza*," "The International *Panza*," and "*Panza Brujería*"), as well as live music by Alexandro Hernández Gutiérrez, the original *flacaso*. This party became rowdy during the performance of "*Panza Brujería*" when Virginia was booed (yes, booed) by a woman in the audience, a Latina no less. As we mention in the script, we use "*Panza Brujería*" to speak out about contemporary issues, politics, and policies that have a direct effect on our collective *panzas*. We also call out a list of people we want to do *brujería* on and name the issues that have forced us to perform *limpias*.[2] This "naming names" list changed from performance to performance based on whatever was—*in our view*—a pressing political concern at that moment.

Breath of Fire held their *Panza* Party just one month after the signing of the controversial (and, um, *anti-immigrant* and, um, *racist*) Arizona Senate Bill 1070.[3] That evening Virginia chose to give *ojo* to Arizona's Republican governor Jan Brewer. Granted, the party was in Orange County (yes, as in *The Real Housewives of Orange County*), but we were also in Santa Ana, the Mexican part of the county known as "the Mexican OC"—you know, the OC you don't see on reality TV. At first Virginia thought the woman who began booing was joining in the protest of Arizona's governor and continued performing. But the woman grew more and more uncomfortable and agitated until she finally blurted out (in the middle of the performance): "I support 1070."

The raucous party atmosphere quickly deflated. At the talkback afterward Virginia explained, "It is not my responsibility to make sure that everyone in this audience leaves happy. As an artist, my responsibility is to my truth. And, yes, to provoke. So I will continue to speak what I know to be true—even if it gets me booed." The heckler stayed for the talkback, but when the house lights went up she was a little less *brava*: she didn't say a word. After the Breath of Fire *Panza* Party, it was Virginia who needed the *limpia* from all that conservative badness. Even when a heckler is just one OC housewife, it leaves an ugly feeling in your *panza*. It's true. Sometimes you *do* have to give *ojo* to protect yourself, especially when dealing with Hispanic reactionaries!

On a different note, in a different county, and a completely different *onda*, a collective of female-identified, queer, and trans activists threw a *Panza* Party at a small infoshop[4] in Riverside to raise money for the fourth annual Ladyfest Inland Empire, a grassroots, DIY (Do It Yourself) feminist festival.[5] The organizers knew that Virginia would be guest teaching at UC Riverside as a visiting artist in the English and theater departments and organized their *Panza* Party around her trip. The *colectiva* decorated the infoshop in true DIY fashion, with handmade signs made from black Sharpies, found paper and glitter, with a punk rock edge. Mari Salinas from Vaya Con Fashion sold a series of ex-voto *panza* prayer cards at the event—an offering to the goddess—thanking her for thickness and an extra curvy body. The night of the party, a band was rehearsing right upstairs, and you could hear the music through the walls. The combination of silver tinsel, handmade signs, balloons, and music reminded Virginia of Daddy O's in Austin—or any other shady bar without windows you might find next to the railroad tracks—the kind of place that helped inspire the writing of "From Cha-Cha to *Panza*." It was a party after all!

Love Your Body Panza Party Invitation by Cristy C. Road © 2012. Courtesy of the artist. Invitation to the "Love Your Body Panza Party" in Riverside, California, February 2012, organized as a fund-raiser by Ladyfest IE 2012! Fourth Annual Ladyfest IE! featuring a screening of *The Panza Monologues* DVD.

These are all examples of different types of events you can create for a *Panza* Party. Through *Panza* Parties—organized by groups of friends or whole families—our *teatro* continues to inch its way into living rooms, *casitas*, and communities, transcending its dependency on money, time, and space. Your *Panza* Party will also help to manifest one of the most ambitious aims of our efforts as theater artists: to circulate (simulated as it may be) theater into our communities to spark collectivity and discussion. But, worthwhile as this aim is, a *Panza* Party does take some planning, preparations, and, of course, creativity. If you want to organize a *Panza* Party DVD screening at your house, cultural center, or theater, we include here the following checklists, which offer advice and tips for successful party planning.

PANZA PARTY SAMPLE INFORMATION FOR AN EMAIL INQUIRY

We recommend you supply all the information in this list and send it in an email to us.

— — — — —

Please Let Us Know about Some of Your *Panza* Party Plans in an Email

- Name of the *Panza* Party host

- Name of the organization (if applicable)

- Your phone number

- Your email address

- Are you hosting a public or private *Panza* Party?

- Date of the *Panza* Party

- Would you consider selling single copies of the DVD at your party?

- Do you want to sell copies of *The Panza Monologues*, 2nd ed., book at your party?

- Would you like further information about possibly inviting one of the artists to your party? (Dependent on artist schedule and availability.)

- Please provide a brief description of your party/theme/occasion for the *Panza* Party.

PANZA CHECKLIST:
PLANNING YOUR *PANZA* PARTY

Before You Start Cooking the *Frijoles*: Pre-Party

☐ Decide what type of *Panza* Party you would like to throw. A private *Panza* Party where you invite only friends or a public *Panza* Party in your community or on your campus?

☐ Decide the date, time, and place of your *Panza* Party.

☐ For community or campus events, gather supporters and allies. Create cross-campus or intracommunity cosponsorships to help coordinate and participate in your party/screening.

☐ Order a copy of *The Panza Monologues* DVD from our website to screen at your party.

☐ Customize your *Panza* Party. Will it be a *Panza* Cocktail Party, a *Panza* Dinner Party, a *Panza* Dance Party, a *Panza* BBQ, a *Panza* Potluck? Even large events can have themes. It's entirely up to you. Every *Panza* Party is different and should be made with your unique *flavor*. Think of ways to make the party reflect your personality.

☐ If you are hosting a public party, identify a venue. Be sure the venue is available for your planned dates. Determine if you need to pay a fee, and be sure that the space meets all your technical and seating needs. If so, reserve the venue.

☐ Send an email to us to let us know you are planning to throw a *Panza* Party. (We always like to learn about *Panza* Parties.) On the previous page, we include a template of information to supply.

☐ Feature an artist. We can't attend all events, but we just might be in your area. We recommend contact at least two months in advance to discuss options.[6]

☐ Selling the book. If you would like to sell the 2nd edition of *The Panza Monologues*, we suggest you contact a UT Press representative directly at www.utexas.edu/utpress/booksellers/booksell.html#sales at least four weeks prior. You should notify your distribution contact that you are organizing a screening with a book-selling event.

☐ Selling the DVD. If you would like to sell copies of *The Panza Monologues* DVD at your event, contact us with inquiries about orders at least four weeks prior to your event.

A Slow Simmer: Preparing to Party

☐ Make your own organizational/shopping list of everything you will need for the party. In addition to seats for all your guests: Do you need to buy, find, trade, borrow, and/or steal any additional groceries? Decorations? Party favors? Do you have enough cups, plates, napkins, and silverware?

☐ Test your DVD. Doing a "test run" a week or so before is a good idea. If your party is in a home, make sure the television and DVD work. If your party is in a public space, check to make sure you understand how to operate the facility's equipment—several days before the screening.

☐ Promote the party. If you are hosting an intimate house party this will most likely only include phone calls, texts to friends, sending out invitations by mail, or creating an email invitation. If you are hosting a public event at a university, cultural center, or theater this could require making and distributing flyers *and* talking to the press or other media outlets. You should begin doing this at least a month in advance. Again, this is your chance to be creative. Page 193 shows the invitation Cristy C. Road created for Ladyfest's party in Riverside.

☐ If you plan to sell our DVD or book, be sure to tell your guests or the public so that they come prepared with cash or checks.

☐ Try to take pictures during your entire process. Marissa Ramirez kept a *Panza* Party scrapbook that included pictures of her and friends shopping at the flea market and at the grocery store, decorating the house, and preparing the brisket, as well as the party itself.

Now You're Cooking: During the Party

☐ Leave plenty of time on the day of the party for set-up and cooking and also for last minute details, emergencies, and calamities. They happen.

☐ Set up well in advance for your guests' arrival. Be ready at least one hour before the party begins. Leave yourself enough time to iron your *traje* or dickies, to put on your *puta* shoes or shine your Stacy Adams—whatever you gotta do to feel *panza* perfect!

☐ If you do plan to sell copies of the DVD or book, have cash on hand to make change for guests. We suggest you ask a friend to volunteer and be responsible for sales at your party—someone other than the party's host. This should be that person's only responsibility. Be sure to create a system for documenting sales before the day of the party and that you have a place set aside at the party for sales.

☐ If you are not selling the DVD or book, we would appreciate if you could let your guests know how they can purchase each of these.

☐ Create a sign-in/email sheet. We'd appreciate adding your guests to our contact lists. Having a sign-in sheet to collect names and emails is one of the best ways to gather this information.[7]

☐ Take pictures! Send them to us in an email, and we can post them on our website to celebrate your party!

☐ Let your guests know that they can host their own screening.

☐ Finally, it's a *pinche* party. Have fun!

Clean Up: The After-Party Aftermath

☐ We hope everyone had a great time, and let us know how your *Panza* Party went via email, Facebook post, or tweet. We encourage you and your guests to share your thoughts about the work. And don't forget to send advertising materials like posters, invites, interviews, press notices, or images of the party to us.

☐ Forward the names and emails of anyone who signed up to join our mailing list.

☐ Return anything borrowed. Return your venue to its hosts/facilitators in pristine condition.

☐ Thank any sponsoring organizations and any volunteers with a personal gesture.

☐ Thank your guests with some thoughts about the experience immediately after the party.

☐ If you sold DVDs or books, coordinate and calculate your book sale monies.

☐ Properly box and return any unsold books to the publisher in a timely manner.

☐ And finally, you did it! Congratulations! We suggest you treat yourself to something nice to celebrate all your work and to avoid the post-party blues.

CONTACT INFORMATION

WEBSITE: www.panzamonologues.com

EMAIL: panzapower@gmail.com

FACEBOOK: www.facebook.com/panzamonologues

TWITTER: https://twitter.com/#!/PanzaMonologues

FIVE/CINCO

PEDAGOGY OF THE *PANZA*
A READING, CREATIVE WRITING, AND DISCUSSION GUIDE
FOR *THE PANZA MONOLOGUES*

INTRODUCTION

While staging a production of our play is a worthy project, we also invite you to explore other ways to engage with both the play and *The Panza Monologues* DVD. In this chapter we offer a variety of discussion topics, activities related to body image and obesity in the United States, investigations of place and identity, creative writing exercises, and ideas to help you think about making your own work of documentary theater. As noted in the "Guidelines, Advice, and Good Wishes for Staging a Production of *The Panza Monologues*," we remain blown over by the many creative ways in which organizations and groups have designed projects that let their *panzas* speak. The suggestions that follow expand on the spirit of those activities.

At their core, these ideas are designed to encourage self-discovery and critical thought. We have both taught in the classroom as full-time middle school teachers in (alternatively) Language Arts, Spanish, ESL, and Special Education and have experience teaching in community settings and working with high school students as well as at the university level in both public and private institutions. We envision that many of the activities could suit a wide variety of populations including middle school and high school populations. For example, to accompany reading or viewing *The Panza Monologues,* teachers could spend one day on the discussion of a particular topic or perhaps design multiple-week units around an activity described below. Our audiences have always included young people, and we believe many of the issues raised by the play are directly relevant to their lives. Therefore, these exercises hope to inspire using the play for higher-level skills such as critical thinking, synthesis, and original thought. As well, we hope college- and university-level instructors will find the activities helpful in deepening their students' critical responses to the work while also encouraging you to activate theory.

Our suggestions are intended to help jump-start your own ideas for class- room conversations and investigations, reading group discussions, or writ- ing circles. We encourage modifications of all kinds depending on your needs. If you have the time (we know teachers and instructors are very busy people), please let us know about your *panza* pedagogy and your work teach- ing *The Panza Monologues* in classroom and community settings.

At the close of this chapter we include a brief bibliography for further reading. Our creative work has been fortified and informed consistently by the work of many luminaries—artistic, activist, and scholarly. We include a brief list of reference works that have imparted knowledge of all kinds to us as socially conscious artists, teachers, Tejanas, Chicanas, and Latinas. We cannot include all the essential writings or thinking that has affected us, but the list provided here is our effort to help set a fire or feed your *panza* or pro- voke you to take up your pen or tinker at your keyboard . . .

TOPICS FOR DISCUSSION AND ACTIVITIES BASED ON *THE PANZA MONOLOGUES*

Before Reading / Screening:

1. Define obesity. List all the factors that you believe can cause someone to become obese.

2. In the past twenty years there has been a dramatic increase in obesity in the United States. Why do you think this has occurred?

3. What does it mean to be healthy? What other types of health exist besides physical health? What types of health concerns affect you, your family, or your community? Do you consider yourself healthy? Why or why not?

After Reading / Screening:

1. Was there a monologue or moment that was particularly surprising, challenging, compelling, or poignant to you personally? Why or why not?

2. Read or view the monologue "My Sister's *Panza*." What types of concerns might a child with diabetes have? What types of concerns might that child's parent/s or caregiver/s have? Have you or anyone in your family ever been diagnosed with an illness that was either life-threatening or caused

major changes in your/their lifestyle? What type of impact did it have on your family?

3. Read or view the monologue "Political *Panza*." What do you think are current laws or legislation that are not *Panza* Positive, and why do you think so? What do you think you can do to change those policies or practices? What do you think would be examples of *Panza* Positive Policies?

4. Read or view the monologue "*Panza Brujería*." Describe a time you have had to "protect yourself" from someone else. Why did you feel that way? What did you do to protect yourself?

Internet Research Activities

1. Read or view the monologue "A Hunger for Justice." Go to www .lafuerzaunida.org to learn about the history and current work of Fuerza Unida in San Antonio. Be sure that you not only read the mission of the organization but also watch videos and interviews with the women of Fuerza Unida. Then do an Internet search for *Fuerza Unida v. Levi Strauss* to find out more information about the 1990 plant closure, the factory's move to Costa Rica, and Fuerza Unida's hunger strike against the company. The website www.peaceworkmagazine.org/worker-solidarity-after-work-gone-story-fuerza-unida provides a great overview. What other sources did you find? How do you think the women felt the day they showed up at work only to find that the factory they worked at had been closed suddenly? What do you think about the actions of Levi Strauss? What challenges do you think the women faced as organizers? Have you or someone in your family ever lost a job unexpectedly? What did you/they do? How did you/they feel? Are there any companies in your local community that have sent work overseas or to another country? How did that affect your community? Write it down. Share with your group. Further Reading: *Sweatshop Warriors: Immigrant Women Workers Take on the Global Factory* by Miriam Chiang Yoon Louie (Boston: South End Press, 2000).

2. Read or view the monologue "International *Panza*." Do an Internet search on U.S.-Cuba relations. www.bbc.co.uk/news/world-latin-america-12159943 offers a time line of major events in the history of U.S.-Cuba relations. What is an embargo? When did the U.S. embargo against Cuba begin? Find an article that takes a position against the embargo. What are

the author's arguments? Find an article that takes a position supporting the embargo. What are the author's arguments? What is the current U.S. position regarding the Cuban embargo? How do you feel the embargo has affected Cuban nationals? How do you think it has affected Cuban Americans? What is your position regarding the embargo? Write it down. Share with your group.

• Use this information to create a class debate about the Cuban embargo. Divide into two teams: one will argue in favor (pro), and the other will argue against (con). In groups, develop a list of main facts that support your argument. After the groups present their positions, each group will form rebuttal arguments to their opponents' position and deliver a closing statement.

3. Read or view the monologue "Praying." Go to www.domesticviolence .org and read the sections of their online *Handbook* titled "What Is Abuse," "Who Are the Victims," and "Who Are the Abusers" (links to the *Handbook* can be found on their homepage). Next, visit the factsheet about domestic violence provided by the National Network to End Domestic Violence at nnedv.org/docs/Stats/NNEDV_DVSA_factsheet2010.pdf. What are the rates of domestic violence in your city? In your state? Report back on how many women, men, and children are subject to or witness domestic violence. Report back on how many calls the National Domestic Violence Hotline received on one single day in 2008 and how many calls went unanswered. How does "Praying" use the *panza* to speak up about domestic violence in this young girl's life? Like the girl in "Praying," what would you say to an abuser if you had the chance? Write it down. Share with your group.

N.B. We caution educators that opening up discussions of domestic violence may elicit participants' own experiences with domestic violence in their families or communities. *Please* be prepared to engage those who may come forward with care and support as well as aid and resources.

Obesity in the United States

1. Read the statistics in our monologue "*Noticias.*"

2. What do you think these statistics have to say about obesity and class? Obesity and race? Obesity and age?

3. Look up statistics about obesity for *your* city and state. We recommend starting at the Centers for Disease Control and Prevention's website, which has figures on adult obesity in the United States (www.cdc.gov/obesity /adult/index.html). Also be sure to look at the CDC's information on childhood obesity (www.cdc.gov/obesity/data/childhood.html). With further Internet investigation, can you find what percentage of your city's residents are considered overweight or obese or have diabetes related to weight? How does your city rate nationally in terms of obesity or obesity-related illnesses? Dig further: how does the United States compare to other countries in terms of body weight or obesity? This data can be made into a pie chart or a bar graph to visually represent the statistics you've found.

4. What social factors do you think contribute to obesity? What cultural factors contribute to obesity? What economic factors contribute to obesity? What gendered factors contribute to obesity?

5. Some activists believe that the war on obesity is actually a war on obese people. What are ways that fat people face discrimination because of their weight? What are ways we can all live healthier lives at any size?

Body Image

1. Find or buy three fashion magazines or find fashion websites on the Internet.

2. Cut out (or print) pictures of women from each one, and paste or tape them on paper or poster board.

3. Study the images closely. What do these pictures say about women? Do the pictures say anything different if the woman is white? Latina? African American? Asian American? How so and why?

4. What do these pictures say about body image? Do you think women have more pressure than men to be a certain body type? Why or why not?

5. When you were looking through the magazines or Internet sites, do you remember seeing different sizes of women represented? Describe what you found overall.

6. Create your own advertisement. What does beauty mean to you? First, do a free-write and create a letter to your body. What do you love about it?

Describe how you appreciate it and what it can do. Then, take a picture of yourself doing something you love to do. Use text from the letter and your picture to create a "counter-ad" to what you find in magazines.

Cultural Mapping

1. Put a large map of your city on a wall.

2. If you are working with a large group or class you might want to break everyone up into small groups, and make each group responsible for one specific part of town (north, south, east, west, and downtown). Identify and mark the following sites on the map (one way to do this is to use different color Post-its):

- grocery stores
- bookstores
- museums
- universities
- cultural centers
- post offices
- public parks
- major highways
- city hall
- courthouses
- jails
- hospitals
- police stations
- gyms
- farmer's markets

3. Consider the locations of different places you have flagged. What do your notations on the map reveal about your city? Do different areas in your city have a larger number of any one kind of place? Does everyone have the same amount of access to food, educational sites, cultural sites, or medical sites? Where do people buy fresh fruits and vegetables in your community?

4. What does public transportation look like in your city? How do people get from one place to another? What types of journeys do people in your city have to make to reach any type of store or site lacking in their neighbor-

hood? Do highways separate neighborhoods? Next identify a major street in your neighborhood, one that has many businesses and is heavily trafficked.

- Count the number of grocery stores on this street.
- Count the number of liquor stores on this street.
- Count the number of fast-food restaurants on this street.
- What other types of businesses are located on this street?
- What do these numbers reveal about this major street in your neighborhood? If you were in a different neighborhood on a different side of town, do you think these numbers would vary? Why or why not?

6. Draw your own map or "counter topography." On a large sheet of paper (butcher paper is great for this), draw a rough sketch of the major streets and highways in your city and neighborhood. Then draw in not only sites and places that are well known or perhaps very famous but also sites that are important *to you*, that make your neighborhood or city special to you or your family. Make your map as personal as you can. Draw each of these sites in its approximate location and label it. Look at the map drawn by Debora Kuetzpal Vasquez at the beginning of Chapter Three/*Tres*, "Tejana Topographies," for inspiration—how does your map compare to hers?

CREATIVE WRITING ACTIVITIES BASED ON *THE PANZA MONOLOGUES*

Some Thoughts on Free-Writing

For many of these creative writing exercises, we suggest beginning with a "free-write." A free-write is just that, writing free from constraints, your own inhibitions, and your self-judgment or the judgment of others. But it is also a focused exercise. It's where you concentrate on the task of writing but not necessarily on how you say it while you are doing it. Here are some best practices to observe during a free-write:

1. Try to write in one sitting for a solid three–five minutes (at first). Don't reject anything that goes onto your paper. Just keep pen to paper, and keep the thoughts moving across the page.

2. Respect how your mind might end up connecting things together! Don't try to "make" connections. Let them come naturally or haphazardly.

3. Don't try to "make" it a monologue or theater during your free-write; just write to tell your truth and reveal your thoughts.

4. Try not to judge your thoughts as they come out—blocking doesn't help. Give in to the rush of ideas that will come, and keep the pen moving across the page.

• The hardest part is often putting those first sentences down on paper!

5. Oftentimes when free-writing, it helps to imagine your listener as you write. This could be a family member, a close friend, or someone completely *unrelated* to the story, or a person *directly connected* to the story.

6. We highly recommend writing by hand rather than on a computer; it's fundamentally different.

7. Don't be afraid to use this imaginative opportunity to make bold choices. Remember, our piece "*Panza Brujería*" addresses U.S. president(s). That's allowed in creative writing!

Creating Monologues

Five prompts to get you started with writing a monologue. First, do a free-write:

1. Write about the first time you felt betrayed or lost trust in your parents.

2. Write about a time you witnessed an injustice.

3. Write about a moment when you felt very deeply for another person's problem or issue.

4. Write your own declaration or manifesto about something that is important to you.

5. What is the most powerful part of your body? Write in the "voice" of this powerful body part. Let it sing out—what's it got to say?

Some tips for writing monologues:

• Be in the moment. In all of these exercises we encourage you to "drop into the moment." Instead of writing about the event as if it were in the past, write about it in the present—as if *you are there right now*. Before you start writing you might close your eyes and see yourself in the moment. Where are you? Who's there with you? What are you wearing? What time of day is it?
• Use all your senses. Don't just describe the event and what you feel but also what you see, hear, smell, and taste.
• Speak from your own voice—don't worry about trying to sound "writ-

erly." What makes your voice unique? What do you hear in your head? How does your voice reflect your personality? Remember that in real life people often do not speak in complete sentences and thoughts. Experiment with language to create your own rhythm, cadence, and musicality.

One-Liners

As we describe in our book's introduction, much of *The Panza Monologues* began with one-line riffs and jokes. The stories behind the one-liners later became entire monologues, but the riff inspired the story. One thought, usually humorous, such as: "I went from cha-cha to *panza*," "That would be my *panza brujería*," "Don't eat at skinny people's houses," or "*Panza* Power!" Here we provide the beginning of one line to help get you started with a one-liner. First, complete each line with your own thought or information. If you want, you can try to make your one-liner both true and funny.

- "When I was a kid I used to . . . "
- "I wasn't always . . . "
- "Perhaps if our government . . . "
- "_____ Power!"

Now, choose one of the one-liners you have created, and do a free-write that elaborates on this start. Write nonstop for three solid, unbroken minutes.

Writing with Personal Photographs

During "A Hunger for Justice" in *The Panza Monologues* performance, we project a series of black-and-white photographs of Mexican American families and people in South Texas taken in the early to mid-twentieth century. We gathered these photographs from the U.S. Library of Congress online photo collections. In these astounding images, the conditions of Mexican Americans' lives in South Texas and, more specifically, San Antonio in the early to mid-twentieth century jump forward through time with powerful clarity. This research led us to mine our families' personal photo archives. As this exercise hopes to demonstrate, photographs from a family's collection can serve as rich writing prompts that yield critical and creative thoughts about history, identity, and place. Here, we suggest writing activities that use photographs for creative work.[1]

• Ask students/participants to bring in older photographs from their family's collections. Here, "old" is relative. For our autogeographies, we both turned to some of the oldest photographs we possess: those that depict our grandparents. Due to our ages, this allowed us to think about the entirety of the twentieth century. To encourage a similar transhistorical perspective, ask students/participants to bring photographs they might have of older family members.

EXERCISE 1: DESCRIPTION
• Study the photograph very closely for at least five minutes.
• In a five-minute free-write, describe the photograph as someone looking in from the outside. Concentrate on describing each element visible in the photograph—everything both in the foreground and in the background. Look on the back of the photograph—is anything written there? This should be only a physical description of what you see in the photo to thoroughly describe it.

EXERCISE 2: RELATIONS
• Study and think about the person(s) in the photograph for at least three to five minutes. What emotions does this photograph evoke in you?
• In a free-write, tell the story of this person's relationship to you. Do you know him or her well? Or do you only know the person from family stories or the photograph itself? Do you wish you knew the person better? Think of this person in the extended relations of your family. Who were the parents of this person? Who were his or her siblings? Who were his or her children? Do you know this person's full name? Where is this person from originally?

EXERCISE 3: THE PERSON
• Study the photograph very closely for at least five minutes.
• Where was this person when their photograph was taken? Why was the person there? What is she or he doing in the photograph? Why?
• How old is the person in this photograph? How did the person earn a living? When did the person stop working, why? How did his or her parents earn their livings?

- Describe in detail the emotions and attitude of the person in this photograph—Happy? Sad? Indifferent? Excited? Somber? Does he or she seem to enjoy having his or her picture taken? Study the person's body language and describe it as well. Does it say something different from the facial expression?

- Do a free-write with the prompt, "I remember . . . ," and write about a specific memory of this person and you.

EXERCISE 4: THE PLACE OF THE PHOTOGRAPH

- Study the photograph very closely and describe the time, place, location, or season when it was taken. Can you locate the house, street, or city where it was taken? If possible, can you find out what this house, street, or location in the photograph looks like now? Do you know who took this photograph?

- Do some historical research either in a library or online about the city or neighborhood where this photograph was taken. How has this place changed over time? How has it remained the same? Every location has defining features—try to discover those connected to the location of your photograph. Write up the details of your research to describe the larger context of where this photograph was taken.

EXERCISE 5: ETHNOGRAPHIC INQUIRY

- If the person in this photograph is still living, ask him or her to tell you about the photograph. What does the person remember? Listen carefully, and take good notes. Then write down and describe what you heard about the story of the photograph. Be sure to write down how you feel about the information relayed to you.

- If the person in this photograph has passed, ask a family member who knew or knew of the person to tell you about the person or the photograph. What do they remember? Listen carefully, and take good notes. Then write down and describe what you heard about the story of the photograph. Be sure to write down how you feel about the information they relayed to you.

ADVANCED WORK: COMBINATION

- Take any of the above exercises you have responded to as source material and combine two pieces of your writing. Begin with the prompt: "When I look at this photograph now . . . "

Autogeography

We use the term *autogeography* to mean auto (self) + geography (space, places, cities, features of space) in order to describe our personal histories. How does space/place help determine your subjectivity, who you are, and how you see things? The following writing prompts are designed to help you begin mapping your own autogeography. Use your responses to them as source material. Looking at places such as your street, your neighborhood, your community, what do your answers reveal about yourself?[2]

WRITING PROMPTS FOR FREE-WRITES:

1. Who are you?

2. Where are you from?

3. Where is your family from?

4. Where do you live? Describe not only your home but also your neighborhood and city.

5. My community is . . .

6. Home is . . .

7. Home sounds like . . .

8. Home tastes like . . .

9. Home smells like . . .

10. Home feels like . . .

11. What is the language of home?

12. Make a list of three places in your neighborhood or city that shaped you. Write about each of these places and its importance. Research the history of these places—what can you learn by looking back?

TEN STEPS FOR CREATING DOCUMENTARY-STYLE THEATER

The simple gestures of this exercise—thinking, free-writing, and interviewing—enfolds three of the basic means we used to write many of the pieces for *The Panza Monologues*. You can do this exercise by yourself to develop work or with a group. In either case, it's designed to kick-start performance work by using the seed of a political idea, issue, situation, or cause to grow a piece for theater or performance. This exercise can be especially effective in group situations because you can use group members as "interviewees" and draw from each other's work for source material and writing support and use all the pieces written to create a larger theater work. Also, writing in a group will reveal many dimensions of an issue because groups always bring multiple perspectives to the subject at hand.

1. To begin, choose a pressing political issue to explore that affects *your daily life*.

2. Take some time to think about the many dimensions of the issue at hand, then ask yourself:
   - *Why* does this issue affect me?
   - *What* do I want others to know about this issue?

3. Find a quiet place to sit down with a pen or pencil and paper and do a "free-write" about this issue. As you write, keep in mind the reasons why the issue affects you and what you want others to know.

4. Only *after* you've completed your free-write, go back, review, and re-write as needed. Look for ways to focus and sharpen your story.

• This takes some time (*writing is often rewriting*), but if the issue is important to you, it should go fast because it's urgent!

5. Now make a list of at least three interview questions about this issue *to ask someone else.*

6. Think, whose perspective(s) would you like to hear talk about your topic/issue?

• Who might be an appropriate choice? Who might offer a surprising, less expected point of view? Both of these perspectives will bring depth to your piece.

7. Conduct an interview with at least one person you have identified in point #6 above.

• Be sure to listen carefully and attentively. Notice not only what they say but also how they say it. Taking a tape recorder or other recording device is extremely helpful.

8. Now, using this person's responses to your questions, in another five- to ten-minute free-write session, compose a separate monologue about your topic.

• Try to incorporate your interview material into this new monologue, in terms of ideas, style of speaking, language, etc. You don't have to use the interviewee's exact words, but you should incorporate her or his point of view to shed light on the issue at hand.

9. Once you've completed this free-write, go back, review, and rewrite as needed. Look for ways to focus and sharpen your story.

10. *You've now generated some materials for a piece!* Think about the best order for the separate pieces you or your group has created and collected; think about what stands out, what needs work, and what is still unclear. The possibilities of what you can do with your stories are endless.

FURTHER READING

Mujeres

Acosta, Teresa P., and Ruth Winegarten. *Las Tejanas: 300 Years of History*. Austin: University of Texas Press, 2003.

Arrizón, Alicia. *Latina Performance: Traversing the Stage*. Bloomington: Indiana University Press, 1999.

Blackwell, Maylei. *Chicana Power: Contested Histories of Feminism in the Chicano Movement*. Austin: University of Texas Press, 2011.

Beauvoir, Simone de, Constance Borde, and Sheila Malovany-Chevallier. *The Second Sex*. New York: Vintage, 2011.

Chabram-Dernersesian, Angie. "I Throw Punches for My Race but I Don't Want to Be a Man: Writing Us—Chica-Nos (Girl, Us) Chicanas—into the Movement Script." In *The Chicana/o Cultural Studies Reader*, edited by Angie Chabram-Dernersesian, 165–182. New York: Routledge, 2006.

Córdova, Teresa. *Chicana Voices: Intersections of Class, Race, and Gender*. Albuquerque: University of New Mexico Press, 1993.

Ensler, Eve. *The Good Body*. New York: Villard, 2004.

———. *The Vagina Monologues*. New York: Villard, 2001.

García, Alma M. *Chicana Feminist Thought: The Basic Historical Writings*. New York: Routledge, 1997.

hooks, bell. *Feminism Is for Everybody: Passionate Politics*. Cambridge, MA: South End Press, 2000.

López, Josefina. *Real Women Have Curves: A Comedy*. Woodstock, IL: Dramatic Publications, 1996.

Martínez, Elizabeth S. *500 Years of Chicana Women's History/500 Años de la Mujer Chicana*. New Brunswick, NJ: Rutgers University Press, 2008.

Mendible, Myra. *From Bananas to Buttocks: The Latina Body in Popular Film and Culture*. Austin: University of Texas Press, 2007.

Moraga, Cherríe. *Loving in the War Years: Lo Que Nunca Pasó Por Sus Labios*. Cambridge: South End Press, 2000.

Moraga, Cherríe, and Gloria Anzaldúa, eds. *This Bridge Called My Back: Writings by Radical Women of Color*. New York: Kitchen Table, Women of Color Press, 1983.

Pérez, Emma. *The Decolonial Imaginary: Writing Chicanas into History*. Bloomington: Indiana University Press, 1999.

Rothblum, Esther D., and Sondra Solovay. *The Fat Studies Reader*. New York: New York University Press, 2009.

Ruíz, Vicki. *From Out of the Shadows: Mexican Women in Twentieth-Century America*. New York: Oxford University Press, 1998.

Ruíz, Vicki, and Korrol V. Sánchez. *Latinas in the United States: A Historical Encyclopedia*. Bloomington: Indiana University Press, 2006.

Wolf, Naomi. *The Beauty Myth: How Images of Beauty Are Used against Women*. New York: W. Morrow, 1991.

History / Cultura

Acuña, Rodolfo. *Occupied America: A History of Chicanos*. New York: Harper & Row, 1988.

Broyles González, Yolanda. *El Teatro Campesino: Theater in the Chicano Movement*. Austin: University of Texas Press, 1994.

Burciaga, José A. *Drink Cultura: Chicanismo*. Santa Barbara, CA: Joshua Odell Editions, Capra Press, 1993.

Castillo, Ana. *Massacre of the Dreamers: Essays on Xicanisma*. Albuquerque: University of New Mexico Press, 1994.

Danielson, Marivel. *Homecoming Queers: Desire and Difference in Chicana Latina Cultural Production*. New Brunswick, NJ: Rutgers University Press, 2009.

González, Juan. *Harvest of Empire: A History of Latinos in America*. New York: Viking, 2000.

Gutiérrez, Ramón A. *When Jesus Came, the Corn Mothers Went Away: Marriage, Sexuality, and Power in New Mexico, 1500–1846*. Stanford, CA: Stanford University Press, 1991.

Huerta, Jorge A. *Chicano Theater: Themes and Forms*. Ypsilanti, MI: Bilingual Press, 1982.

Kanellos, Nicolás. *Hispanic Theatre in the United States*. Houston, TX: Arte Público Press, 1984.

———. *Mexican American Theatre: Then and Now*. Houston, TX: Arte Público Press, 1983.

Moraga, Cherríe. *The Last Generation*. Boston, MA: South End Press, 1993.

Moraga, Cherríe, and Celia H. Rodriguez. *A Xicana Codex of Changing Consciousness: Writings, 2000–2010*. Durham, NC: Duke University Press, 2011.

Muller, Lauren, and June Jordan. *June Jordan's Poetry for the People: A Revolutionary Blueprint*. New York: Routledge, 1995.

Orozco, Cynthia. *No Mexicans, Women, or Dogs Allowed: The Rise of the Mexican American Civil Rights Movement*. Austin: University of Texas Press, 2009.

Rivera-Servera, Ramón. *Performing Queer Latinidad: Dance, Sexuality, Politics*. Ann Arbor: University of Michigan Press, 2012.

Sandoval, Chela. *Methodology of the Oppressed*. Minneapolis: University of Minnesota Press, 2000.

Sandoval-Sánchez, Alberto. *José, Can You See? Latinos On and Off Broadway*. Madison: University of Wisconsin Press, 1999.

Soto, Sandy. *Reading Chican@ Like a Queer: The De-Mastery of Desire*. Austin: University of Texas Press, 2010.

Vargas, Deborah R. *Dissonant Divas in Chicana Music: The Limits of La Onda*. Minneapolis: University of Minnesota Press, 2012.

Tejas

Anzaldúa, Gloria. *Borderlands/La Frontera*. San Francisco: Aunt Lute Books, 1999.

Arreola, Daniel D. *Tejano South Texas: A Mexican American Cultural Province*. Austin: University of Texas Press, 2002.

Berriozabal, María Antonietta. *María, Daughter of Immigrants*. San Antonio, TX: Wings Press, 2012.

Brear, Holly B. *Inherit the Alamo: Myth and Ritual at an American Shrine.* Austin: University of Texas Press, 1995.

de la Teja, Jesús F. *San Antonio de Béxar: A Community on New Spain's Northern Frontier.* Albuquerque: University of New Mexico Press, 1996.

de León, Arnoldo. *The Tejano Community, 1836–1900.* Albuquerque: University of New Mexico Press, 1982.

———. *They Called Them Greasers: Anglo Attitudes toward Mexicans in Texas, 1821–1900.* Austin: University of Texas Press, 1983.

Esparza, Laura. "I DisMember the Alamo: A Long Poem for Performance." In *Latinas on Stage,* edited by Alicia Arrizón and Lillian Manzor, 70–89. Berkeley, CA: Third Woman Press, 2000.

Flores, Henry. *The Evolution of the Liberal Democratic State with a Case Study of Latinos in San Antonio, Texas.* Lewiston, NY: Edwin Mellen Press, 2003.

Flores, Richard R. *Remembering the Alamo: Memory, Modernity, and the Master Symbol.* Austin: University of Texas Press, 2002.

Lack, Paul D. *The Texas Revolutionary Experience: A Political and Social History, 1835–1836.* College Station: Texas A&M University Press, 1992.

Limón, José. *Dancing with the Devil: Society and Cultural Poetics in Mexican-American South Texas.* Madison: University of Wisconsin Press, 1994.

Miller, Char. *On the Border: An Environmental History of San Antonio.* Pittsburgh: University of Pittsburgh Press, 2001.

Montejano, David. *Anglos and Mexicans in the Making of Texas, 1836–1986.* Austin: University of Texas Press, 1987.

Orozco, Cynthia, Emilio Zamora, and Rodolfo Rocha, eds. *Mexican Americans in Texas History.* Austin: Texas State Historical Association, 2000.

Rosales, Rodolfo. *The Illusion of Inclusion: The Untold Political Story of San Antonio.* Austin: University of Texas Press, 2000.

San Miguel Jr., Guadalupe. *Let All of Them Take Heed: Mexican Americans and the Campaign for Educational Equality in Texas, 1910–1981.* Austin: University of Texas Press, 1987.

Tijerina, Andrés. *Tejanos and Texas under the Mexican Flag, 1821–1836.* College Station: Texas A&M University Press, 1994.

Tyler, Ronnie C., Douglas E. Barnett, and Roy R. Barkley. *The New Handbook of Texas.* Austin: Texas State Historical Association, 1996.

PANZA PILÓN
A MANIFESTO FOR *PANZA* POSITIVE
CHICANA CULTURAL PRODUCTION

The *pilón*, the baker's dozen, the sweet bonus, the unexpected extra bit. While our play closes with the heartfelt, spirited declarations in "*Panza* Girl Manifesto," as a result of our experiences with making, performing, and producing The Panza Monologues, we have written an additional manifesto. This one has more serious-minded recommendations that we believe would encourage the propagation of *panza* positive cultural production. In this manifesto, we also speak specifically as Latinas, as women of color theater artists.

Like "*Panza* Positive Politics," the idea of *panza* positive cultural production suggests a more holistic approach to living and society, art making and caretaking, especially for producing theater. As Chicana theater artists, we have traveled between multiple kinds of producing spaces—Latina/o-specific and mainstream. Each space has yielded its particular lessons. Thus some of our thoughts that follow address the condition of making art as women, while others more directly think about the function and possibilities of Latina/o cultural organizations and producers. For all contexts, the recommendations we articulate consider the whole artist's care, not only the care of her creative projects, which in and of themselves always need considerable attention. For "*panza* positive practices," to take care of the whole person would be to consider all the aspects of a woman's life, from body to family to community, and also her larger situations in cities, states, regions, and nations.

Thus in the tradition of a Chicana/o plan for action, we offer the following recommendations for the future, indeed an appeal, for the best working conditions we might hope for in order to create more theater by U.S. Latina/os that resolutely and radiantly continues to enunciate our stories of struggle, belonging, injustice, and vexations, as well as our dreams.

A Manifesto for *Panza* Positive Chicana Cultural Production

UNO: *Cultural producers, cultural centers, presenters, and producing nonprofit organizations need to create commitments to both developing and presenting theater. These entities need to think in layers and know that part of making art, and thus nurturing artists' creative activity, is process as well as product.*

For theater, we believe a multilayered strategy among cultural institutions would embrace the following tenets:

- In addition to offering fully made productions, invite artists to residencies where their *only* task at your organization is to develop work—not teach, not deliver a finished production for public viewing (formal or "in progress," free or otherwise), not lead a workshop or perform duties such as facilitate a seminar. Invite theater artists to your space/institution because you believe in their work and because your sole investment is to develop new work in order to help move it forward. Therefore, don't occupy creative time with tasks that are not about creating/developing the work. Often, art making needs the grace of isolation and solitude to bring it to its brightest fruition.

- However, at specific moments in its development, theater also needs an audience in order to move forward. We suggest working vigorously with artists to configure the best opportunities for them to show their work at *different* stages of development—including table readings, workshop readings, staged readings, and full productions. This strategy makes their experience in your community truly supportive to artists' creative needs. And this type of variety makes the institution's intersections with and offerings to audiences more innovative and meaningful for all parties involved in the process.

- We believe the axiom that all theater is local. If you invite an outside artist into your community or to your institution (i.e., someone from a different geographic location), first make sure that you are also actively—and in equal measure (in terms of time and budget)—nurturing local talent. Here we are not speaking of youth programs, which have a specific place and function for many institutions. We are specifically advocating for new (adult) emerging artists of all kinds and especially emerging women theater artists. Discover *and develop* the talent that lies right outside the door of your institution. Don't spend the entirety of your budget to bring in a big name at the expense of your local responsibilities. Interrogate why you want to present nonlocal artists as opposed to creating opportunities and/or collaborations with local artists.

Redirection of this kind will often involve spending time and resources to nurture artists in different stages of their careers. Yet we believe this is one of the most radical and responsible practices an institution can enact toward the end of directly affecting their communities' artistic growth—and responding to their local circumstances. See the first bullet point.

- Spread the wealth of your attention, care, and resources to many different artists. Interrogate how regularly you offer opportunities to any one artist. Interrogate how often women versus men are featured in your organization's fully staged productions versus "development" opportunities.

DOS: *While we invite opportunities for conversations about our art-making process and political/creative visions, don't force artists into sessions or encounters where feedback serves a compulsory function or becomes de rigueur as part of the artist's obligations for the privilege of presenting or producing her work at your organization or institution. It's not always helpful for the artist.*

At the nationally acclaimed Eugene O'Neill Theater Center's Playwright's Conference they subscribe to a creative rule whereby no one may offer feedback to a playwright's work—unless the playwright specifically asks for thoughts—because often the feedback is not always helpful to what the artist is trying to accomplish in a particular moment of development. We also encourage cultural producers, cultural centers, presenters, and producing nonprofit organizations to think about creating models of feedback that expand beyond traditional audience talkback models, which all too often devolve into harmful and unproductive free-for-all critiques unhelpful for the artist.

Speaking more specifically as Latina theater makers, no one Latina/o-authored play can possibly address the immense complexity of Latina/o contexts and experiences. We often find that there are so many stories lacking representation in the Latina/o theater experience and that an audience wants a play to speak in so many ways, the play loses its own voice in its quest to satisfy "feedback" to speak more expansively. This dilutes work. Here the double standard of theater practice for artists of color becomes clear: theater producers and audiences do not ask this of white playwrights or plays. Instead, we need more people of color theater artists articulating all of our different and varied ethnic, racialized, and regional experiences—not a few representative playwrights burdened with the task of capturing the totality of, for example, the Latina/o experience in the United States through their work.

We believe that any approach to talking about work with an artist should be artist and not audience centered. Make sure to begin with the question: what does *the artist* want/need to move her work forward in regard to feedback?

THREE: *As women, we need to stop giving our creative work away for free.*

We believe women need to cease reckless donations of our creative energy and labor, which has come to be an expected practice by cultural producers, cultural centers, presenters, and producing nonprofit organizations solely because we are female artists. This plays on gendered stereotypes that position women as caretakers of many kinds—and includes all levels and tasks performed by women in producing organizations. While it has become a practice of social change art making and is appropriate at certain junctures or for certain purposes, we do not believe that women should continually donate their creative labor to the point where we no longer validate or financially sustain ourselves as working artists in this country.

In the United States—where women earn only seventy-eight cents for every dollar that men make (and remember that for women of color the disparity is even greater: Latinas earn sixty-five cents) and most nonprofits are government or foundation funded—women need to refrain from serving as accommodating, passive, "donation tick marks" for organizations. We need to teach women artists that we are used as a commodity—a form of gendered and often racialized capital—on grant requests, grant reports, and other sources of finance—seeking documents by institutions who receive federal or foundation monies. Nonprofit producing organizations can gain a better profile for receiving funds by listing the participation of women artists and, especially, gain financial merit by listing the "participation" of underrepresented women artists such as Chicanas. Women need to become aware of how they are made use of within an organization at all levels of their participation.

- Likewise, cultural centers, community, and nonprofit organizations need to stop directly asking artists, especially female artists, to donate their work—especially when often their seasons or presenting calendars host a plethora of (paid) male artists, living or dead.
- Instead, cultural centers, community, and nonprofit organizations need to become more conscious of formally and legibly fostering woman-centered work *by women* and queer women of color work. They also need to be brave: resist the thought that work by women of color is not representative of the totality of their audience and, therefore, unworthy of time, space, or funding and development. Are you making art only *for profit* as a nonprofit?

CUATRO: *Change in any nonprofit organization that desires to make itself a better home for artists needs to begin from the top down.*

The culture and ethos of the organization is not derived from its carefully crafted mission statement but always from the attitudes, beliefs, and behaviors of its leaders. Although we admire organizations that seek to situate themselves as egalitarian, we have yet to see a truly democratically run nonprofit. So first we need to realize that this nonhierarchical ideal has been cast aside. Second, far too often executive directors of organizations are required to possess a host of knowledge areas that are widely (and wildly) divergent. This is particularly true for smaller organizations, which have fewer resources to provide salaries. We believe organizations need both financial stewards (managing directors, as they are often called) and artistic managers at the helm, and this very rarely comes in the package of one and the same person. As we have observed, often organizations falter in their leadership because they insist on this combination gold mine in their hiring practices.

Even more rarely do women of color have the opportunity to receive the training, resources, and experience to develop skills and abilities *in the arts* that would make them viable candidates for either of these positions because they have often been underdeveloped or absent altogether from nonprofit arts organizations (both as artists and as top-tier administrators).

Unfortunately, Latina/o organizations seem to bear witness to this circumstance most particularly. And even when this combination does come in the package of one person, the individual is often so overworked and (most commonly with people of color organizations) underpaid that not only does the environment that they manage suffer, but also the work they produce is done at the expense of their own sense of self and/or private life (*panza* positive care).

> • In addition, we must discontinue the misinterpretation of critique of an organization—reflections on its working structure or practices— as a personal attack. Organizations' leaders and upper-tier administrators must be more willing to listen to feedback and different ideas from their artists and staff that specifically address how to make the organization more livable and thus *panza* friendly.
> • On the other hand, as women in the arts, we need to learn to articulate our needs and desires for holistic care as artists without shame, fear of retribution, or, worse, castigation for having the ability to ar-

ticulate our needs and desires. Stating one's desire for institutional change that seeks innovative, creative solutions toward creating *panza* positive policies in an arts organization of any kind should not be considered anathema to the organization's growth and betterment.

FIVE: *For the sake of advancing a Chicana/o and Latina/o theater that reflects our experiences of the world in terms of form and content, we need to create more Latina/o dramaturgs and directors—and at least half of them need to be women, who are some of the least likely people to perform these two specific and essential tasks in U.S. theater.*

We need to prioritize the growth of these types of artists, nurture them, collectively raise them in cultural centers, community, or nonprofit organizations that foster and support new work where these artists can test their wings before their wings are then possibly clipped and pruned by the thresher of professional theaters or the incubators of graduate schools. We also need to fund them and their projects. For the sake of our cultural production, we need to insist that new play production of any kind will benefit from a dramaturg's deep knowledge or a director's participation in the creative process of theater making. In particular, our cultural centers that seek to produce theater need to become more responsible about learning what these two positions can mean to theater production, to the betterment of work, and to the audiences their productions engage.

SEIS: *One of the most valuable things that you can give emerging theater artists today is space and time.*

A free space, unfettered, such as a big room without anything in it. Often we would have given almost anything for this simple privilege. Instead, we have rehearsed *The Panza Monologues* in cramped living rooms, empty houses, and out-of-the-way places like backyards. Theaters should not sit dark when there is so much need for them beyond formal presenting opportunities—especially when artists are willing to offer an exchange of services to gain access to resources. We realize that there are always operational costs to consider, but how can organizations take the lead in fostering new working methodologies that hinge on concepts of fair trade or other types of equal exchange to the benefit of their organization in the effort of opening up a resource?

We also strongly encourage universities (whose academic labor and careers often depends on the artistic output of cultural producers) to become more creative in opening up the resources of their institutions. In addition to simply presenting work, for example, create visiting artist positions or residencies (short and long term); produce new work from page to stage; offer big, unused areas as rehearsal space; or offer crucially needed IT support/technology. Of course, the resources of academic institutions are limited, and it will take effort to fundamentally rethink your institution's possibilities, yet at the same time we have witnessed too many wasted opportunities (and walked by too many empty rooms in academic institutions at night). We urge creative thinking in how to integrate artists and their development into the lifeworld of the academy.

— — — — —

These are just a few suggestions gathered from the travels of our life experiences as artists. They form opening remarks to a very important conversation we have yet to see engaged fully—yet the need for this conversation has been evident to us time and again throughout the years. We strongly encourage artists, artistic directors and administrators, and all levels of staff at producing organizations to embark on conversations about what *panza* positive cultural production could look like in manifestations of practice. Place the well-being of people at the center of that conversation, and take particular care to notice the *panzas* of women. Actively ask, what do we need to keep the artistic *panza* fed *and* healthy? How can we refigure the way in which we work to engage imagination and play and also engender the arguments for social justice that theater productions so often describe? We hope our articulations help with the task of growing, nurturing, and holistically empowering the next generation of theater makers and producers with *panza* positive approaches to cultural production.

c/s

NOTES

Introducción to the Second Edition

1. Daniel D. Arreola, *Tejano South Texas: A Mexican American Cultural Province* (Austin: University of Texas Press, 2002), 2.

2. For a more detailed explanation of our dramaturgy, please see Chapter One/ *Uno*.

3. We describe the larger story of the collaborative effort to create the script in Chapter One/*Uno*.

4. An exacting description we borrow from the theater director Anne Bogart that carefully describes the type of theater she (and we) seeks to make.

5. This desire for something to hold on to after the play is also why we take care to make beautiful programs for our audiences to carry home—even if they're only black-and-white photocopies.

The Panza Monologues: From Cuentos to DVD

1. During my employment the EPJC had one or two male staff members at different and various times.

2. Bill Miller's "Fun Facts" website attests to their phenomenal popularity: "In 2001, sold 4.5 MILLION pounds of Brisket. (4 & 1/2 lbs. for every man, woman, and child in San Antonio)." "Fun Facts," Bill Miller Bar-B-Q, www.billmillerbbq.com/ (accessed February 27, 2012).

3. Virginia used to bring her wok to the receptions for our many events and attempt to feed hundreds from the service of one sizzling wok in motion. Impossible as it may seem, she succeeded. I still kid her about trying to feed the world with her wok—and she still tries to do it.

4. Who knew that the area would one day raze some of the older buildings and replace them with new gas stations, a Walgreens, and even a Starbucks and a vegetarian restaurant down the street?

5. Notice here how the city belongs to the Alamo, not vice versa—another indication of the structure's organizing power. In March 2011 mysanantonio.com ran an update story with new details about San Antonio's obesity epidemic: "The 2010 Bexar County Community Health Assessment—created by the county's Health Collaborative—reported that 85 percent of Southside residents are overweight or obese, followed by residents in Southeast San Antonio at 80 percent." Clearly since this type of health data was first identified in the early 2000s, the problem has intensified. Moreover, the article went on to articulate other alarming socioeconomic factors concerning the Mexican American majority south side: "The median family income on the Southside is $31,000 annually, compared to $73,500 in North Central San Antonio. Some 45.5 percent of Southside residents do not have a high school diploma, followed by Southeast residents at 35.7 percent. About 16 percent of Southside residents were diagnosed with diabetes, compared to 7 percent and 8 percent in Northwest and Northeast San Antonio." Noi Mahoney, "Health Data Grim for Southside Residents," *San Antonio Express-News,* March 3, 2011 (accessed March 14, 2012), www.mysanantonio.com/community/southside/news/article/Health-data-grim-for -Southside-residents-1036381.php.

6. "The Austin Project (tAP) is an art-based process for social change that engages the primary principles of the Jazz Aesthetic: rigorous honesty, presence, virtuosity, and community accountability. Descended from the explorations of Dianne McIntyre's Sounds in Motion Studio and the writing of Aishah Rahman, and enriched by the teaching practice known as Unlearning Racism, the Jazz Aesthetic is a way of making work that insists on the importance of Spirit to activism, scholarship and artistic creation. It puts the artist in the service of meeting the community's deepest needs, community organizers in the service of their calling as artists, and scholars in the service of an engaged pedagogy." Virginia first participated in tAP in 2003 and continues to be an ensemble member. Her writings for the project can be found in the Austin Project's book *Experiments in a Jazz Aesthetic: Art, Activism, Academia and the Austin Project,* edited by Omi Osun Joni L. Jones, Lisa L. Moore, and Sharon Bridgforth. See http://e-tap.org/history.htm for further information about tAP.

7. I believe "From Cha-Cha to *Panza*" offers a good example of this transposition, re-presented for formal staging.

8. For more information on MALCS and its activities, visit www.malcs.org.

9. *Texas Monthly* is a leading popular magazine concerning all things Texas. As the magazine states on its website: "As a leisure guide, TEXAS MONTHLY continues to be the indispensable authority on the Texas scene, covering music, the arts, travel, restaurants, museums, and cultural events with its insightful recommendations." Its readership across the state is wide and devoted, and, I suspect, more often than not Anglo and upper middle class—even though there are curious Tejanas like me who read the mag as well—just to keep an eye on its offerings. Thus the magazine's ideas (such as lists of who counts in Texas) are constitutive for Texas histo-

ry or careers and offer a measure of prevalent Texan sensibilities. A web version of their article "30 Texas Women" is available at www.texasmonthly.com/2003-02-01/webextra2.php.

10. Theater made by Latina/os in the United States has long functioned as a means to articulate racial discrimination and inequities—inter- and intracultural. There is the internationally recognized precedent of Luis Valdez and El Teatro Campesino as well as the feminist poetics set forth by contemporary Chicana/Latina playwrights. These precedents are invaluable. However, our concerns centered on the atrophy of new works by Chicana/os in our city; creating new work about our city served as a strong motivator for us. Admittedly, this is a local concern but one that is important—especially when thinking about the prominent position theater once held in San Antonio: professional Spanish-language theater companies flourished in the city in the early and mid-twentieth century. See Nicolás Kanellos, *Two Centuries of Hispanic Theatre in the Southwest* (Houston: Arte Público, 1983). Kanellos's work is an invaluable historical survey of the development of early-twentieth-century U.S. Latina/o theater. For midcentury Mexican Americans caught in a city like San Antonio, besieged by apartheid-like conditions and bigotry, Spanish-language theater served as a community-based vehicle to help preserve Mexican culture, customs, and mores. Early in the century, performers commonly used the stage to call out or comment on political issues of the day through satire, lampoon, and humor—strategies we also employ for many of the same reasons. As Kanellos has noted, "The community felt that its culture was threatened and that the theatre had a definite role to play in its protection and survival." Nicolás Kanellos, *Mexican American Theater: Legacy and Reality* (Pittsburgh: Latin American Literary Review Press, 1987), 119–120. In our contemporary fashion, we have worked with a parallel philosophy.

11. Cherríe Moraga and Gloria Anzaldúa, eds., *This Bridge Called My Back: Writings by Radical Women of Color* (New York: Kitchen Table, Women of Color Press, 1983), xxiv.

12. See "*Panza Pilón*" for further thoughts about development.

13. Café Latino, a locally owned, small coffeehouse/restaurant in San Antonio. Unfortunately, it has now closed.

14. A young America Ferrera played the lead character, a Tejana, in this workshop production of the play. She had already starred in the film *Real Women Have Curves* and had yet to appear on TV's *Ugly Betty*.

15. In 2004, Lorenzo Herrera y Lozano served as the interim executive director of ALLGO. We staged our work with ALLGO just before they redesigned their name and refocused their mission. They now use the acronym *allgo*, lowercase italics, to honor their original name but also to signify their reconceptualization from 2005 on.

16. allgo now functions as "a statewide queer people of color organization" with programs and organizing for LGBTQ communities in Texas. For more information about allgo and its activist work, see allgo.org/allgo/about.

17. During tech week, the final three to five rehearsals are held. The show is performed in its entirety, with all technical aspects in place (lights, music, and staging), to prepare for its first public performance.

18. Founded in 1980, the Guadalupe Cultural Arts Center is a Latina/o nonprofit, multidisciplinary arts organization. As stated on its website: "Located in the heart of San Antonio's west side, the Guadalupe is the largest community-based, multidisciplinary organization in the United States." Its mission is "to preserve, promote and develop the arts and culture of the Chicano/Latino/Native American peoples for all ages and backgrounds through public and educational programming in six disciplines: Dance, Literature, Media Arts, Theater Arts, Visual Arts and Xicano Music." The Guadalupe served as the site for the historic TENAZ International Theatre Festival in 1992.

19. This is true, with the lone exception of Cara Mía Theatre Company in Dallas (*mil gracias*).

A Chronological Production History of *The Panza Monologues*

1. Cara Mía Theatre, led by Artistic Director David Lozano, serves as an exception. To David's credit, word of our piece reached him as a possibility for their season at the urging of a former Chicana actor who had worked with his company. David invited us on this enthusiastic behest, for which we are extremely grateful.

2. Front-of-house management includes important tasks such as ticket sales and facilitating the audience's arrival and seating.

3. For more information on MALCS and its activities, visit www.malcs.org.

San Antonio Paint(ed) by Numbers

1. Raquel R. Márquez, Louis Mendoza, and Steve Blanchard, "Neighborhood Formation on The West Side of San Antonio, Texas," *Latino Studies*, 5, no. 3 (2007): 208–316.

2. David Montejano, *Anglos and Mexicans in the Making of Texas, 1836–1986* (Austin: University of Texas Press, 1987), 182; emphasis added. The infamous Texas Rangers were responsible for 5,000 Tejana/o deaths between 1914 and 1919.

3. Richard A. Buitron, *The Quest for Tejano Identity in San Antonio, Texas, 1913–2000* (New York: Routledge, 2004). Buitron provides an excellent description of these tensions.

4. U.S. Census Bureau, "DP03: Selected Economic Characteristics, 2008–2010 American Community Survey 3-Year Estimates, San Antonio City, Texas," accessed July 4, 2012, http://factfinder2.census.gov. This figure reflects a data set of the population sixteen years of age and older. In the "City of San Antonio, Texas Comprehensive Annual Financial Report Fiscal Year Ended September 30, 2011" (a report by the city's government), the unemployment rate for the city was noted at a (seasonally adjusted) 8.1 percent.

5. U.S. Census Bureau, "DP02: Selected Social Characteristics in The United States, 2008–2010 American Community Survey 3-Year Estimates, San Antonio City, Texas," accessed July 4, 2012, http://factfinder2.census.gov. By way of comparison, Phoenix, Arizona—the sixth largest city in the United States—maintains a 38.6 percent birthrate.

6. U.S. Census Bureau, "M0209. Percent of the Total Population Who Are White Alone, Not Hispanic or Latino, 2009 American Community Survey, San Antonio City, Texas," accessed December 16, 2010, http://factfinder.census.gov.

7. Henry Flores, *The Evolution of the Liberal Democratic State with a Case Study of Latinos in San Antonio, Texas* (Lewiston, NY: Edwin Mellen Press, 2003), 119. Flores's book is an enlightening study of the city; see chapter 4 for pertinent research on economic development.

8. This included the creation of the Good Government League (GGL) in the mid-1950s, a coalition/political machine of powerful wealthy business figures in the city who organized and financially supported a groomed slate of candidates to run for all aspects of city government, in effect, fully controlling the outcome of city elections from behind the scenes for nearly eighteen years in order to create the best environment possible for their businesses. See Rodolfo Rosales, *The Illusion of Inclusion: The Untold Political Story of San Antonio* (Austin: University of Texas Press, 2000). Chapter 3, "The Shaping of a Political Agenda and Its Consequences," is particularly helpful.

9. Flores, *The Evolution of the Liberal Democratic State,* 125 (chart).

10. Figures here are averaged from area data and maps provided by the San Antonio Economic Development Foundation, a nonprofit that "assists business and industry relocating or expanding into the San Antonio area." "Housing," San Antonio Economic Development Foundation, last modified May 2011, accessed June 20, 2012, www.sanantonioedf.com/living-here/housing.

11. "Books in the Barrio" eventually convinced Walden Books to set up a storefront in the south side's largest indoor mall, but in the recent economic downturn the franchise pulled the store, yet again, leaving the area without a bookstore.

12. Quoted in Cynthia E. Orozco, "*Rodríguez v. San Antonio ISD,*" in *Handbook of Texas Online, Texas State Historical Association,* n.d., accessed December 12, 2010.

13. Teresa Palomo Acosta, "*Edgewood ISD v. Kirby,*" in *Handbook of Texas Online, Texas State Historical Association,* n.d., accessed December 12, 2010.

14. Ibid.

15. See Acosta's excellent entry, "*Edgewood ISD v. Kirby,*" in *Handbook of Texas Online,* for further details.

16. "About UTSA, UTSA's History," University of Texas at San Antonio, n.d., accessed December 10, 2010.

17. Ibid.

18. In 1997 UTSA finally opened a "downtown" campus in San Antonio. However, the northwest campus is its "main" one.

19. Patricia Glenn and Clint Rodenfels, "Beyond First Year Retention: The Graduation Initiative," University of Texas at San Antonio, last modified 2008, accessed November 24, 2010, http://www.utsa.edu/gi/documents/glenn_rodenfels_csrde_presentation_0809.pdf.

20. U.S. Census Bureau, "M1502: Percent of People 25 Years and Over Who Have Completed a Bachelor's Degree, 2009 American Community Survey, San Antonio City, Texas," accessed December 16, 2010, http://factfinder.census.gov. For com-

parison, the United States in total has roughly a 31 percent college-degree-attaining population.

21. U.S. Census Bureau, "2010 Population Finder," accessed July 4, 2012, http://www.census.gov/popfinder/. Population statistics for both cities can be found on this webpage.

22. U.S. Census Bureau, "Selected Social Characteristics in the United States: 2009, 2009 American Community Survey, Austin City, Texas," accessed December 16, 2010, http://factfinder.census.gov. Austin has a 7.9 percent population that did not complete high school.

23. U.S. Census Bureau, "DP02: Selected Social Characteristics in the United States, 2010 American Community Survey 1-Year Estimates, San Antonio City, Texas," accessed December 16, 2010, http://factfinder.census.gov. All figures in this paragraph have been culled from this source.

24. Ibid.

25. Ibid.

26. Ibid.

27. U.S. Census Bureau, "M1701: Percent of People below Poverty Level in the Past 12 Months (for Whom Poverty Status Is Determined), 2009 American Community Survey, San Antonio City, Texas," accessed December 16, 2010, http://factfinder.census.gov. All statistics cited concerning poverty have been culled from this data.

28. U.S. Census Bureau, "DP03: Selected Economic Characteristics, 2010 American Community Survey 1-Year Estimates, San Antonio City, Texas," accessed December 16, 2010, http://factfinder.census.gov.

29. U.S. Census Bureau, "DP03: Selected Economic Characteristics, 2008–2010 American Community Survey 3-Year Estimates, San Antonio City, Texas," accessed December 16, 2010, http://factfinder.census.gov.

30. Ibid.

31. "City of San Antonio, Texas Comprehensive Annual Financial Report Fiscal Year Ended September 30, 2011," City of San Antonio Department of Finance, last modified 2011, accessed June 20, 2012, http://www.sanantonio.gov/ir/cafr/FY%20 2011%20CAFR%20FINAL%20for%20Website.pdf.

32. Ibid., 17. The report cites a formal study conducted by Richard V. Butler and Mary Stefl, scholars at Trinity University located in San Antonio, for its figures.

33. Gregg Eckhardt, "The Edwards Aquifer Website," accessed December 15, 2010, http://www.edwardsaquifer.net.

34. Gregg Eckhardt, "Edwards Aquifer News for 2010," accessed December 15, 2010, http://www.edwardsaquifer.net/news.html.

Autogeographies

1. I can remember encountering very few women who served as soldiers when I was a child.

2. Places similar to a giant Wal-Mart in merchandise with a separate store called "the commissary," which was the military's version of a large grocery store.

3. Unbeknownst to us until we came to know each other's stories more thoroughly, both Virginia and my family settled on the northeast side of town—near Fort Sam and Randolph Air Force Base. However, this is a large area. While my family was first situated in the southern and eastern side of the northeast area, Virginia's family was located farther east. I attended high school in the Northeast Independent School District. Virginia attended high school in the Judson Independent School District. So while we both speak of the northeast, we were actually located very far apart in the area. However, when my parents purchased their home, as we also later came to find, it was less than two miles away from where Virginia's family lived. Our subdivisions were right by each other.

4. Chicago native Sandra Cisneros purchased a home in San Antonio's historic (and rather wealthy) King Williams district. In refurbishing the home, she decided to paint the exterior a shade of violet that drew its origins from a Mexican-inspired color palette. The historic district (and very cranky neighbors) objected, claiming that her color choice did not fit the "historic" decorum of the neighborhood's stately homes. Cisneros argued, successfully, that her color was indeed historical and accurate. Her color drew from the *Mexican* history of the area and the city. The battle quickly exposed the tenets of Eurocentricism that underlie many Anglo residents' actions in the city. The whole controversy played out loudly in both national and local media.

5. My school was a Catholic women's college that worked in coordination with a Catholic men's college, located about four miles away. All classes were coed, as were some clubs. But the two schools were separate incorporated institutions that maintained their own traditions, governance, monies, and identity, even as their student bodies converged at opportune moments—as in play productions. It seemed an ingenious compromise for single sex institutions' sustainability: have coed classes and activities, yet maintain distinct and separate entities.

6. In terms of racial identity, I appear to be of Chinese, Japanese, Filipina, or Korean origin. But as I hope this autogeography makes clear, I am of wholly Mexican descent. When I was born, my eyelids were what doctors referred to as "underdeveloped." This meant that I lacked the ability to raise them. Janie caught this when I was very young, and I used to lift my whole head to look at something—I still do, kinda. To correct this, when I was an infant, I had surgery that in effect raised my eyebrows, which raised my eyelids and eliminated their folds—a move that granted me the ability to see, for which I am extremely grateful. However, as a result, it drastically changed the shape of my eyes—and has always confounded people's ability to "place" me.

7. Charles Lyons, Harry Elam Jr., Alice Rayner, Carl Weber, and Yvonne Yarbro-Bejarano—notable scholars who granted me a great deal of their time and rigorous instruction.

Guidelines, Advice, and Good Wishes for Staging a Production of *The Panza Monologues*

1. In some cases, we have waived our royalty fees to support producers who donate the proceeds from their event to organizations that have a discernible commit-

ment to a feminist philosophy (pro-women, pro-*panza*-positive politics, which includes access to *all* forms of preventive health care, support, education, and other services for women).

2. Please see our epilogue, "*Panza Pilón:* A Manifesto for *Panza*-Positive Chicana Cultural Production," for elaboration.

3. Julio Salgado is an activist and artist based in California's Bay Area. He is also a cofounder of DreamersAdrift.com. As the *Huffington Post* notes, "His activist artwork has become a staple of the DREAM Act movement. His status as an undocumented, queer artivist has fueled the contents of his illustrations, which depict key individuals and moments of the DREAM Act movement." Julio was an ally of Conciencia Femenil and also a fellow student at Cal State Long Beach. Please visit juliosalgado83.tumblr.com for more info.

4. Cal State Long Beach has an undergraduate enrollment of approximately 35 percent Latina/o students and is the second largest campus of the California State University (CSU) system. It is the third largest university in the state of California by enrollment.

5. "Movimiento Estudiantil Chicano de Aztlán (MEChA) is a student organization that promotes higher education, *cultura*, and *historia*. MEChA was founded on the principles of self-determination for the liberation of our people (Chicana/os). We believe that political involvement and education is the avenue for change in our society." For further historical information on MEChA, visit www.nationalmecha.org.

6. One of the most powerful, badass Chicana Heavyweights to emerge from the Movement, Anna Nieto Gómez attended Cal State Long Beach where she also helped to found UMAS, which later became MEChA. She went on to found Las Hijas de Cuauhtémoc. She coedited the first Chicana scholarly journal, *Encuentro Femenil* and worked for the Chicana Service Action Center. Nieto Gómez is the author of numerous articles on Chicana rights, labor, community organizing, education, and history. She also attended UCLA and taught at California State University, Northridge, where she developed classes about Chicanas and community organizing. After being denied tenure, she left Cal State Northridge and earned her MSW at the University of Southern California. She is a licensed clinical social worker and has worked for the state of California in the Departments of Health and Mental Health. To read just a few of her insightful writings, see Alma M. García's book, *Chicana Feminist Thought: The Basic Historical Writings* (New York: Routledge, 1997).

7. "Conciencia Femenil," *Facebook,* accessed March 16, 2012.

8. "The President's Commission on the Status of Women serves the campus community through initiating, advocating and implementing action that addresses the concerns of CSULB women students, faculty, staff and administrators." www.csulb.edu/org/women.

9. Decorated sugar skulls. A Mexican tradition usually made for Día de los Muertos or to honor the dead.

10. At Stanford University, poet/playwright/teacher Cherríe Moraga served as a mentor to Irma. In 2010 Virginia performed as an actor in her premiere production of *Digging Up the Dirt.* She remains a powerful influence in both our lives.

11. See the *"Introducción"* for thoughts on the need for public naming.

Tupperware Meets Telenovela: How to Organiza a *Panza* Party

1. The National Organization for Women Foundation launched its Love Your Body campaign in 1998, designed to challenge media images of beauty and to promote positive body images for women and young girls. For more information, see loveyourbody.nowfoundation.org.

2. See in the glossary *"Panza Brujería"* for definitions of *brujería* and *limpias*.

3. In 2010 Arizona Republican state senator Russell Pearce introduced into the Arizona legislature the Support Our Law Enforcement and Safe Neighborhoods Act (SB 1070). In short, SB 1070 not only attacked undocumented peoples but also made the act of being brown (Mexican) suspect. Or, as Virginia's mother would say, *"Donde nos chingaron* real, real good." The legislation makes it a misdemeanor to be undocumented in Arizona (*sin papeles*), allows law enforcement to question any person's immigration status at any time, and punishes those who hire or aid undocumented peoples. The bill became Arizona law in April 2010 and was met with widespread opposition, including a national call to boycott the state of Arizona. In June 2012, on hearing arguments in *Arizona v. the United States,* the U.S. Supreme Court struck down three of four provisions in SB 1070; however, the Court upheld a provision that allowed state law enforcement officers who had "reasonable suspicion" to question any person's immigration status.

4. Part of a long-standing anarchist tradition, an infoshop is a site for the distribution of political information—often through political and cultural events, meetings, zines, and books.

5. From the Facebook page of "Ladyfest IE 2012! Fourth Annual Ladyfest IE!": "Ladyfest is a global celebrated festival and was brought to the IE [Inland Empire of California] three years ago in 2009. Ladyfest IE is a grassroots, D.I.Y, feminist festival. It consists of workshops, music, vendors, speakers, poetry, art, & the participation of the community. Ladyfest's goal is to inspire women & to bring awareness on local and global struggles." Accessed June 27, 2012.

6. See contact information at the end of this chapter.

7. See contact information at the end of this chapter.

Creative Writing Activities Based on *The Panza Monologues*

1. Exercises for this activity were inspired in part by Laura Davis's "Using Photos as Writing Prompts," in *The Writer's Journey Roadmap*, last modified July 5, 2011; accessed July 7, 2012.

2. Prompts for this activity were inspired in part by Sharon Bridgforth's Finding Voice Facilitation Method. For more information, see www.sharonbridgforth.com.

ADDITIONAL ART CREDITS

INDEX